JAMES, PETER, JOHN AND JUDAH
for
EVERYONE

20TH ANNIVERSARY EDITION WITH STUDY GUIDE

NEW TESTAMENT FOR EVERYONE
20TH ANNIVERSARY EDITION WITH STUDY GUIDE
N. T. Wright

Matthew for Everyone, Part 1
Matthew for Everyone, Part 2
Mark for Everyone
Luke for Everyone
John for Everyone, Part 1
John for Everyone, Part 2
Acts for Everyone, Part 1
Acts for Everyone, Part 2
Romans for Everyone, Part 1
Romans for Everyone, Part 2
1 Corinthians for Everyone
2 Corinthians for Everyone
Galatians and Thessalonians for Everyone
Ephesians, Philippians, Colossians and Philemon for Everyone
1 and 2 Timothy and Titus for Everyone
Hebrews for Everyone
James, Peter, John and Judah for Everyone
Revelation for Everyone

JAMES, PETER, JOHN AND JUDAH

for

EVERYONE

20TH ANNIVERSARY EDITION WITH STUDY GUIDE

N. T.
WRIGHT

STUDY GUIDE BY MICHAEL KIRKINDOLL

WESTMINSTER
JOHN KNOX PRESS
LOUISVILLE • KENTUCKY

First published in Great Britain in 2011 by the
Society for Promoting Christian Knowledge
36 Causton Street
London SW1P 4ST
www.spckpublishing.co.uk

and in the United States of America
by Westminster John Knox Press,
100 Witherspoon Street, Louisville, KY 40202

20th Anniversary Edition with Study Guide
Published in 2023
by Westminster John Knox Press
Louisville, Kentucky

23 24 25 26 27 28 29 30 31 32—10 9 8 7 6 5 4 3 2 1

Cover design by Alllison Taylor

Library of Congress Cataloging-in-Publication Data

Names: Wright, N. T. (Nicholas Thomas) author. | Kirkindoll, Michael L., 1953-
Title: James, Peter, John and Judah for everyone / N. T. Wright ; study guide by Michael Kirkindoll.
Other titles: Early Christian letters for everyone
Description: 20th anniversary edition with study guide. | Louisville : Westminster John Knox Press, 2023. | Series: New Testament for everyone | Revised edition of: Early Christian letters for everyone / N. T. Wright. Great Britain : Society for Promoting Christian Knowledge, 2011. | Summary: "This expanded edition contains Wright's updated translation of the biblical text, a new introduction, and a study guide designed for use in Bible study classes and individual reflection. Helpful summaries and insightful questions assist group leaders, study participants, and solo learners to encounter these early Christian writings in exciting and enriching new ways"-- Provided by publisher.
Identifiers: LCCN 2023031444 (print) | LCCN 2023031445 (ebook) | ISBN 9780664266523 (paperback) | ISBN 9781646983506 (ebook)
Subjects: LCSH: Bible. Catholic Epistles--Criticism, interpretation, etc.
Classification: LCC BS2777 .W75 2023 (print) | LCC BS2777 (ebook) | DDC 227/.906--dc23/eng/20230721
LC record available at https://lccn.loc.gov/2023031444
LC ebook record available at https://lccn.loc.gov/2023031445

For
Sam

CONTENTS

CONTENTS

INTRODUCTION TO THE
ANNIVERSARY EDITION

It took me ten years, but I'm glad I did it. Writing a guide to the books of the New Testament felt at times like trying to climb all the Scottish mountains in quick succession. But the views from the tops were amazing, and discovering new pathways up and down was very rewarding as well. The real reward, though, has come in the messages I've received from around the world, telling me that the books have been helpful and encouraging, opening up new and unexpected vistas.

Perhaps I should say that this series wasn't designed to help with sermon preparation, though many preachers have confessed to me that they've used it that way. The books were meant, as their title suggests, for everyone, particularly for people who would never dream of picking up an academic commentary but who nevertheless want to dig a little deeper.

The New Testament seems intended to provoke all readers, at whatever stage, to fresh thought, understanding and practice. For that, we all need explanation, advice and encouragement. I'm glad these books seem to have had that effect, and I'm delighted that they are now available with study guides in these new editions.

N. T. Wright
2022

INTRODUCTION

On the very first occasion when someone stood up in public to tell people about Jesus, he made it very clear: this message is for *everyone*.

It was a great day – sometimes called the birthday of the church. The great wind of God's spirit had swept through Jesus' followers and filled them with a new joy and a sense of God's presence and power. Their leader, Peter, who only a few weeks before had been crying like a baby because he'd lied and cursed and denied even knowing Jesus, found himself on his feet explaining to a huge crowd that something had happened which had changed the world for ever. What God had done for him, Peter, he was beginning to do for the whole world: new life, forgiveness, new hope and power were opening up like spring flowers after a long winter. A new age had begun in which the living God was going to do new things in the world – beginning then and there with the individuals who were listening to him. 'This promise is for *you*', he said, 'and for your children, and for everyone who is far away' (Acts 2.39). It wasn't just for the person standing next to you. It was for everyone.

Within a remarkably short time this came true to such an extent that the young movement spread throughout much of the known world. And one way in which the *everyone* promise worked out was through the writings of the early Christian leaders. These short works – mostly letters and stories about Jesus – were widely circulated and eagerly read. They were never intended for either a religious or intellectual elite. From the very beginning they were meant for everyone.

That is as true today as it was then. Of course, it matters that some people give time and care to the historical evidence, the meaning of the original words (the early Christians wrote in Greek), and the exact and particular force of what different writers were saying about God, Jesus, the world and themselves. This series is based quite closely on that sort of work. But the point of it all is that the message can get out to everyone, especially to people who wouldn't normally read a book with footnotes and Greek words in it. That's the sort of person for whom these books are written. And that's why there's a glossary, in the back, of the key words that you can't really get along without, with a simple description of what they mean. Whenever you see a word in **bold type** in the text, you can go to the back and remind yourself what's going on.

INTRODUCTION

There are of course many translations of the New Testament available today. The one I offer here is designed for the same kind of reader: one who mightn't necessarily understand the more formal, sometimes even ponderous, tones of some of the standard ones. I have of course tried to keep as close to the original as I can. But my main aim has been to be sure that the words can speak not just to some people, but to everyone.

Let me add a note about the translation the reader will find here of the Greek word *Christos*. Most translations simply say 'Christ', but most modern English speakers assume that that word is simply a proper name (as though 'Jesus' were Jesus 'Christian' name and 'Christ' were his 'surname'). For all sorts of reasons, I disagree; so I have experimented not only with 'Messiah' (which is what the word literally means) but sometimes, too, with 'King'.

The 'early Christian letters' in this book are short, sharp and to the point. They are full of clear practical advice for Christians taking their early steps in the faith and needing to know where the problems were going to come and what resources they could find to cope with them. But they also breathe the fresh air of delight in a new-found faith, hope and life. They are full of wonder at the fact of Jesus himself, at what he'd done in giving his life to rescue people, at what he had revealed about who God himself is. They are realistic in facing the dangers a Christian community will meet in the world around, trying to squash the church into its own ways of life and to stifle the rumour that the living God might be on the loose. And they are equally realistic in highlighting difficulties which may arise within the community itself. They draw richly on the ancient scriptures of Israel to help give the young Christians that all-important sense of depth in discovering who they really are within God's love and purposes; and they range widely across issues of everything from politics to private life. They are a vital resource for every church and every Christian. So here they are: James, Peter, John and Judah for everyone!

Tom Wright

Black Sea

Byzantium

BITHYNIA-PONTUS

GALATIAN
PONTUS

Troas
MYSIA

Ancyra

ASIA

GALATIA

CAPPADOCIA

PHRYGIA

LYDIA

LYCAONIA

Ephesus

Antioch

Colossae

Iconium

CARIA

PISIDIA
Lystra

Derbe

CILICIA

LYCIA-PAMPHYLIA

Tarsus

Aegean
Sea

Mediterranean Sea

| 0 | 100 | 200 miles |
| 0 | 100 | 200 kms |

GALATIA Roman province
MYSIA Other region

JAMES

JAMES 1.1-8

The Challenge of Faith

¹James, a slave of God and of the Lord Jesus the Messiah, to the twelve dispersed tribes: greeting.

²My dear family, when you find yourselves tumbling into various trials and tribulations, learn to look at it with total joy, ³because you know that, when your faith is put to the test, what comes out is patience. ⁴What's more, you must let patience have its complete effect, so that you may be complete and whole, not falling short in anything.

⁵If any one of you falls short in wisdom, they should ask God for it, and it will be given them. God, after all, gives generously and ungrudgingly to all people. ⁶But they should ask in faith, with no doubts. A person who doubts is like a wave of the sea which the wind blows and tosses about. ⁷Someone like that should not suppose they will receive anything from the Lord, ⁸since they are double-minded and unstable in everything they do.

I used to think the waves had come from far away. Standing by the sea and watching the grey-green monsters roll in, it was easy to imagine that this wave, and then this one, and then the one after that, had made the journey from a distant land. Here they were, like the magi, arriving at last to deposit their gifts.

But of course it isn't like that. Waves are what happens when wind and tide take hold of the waters that are there all the time and make them dance to their tune. Just yesterday I stood in the bright sunshine and watched them sparkling and splashing around a little harbour, making the boats dip and bob. A fine sight; the waves seem to have character and energy of their own. But they don't. They are the random products of other forces.

The challenge of **faith** is the challenge not to be a wave. There are many winds and tides in human life, and it's easy to imagine ourselves important because we seem, from time to time at least, to dance and sparkle this way and that. The question is whether the character that develops within us is the real thing, or whether, as James says in verse 6, we are simply double-minded and unstable, blown and tossed about by this wind or that.

We don't know for sure, by the way, who James was. It was as common a name in the first century as it is today. But there is a strong chance that this letter was from the best-known James in the early church: James the brother of Jesus, the strong central leader in the Jerusalem church over the first thirty years of Christianity. Peter and Paul and the others went off around the world, but he stayed put, praying and teaching and trusting that the God who had raised his beloved brother from the dead would complete what he had begun. This letter, then, would be part of that work, written to encourage Christians across the world – whom he sees as the new version of the 'twelve dispersed tribes' of Israel – to face up to the challenge of faith.

Quite a challenge it was then, as it is now and always has been. The moment you decide to follow Jesus is the moment to expect the trials to begin. It's a bit like opening the back door to set off on a walk and finding that the wind nearly pushes you back inside before you've even started. And James tells us we should celebrate such moments (verse 2)! We should learn to look at them with joy. What can he mean?

When a Christian is tested it shows something real is happening. There are many kinds of tests: actual persecution, which many face today; fierce and nasty temptations, which can strike suddenly when we're not expecting them; physical sickness or bereavement; family or financial troubles; and so on. But you wouldn't be tested unless you were doing something serious. Mechanics don't test scrap metal; they test cars that are going to face tough conditions. Those who follow Jesus the **Messiah** are not simply supposed to survive. They are supposed to count, to make a difference in the world, whether through the quiet daily witness of a faithful and gentle life or the chance, given to some, to speak and act in a way which reveals the **gospel** to many others. For all of that we need to become strong, to face up to the challenge.

So James draws attention to the result of the test: patience. Don't panic. Don't overreact. Don't turn a problem into a crisis. Be patient. This is one of the great themes of this letter (see 5.7). And, says James, you should let patience have its complete effect. Let it work right through your system (verse 4). Imagine your life like a house. Faith is what happens when you look out of the window, away from yourself, to the God who is so much greater than you. Patience is what happens inside the house when you do that.

One of the other great themes of the letter comes here at the beginning, in parallel with patience. Wisdom! James is the most obvious representative in the New Testament of what in the ancient Israelite scriptures (the Old Testament) we think of as 'wisdom literature': the sifted, tested and collected wisdom of those who learned to trust God for everything and to discover how that trust would work out in every aspect of daily life. How should I cope with this situation, with that tricky moment? You need wisdom – and you should ask for it.

But how do I know that God will give it to me? Here, as the secret of faith, patience and wisdom combined, we have the heart of what James wants to say. God gives generously and ungrudgingly to all people (verse 5). How easy it is for us to imagine that God is stingy and mean.

We project on to the maker of all things the fearful, petty or even spiteful character we meet so often in real life, sometimes even when we look in the mirror. Learning who God really is and what he's truly like – and reminding ourselves of it regularly – is the key to it all. Without that, you'll be double-minded, swept this way one minute and that way the next. You'll just be another wave. With it, you will have a settled character. Wisdom. Patience. Faith.

JAMES 1.9–18

The Snares of the World and the Gift of God

⁹Brothers and sisters who find themselves impoverished should celebrate the fact that they have risen to this height – ¹⁰and those who are rich that they are brought down low, since the rich will disappear like a wild flower. ¹¹You see, the rich will be like the grass: when the sun rises with its scorching heat, it withers the grass so that its flower droops and all its fine appearance comes to nothing. That's what it will be like when the rich wither away in the midst of their busy lives. ¹²God's blessing on the man who endures testing! When he has passed the test, he will receive the crown of life, which God has promised to those who love him. ¹³Nobody being tested should say, 'It's God that's testing me', for God cannot be tested by evil, and he himself tests nobody. ¹⁴Rather, each person is tested when they are dragged off and enticed by their own desires. ¹⁵Then desire, when it has conceived, gives birth to sin; and when sin reaches maturity it gives birth to death. ¹⁶Don't be deceived, my dear family. ¹⁷Every good gift, every perfect gift, comes down from above, from the father of lights. His steady light doesn't vary. It doesn't change and produce shadows. ¹⁸He became our father by the word of truth; that was his firm decision, and the result is that we are a kind of first fruits of his creatures.

'Listen for the echo', said my friend. We were standing at the back of a great cathedral, and the choir was about to sing a powerful, beautiful anthem. Sure enough: the conductor knew what he was doing. As each part of the anthem developed, the building seemed to pick it up, cherish it, play with it, and use it as the background to the next part. After a while it was hard to tell what was actual echo and what was in our memory, in our mind, while we were listening to the next bit. When, finally, the choir fell silent, there was a full ten seconds in which we could savour the last chord. The whole building was designed that way, so as to give the impression that, along with the human choir, there were other, older voices, hundreds of years of worship on earth, joining in. Not to mention the heavenly host themselves.

Listen for the echo! The early Christians lived and worked within a massive echo chamber, more vast than any cathedral. It was, of course, the Old Testament, the ancient scriptures of Israel, which the followers of Jesus believed had all come rushing together with new meaning in the life, death and **resurrection** of their lord and master. Here, as often happens in early Christian writings, we find a clear echo of a famous passage. 'The grass withers,' wrote the prophet, 'the flower fades, but the **word** of our God will stand for ever.' You'll find that in Isaiah 40.7–8. It might be worth looking up the whole passage; it's one of the greatest biblical chapters of all time. James is encouraging us to hear the particular teaching he is giving within this much larger echo chamber, to allow the ancient echoes to colour the way we think about what he's saying.

What he is saying is that we must learn to trust God and his word rather than the snares of the world. He has two kinds of snares in mind: the snare of wealth, and the snare of actual temptation. (The two often go together, of course, as when someone is tempted to cheat or steal to become rich.) And he is warning that these powerful impulses are deeply deceptive. They are like the wonderful wild flowers which spring up out in the open country: here today, gone tomorrow, or even sooner if the sun is hot. The question is, what is going to last? What is permanent? And his answer is clear: God and his word. And the 'word' is not merely the word that conveys true information. When God speaks, things happen. Things happen *to us*. Things happen *in us*. The word of God is like medicine which goes down deep inside, healing our inner hurts and changing our inner motivations, so that we become different people (verse 18).

That is urgently needed, because without it we will look (metaphorically) at the glorious wild flowers and think they are what matters. We will see people becoming rich and famous, with fine houses, big cars and luxurious holidays. Today's celebrity culture tells its own story. A famous footballer one day, out on the street the next; a flashy wedding one day, a messy divorce the next. We know these stories, and yet we are seduced by the glitter of it all.

James has sharp, even sarcastic, words to say about it. When you find you're poor, you should celebrate, because that is actually the height to which you should aspire! When you find you're rich, celebrate the fact that you're being humbled, because it will all be swept away! Learn (in other words) to look at the world inside out and upside down, as Jesus constantly taught. Don't allow your imagination to be drawn into the snare. See things as God sees them.

In particular, recognize what's happening when you are tempted. Developing what he said about 'trials and tribulations' in verse 2, he warns us not to imagine that God is responsible for the temptation itself. The testing comes from within (Jesus made that clear, too). None of us starts off with a pure internal 'kit' of impulses, hopes and fears. If you are true to 'yourself', you will end up a complete mess. The challenge is to take the 'self' you find within, and to choose wisely which impulses and desires to follow, and which ones to resist.

Some desires, says James, start a family tree of their own (verse 15). Desire is like a woman who conceives a child, and the child is sin: the act which flows directly from that part of the 'self' which pulls us away from the genuine **life** which God has for us. And when the child, sin, grows up and becomes mature, it too has a child. That child is death: the final result of following those desires which diminish that genuine human life. The contrast could hardly be sharper: God promises 'the crown of life' (verse 12), but those desires lead in exactly the opposite direction. Here, as so often in scripture, the teaching of 'wisdom' fits together with what the ancient Israelites saw as God's '**covenant**' promise, requiring the choice between life and death.

So, once again, James grounds his teaching in what is true about God himself, God the generous giver, the 'father of lights'. Everything that truly lights up the world is a gift from him; but, whereas the sun, the moon and the stars all come and go in their shining, God's light is constant. And – back to the echo of Isaiah 40 – 'he became our father by the word of truth'. God has started his own fresh family tree, the new birth that brings new life, through the powerful word of the **gospel** of Jesus.

It doesn't stop with us. Those in whose lives the word is doing its work are just the start. We, says James, are 'a kind of first fruits of his creatures'. Another echo, this time of the early harvest festival in the **Temple**. You bring the 'first fruits', the beginning of the crop, as an offering to God, as a sign that there is much more to come. One day, God's word will transform the whole creation, filling **heaven** and earth with his rich, wonderful light and life. Our lives, transformed by the gospel, learning to look at the world differently, standing firm against temptation, are just the start of that larger project.

JAMES 1.19–27

The Word that Goes to Work

[19]So, my dear brothers and sisters, get this straight. Every person should be quick to hear, slow to speak, slow to anger. [20]Human anger, you see, doesn't produce God's justice! [21]So put away everything that is sordid, all overflowing malice, and humbly receive the word which has been planted within you and which has the power to rescue your lives.

²²But be people who do the word, not merely people who hear it and deceive themselves. ²³Someone who hears the word but doesn't do it, you see, is like a man who looks at his natural face in a mirror. ²⁴He notices himself, but then he goes away and quickly forgets what he looked like. ²⁵But the person who looks into the perfect law of freedom, and goes on with it, not being a hearer who forgets but a doer who does the deed – such a person is blessed in their doing.

²⁶If anyone supposes that they are devout, and does not control their tongue, but rather deceives their heart – such a person's devotion is futile. ²⁷As far as God the father is concerned, pure, unsullied devotion works like this: you should visit orphans and widows in their sorrow, and prevent the world leaving its dirty smudge on you.

Human wisdom regularly produces proverbs. 'A stitch in time saves nine.' 'A rolling stone gathers no moss.' And so on. One of the proverbs I learned very early in life went like this: 'Sticks and stones may break my bones, but words will never hurt me.' I think we boys at school used to chant it to one another as a response to a silly playground insult.

But of course that proverb is very misleading. You can recover from a broken leg or arm. But if someone smears your good name – if someone tells lies about you, and other people believe them – it may be much, much harder. You may never get the job you want. People may never quite trust you. Friends, even family, may turn away. Words can be terrible things. They can leave lasting wounds.

Here James introduces another of his key themes: the dangerous power of the human tongue. This is all of a piece with what he has just said about God's **word**. It isn't just conveying information; it actually does things, changes things, brings about a new and lasting state of affairs. So in this passage we see God's word going to work, at the same time as we hear a warning about our human words going to work in a rather different direction. As so often in James, when you hold what seem to be different ideas side by side, from one paragraph to another, a much bigger picture emerges.

So we begin with a theme which many early Christian writers emphasized: the danger of human anger. James has been emphasizing the need for patience; anger is, of course, one of the things that happens when patience reaches its limit. In verses 19–21 he applies his teaching about patience in a particular direction: we always imagine that when the world is out of joint a little bit of our own anger will put things straight. Paul, in Ephesians 4.26, allows that there may be a type of anger which is appropriate, but insists that it must be kept severely in its place. James hints at a similar concession when he says we should be 'slow to anger' as we are slow to speak. But the point is this. If what we want is God's justice, coming to sort things out, we will do better to get entirely out of the way and let God do his own work, rather than supposing our burst of anger (which will most likely have all sorts of nasty bits to it, such as wounded pride, malice and envy) will somehow help God do what needs to be done.

The way God works in us and through us is not by taking our nasty or malicious anger and somehow making it all right. The way God works is, again, through his *word*. In the previous passage James spoke of that word in terms of God giving birth to us as new creatures, as the beginning of his whole new creation. Here, with help from another passage in Isaiah (55.10–11), he sees God's word in terms of something being sown or planted, producing a beautiful shrub or a fruitful harvest.

But how does this happen? Every generation in the church worries, rightly, about people who just glide along, seeming to enjoy what they hear in church but without it making any real difference. 'Nominal Christians', we sometimes say. It is comforting, in a way, to know that James faced exactly the same problem in the very first generation: people who were happy to listen to the word (this presumably means both the teaching of the Old Testament and the **message** about Jesus) but who went away without it having affected them very much.

Here he uses an interesting illustration. In his day there were, of course, no photographs. Hardly anyone had their portrait painted. Not many people possessed mirrors, either. So if you did happen to catch sight of yourself, you might well forget at once what you looked like. That's what it's like, says James, for some when they hear God's word. A quick glance – 'Oh, yes,' they think, 'that's interesting' – and then they forget it straight away and carry on as before.

James's remedy for this is to remind us what the word of scripture, and the message about Jesus, really is: it is 'the perfect **law** of freedom'. To us that sounds like a contradiction in terms. How can a 'law' be part of 'freedom'? Isn't a law something which restricts your freedom, which stops you doing what you want?

Yes and no. Supposing we didn't have a law about which side of the road we were supposed to drive on. Everyone would set off and do their own thing. It would be chaos: accidents, near-misses, and nobody able to go at any speed for fear of disaster. The law that says you drive on the left (in Britain and elsewhere) or the right (in America and elsewhere) sets you free. That's what God's law is like: by restricting your 'freedom' in some ways, it opens up far greater, genuine freedoms in all other ways. And the point is this: when you look into this 'law', the word of God, it is supposed to change you. The word must go to work. When that happens, God's blessing – that is, God's enrichment of your **life** in all kinds of new ways – will surely follow.

James is nothing if not practical. After this flash of glorious theological theory he comes back to earth with a bump. A pious person with a foul mouth is a contradiction in terms (verse 20). Such a person is deceiving themselves – but nobody else. James doesn't immediately say what the remedy is, but he says, in effect, 'All right: you want to follow in God's way? Here's how! There are people out there who need your help; and there is a messy world out there that will try to mess up your life as well. Make sure you focus on the first and avoid the second.' Good, brisk teaching. Almost like a set of proverbs.

JAMES 2.1–13

No Favourites!

¹My brothers and sisters, as you practise the faith of our Lord Jesus, the anointed King of glory, you must do so without favouritism. ²What I mean is this: if someone comes into your assembly wearing gold rings, all dressed up, and a poor person comes in wearing shabby clothes, ³you cast your eyes over the person wearing fine clothes and say, 'Please! Have a seat up here!' but then you turn to the poor person and say, 'Stand there!' or, 'Get down there by my footstool!' ⁴When you do this, are you not discriminating among yourselves? Are you not turning into judges with evil thoughts? ⁵Listen, my dear brothers and sisters. Isn't it the case that God has chosen the poor (as the world sees it) to be rich in faith, and to inherit the kingdom which he has promised to those who love him? ⁶But you have dishonoured the poor man. After all, who are the rich? The rich are the ones who lord it over you and drag you into court, aren't they? ⁷The rich are the ones who blaspheme the wonderful name which has been pronounced over you, aren't they?

⁸Supposing, however, you keep the royal law, as it is written, 'You shall love your neighbour as yourself'; if you do this, you will do well. ⁹But if you show favouritism, you are committing sin, and you will be convicted by the law as a lawbreaker. ¹⁰Anyone who keeps the whole law, you see, but fails in one point, has become guilty of all of it. ¹¹For the one who said, 'Do not commit adultery', also said, 'Do not murder'. So if you do not commit adultery, but do murder, you have become a lawbreaker. ¹²Speak and act in such a way as people who are going to be judged by the law of freedom. ¹³Judgment is without mercy, you see, for those who have shown no mercy. But mercy triumphs over judgment.

I have often been embarrassed in church, but one of the worst moments was on Easter morning many years ago. I had arrived at the service in what I thought was good time, but there was already a large queue

10

outside and it wasn't moving. Clearly the place was already packed. I was wondering what to do when a familiar voice greeted me. I turned round and saw a man I knew a bit, a very senior and distinguished person in the city. I was flattered to be recognized and singled out. But then came the moment. 'Come with me', he said conspiratorially. He led me forward, past the queue, to one of the ushers.

'I am Lord Smith', he said to the man (I use 'Smith', of course, as a pseudonym). 'I would be grateful if you could find my friend and myself somewhere to sit.'

Before I had time to think, the two of us were escorted right to the front of the church, where we were given excellent seats with a full view of the service.

But I didn't enjoy it. I was thinking of James chapter 2, and wondering if either my acquaintance or the usher had read it recently. Of course, the same chapter tells me I shouldn't be judgmental (verse 13). But the whole passage simply rules out any question of pulling social rank in church.

This is part of what James means at the end of the previous chapter by not letting the world leave its dirty smudge on you. The world is always assessing people, sizing them up, putting them down, establishing a pecking order. And God, who sees and loves all alike, wants the church to reflect that generous, universal love in how it behaves. In some parts of the early church they had a rule that if a regular member of the congregation came into church the usher would look after them, but that if a stranger came in, particularly a poor stranger, the bishop himself would leave his chair and go to the door to welcome the newcomer. I have often wished I had the courage to do that.

But James goes further than simply insisting on equality of treatment. He hints at something he will develop later: that the rich are likely to be oppressors, and even persecutors, of the church. In every society, unless it takes scrupulous care, the rich can operate the 'justice' system to their own advantage. They can hire the best lawyers; they can, perhaps, even bribe the judges. They can get their way, and the poor have to put up with it. And in James's society 'the rich' may be more sinister still. As verse 7 indicates, in the first century it was most likely 'the rich' who were anxious about the dangers of this new **messianic** movement, these raggle-taggle Jesus-followers, making a fuss about an executed madman and thinking that God's new world had already been born. Don't they know who's in charge around here?

And James is ready with his answer: Yes, it's King Jesus who's in charge. He is the Lord, the anointed one, the King of glory (verse 1)! All human status, all pride of wealth and fine clothing, pale into insignificance before him. And he, Jesus, has re-emphasized one of the most central passages of Israel's ancient **law**: 'Love your neighbour as yourself'. That was central to Jesus' teaching, and it remained central in early Christianity. But it needed to be spelled out and applied, as here, to one situation after another. This is the 'royal **law**', by which James presumably means 'the law which King Jesus himself endorsed and insists upon'. This passage, incidentally, is one of several which make it quite clear that the early church really did see Jesus as 'king', as '**Messiah**'. They believed that God had established his '**kingdom**' in and through Jesus, and they were determined to live under that rule, whether or not the rest of the world – and the rest of the Jewish people whose Messiah Jesus was! – took any notice.

If this is the royal law, the 'law of freedom' (verse 12 looks back to chapter 1 verse 25), then to break this law is indeed to be a lawbreaker. And, as one wise writer put it a long time ago, the law is like a sheet of glass: if it's broken, it's broken. It's no good saying it's only a little bit broken. A sheet of glass can no more be only partly broken than a car tyre can be only partly flat. If it's flat, it's flat. James sees already, even in these early days of the movement, that some people were trying to drive on the flat tyre of social prestige rather than the full tyre of loving one's neighbour as oneself.

Here is the paradox, to which James returns in verse 13. God's mercy is sovereign. It will triumph. But the minute you say 'Oh well, that's all right then; God will forgive, so it doesn't matter what I do' – and, in particular, when 'what I do' includes discriminating against the poor – then, precisely because God is the God of mercy, he must act in judgment. He will not for ever tolerate a world in which mercy is not the ultimate rule of life. 'Mercy' isn't the same as a shoulder-shrugging 'tolerance', an 'anything goes' attitude to life. 'Anything' doesn't 'go'. 'Anything' includes arrogance, corruption, blasphemy, favouritism and lawbreaking of all kinds. If God was 'merciful' to that lot, he would be deeply *un*merciful to the poor, the helpless, the innocent and the victims. And the whole **gospel** insists that in precisely those cases his mercy shines out most particularly. So must ours.

JAMES 2.14–26

Faith and Works

[14]What use is it, my dear family, if someone says they have faith when they don't have works? Can faith save such a person? [15]Supposing a brother or sister is without clothing, and is short even of daily food, [16]and one of you says to them, 'Go in peace; be warm, be full!' – but doesn't give them what their bodies need – what use is that? [17]In the same way, faith, all by itself and without works, is dead.

¹⁸But supposing someone says, 'Well: you have faith, and I have works.' All right: show me your faith – but without doing any works; and then I will show you *my* faith, and I'll do it by my works! ¹⁹You believe that 'God is one'? Well and good! The demons believe that, too, and they tremble! ²⁰Do you want to know, you stupid person, that faith without works is lifeless? ²¹Wasn't Abraham our father justified by his works when he offered up his son Isaac on the altar? ²²You can see from this that faith was working together with the works, and the faith reached its fulfilment through the works. ²³That is how the scripture was fulfilled which says, 'Abraham believed God, and it was reckoned to him as righteousness', and he was called 'God's friend'. ²⁴So you see that a person is justified by works and not by faith alone. ²⁵In the same way, wasn't Rahab the prostitute justified by works when she gave shelter to the spies and sent them off by another road? ²⁶Just as the body without the spirit is dead, you see, so faith without works is dead.

That's the wrong way round, isn't it? That's what we are inclined to think as we read that final verse. If I were to use 'the body and the **spirit**' as a picture for '**faith** and works', I would make 'faith' correspond to the 'spirit' and 'works' to the 'body'. After all, faith happens in the spiritual dimension, and works in the bodily dimension, doesn't it?

Well, yes, in a sense. But as so often when scripture says something we find puzzling, there is a deeper truth waiting to be discovered. James is very concerned about a problem which was already arising in the earliest church and which is with us to this day. He has already begun to address this problem in the previous chapter, when he spoke about being 'people who do the **word**, not merely people who hear it'. He has heard people talking about 'faith', not meaning a rich, lively trust in the loving, living God, but rather a shell, a husk, an empty affirmation, a bare acknowledgement. A body without a spirit.

You can see this clearly in verse 19. James goes back to one of the most basic points of ancient Judaism, the confession that 'God is one'. That was, and still is, at the heart of Jewish daily prayer: 'Hear, O Israel: the Lord our God, the Lord is One; and you shall love the Lord your God with all your heart, and mind, and **soul** and strength.' It was at that point that Jesus himself added what James has earlier called 'the royal **law**', 'Love your neighbour as yourself.'

But simply saying 'God is one' doesn't get you very far if it doesn't make a difference in your life. After all, as James points out, the **demons** know all this too, and it doesn't do them any good; it merely scares them out of their wits. So it becomes clear that what James means by 'faith' in this passage is not what Paul and others developed as a full, Jesus-shaped meaning; it is the basic *ancient Jewish* meaning, the confession of God as 'one'. This, he says, needs to translate into action, into Jesus-shaped action, if it is to make any significant difference. At this point, he is actually on the same page as Paul, who in his fiercest letter about faith and works defines 'what matters' as 'faith working through love' (Galatians 5.6).

The same point emerges in the earlier illustration James uses, in verses 15 and 16. Actually, this isn't just an 'illustration', because (as we see throughout the letter) one of the key 'works' that James expects followers of Jesus to be doing is caring for the poor. But at the level of illustration this is how it works: there is no point in saying to someone without clothes or food, 'be warm and full'. Those words won't do anything to help. They need to be translated into action. The 'faith' which isn't enough is a mere verbal formula. It won't do simply to tick the box saying 'I believe in one God' and hope that will do. It won't. Without a radical change of life, that 'faith' is worthless, and will not rescue someone from sin and death.

At this point James refers to two famous characters in scripture. Like Paul, he first mentions Abraham, the father of the Israelite people. He brings together two key passages: Genesis 15, where Abraham believes in God's promise to give him an enormous family even though he is childless, and Genesis 22. In the latter passage, following the awful episode about Abraham fathering a son on his slave-girl Hagar, and then sending them away, Abraham faces a stern test. He is commanded to **sacrifice** Isaac, his son by Sarah, the son through whom those great promises were to be fulfilled. It's a dark episode, but Abraham stands the test. The faith he had at the beginning was translated into action. He had believed that God would do what he promised, and he was prepared to put that faith into practice. That's what counts.

That was a living faith. It wasn't a bare acknowledgement of God, but rather an active friendship (verse 23, referring to passages like Isaiah 41.8). That friendship, embodied in the '**covenant**' which God established in Genesis 15.7–20 and reaffirmed in 22.15–18, is the basis for what James, like Paul, calls '**justification**', God's declaration that a person is a member of the covenant, is 'in the right', is part of God's forgiven family.

The second person James mentions is Rahab. She appears, initially, to be an unlikely example of faith, since she was a pagan prostitute. She lived in the city of Jericho at the time when the Israelites, on their way to the promised land, were about to cross the river Jordan with Jericho as their first target. In the story, Joshua sent two men, ahead of his invasion, to spy out the city. They stayed the night in Rahab's house. She protected them from the troops who were looking for them, explaining that she had come to believe in Israel's God as the only true God in **heaven** and earth (Joshua 2.11). The point is that *she translated that belief into action*, even though it was risky. In return, Joshua spared her and her family when the invasion took place. She seems to have married an Israelite, and became, remarkably enough, the great-great-grandmother of King David, and hence part of the family tree of Jesus himself (Matthew 1.5).

Translating belief into action, even when it seems impossible or downright dangerous. That is the faith that matters. That is the faith that justifies (verse 24). That is the faith that saves (verse 14). This is near the heart of the **message** of James: the challenge to make sure that faith is the real thing, that it does what it says on the packet.

JAMES 3.1-12

Taming the Tongue

¹Not many of you should become teachers, my brothers and sisters; you know that we will be judged more severely. ²All of us make many mistakes, after all. If anyone makes no mistakes in what they say, such a person is a fully complete human being, capable of keeping firm control over the whole body as well. ³We put bits into the mouths of horses to make them obey us, and then we can direct their whole bodies. ⁴Consider, too, the case of large ships; it takes strong winds to blow them along, but one small rudder will turn them whichever way the helmsman desires and decides. ⁵In the same way, the tongue is a little member but boasts great things. See how small a fire it takes to set a large forest ablaze! ⁶And the tongue *is* a fire. The tongue is a world of injustice, with its place established right there among our members. It defiles the whole body; it sets the wheel of nature ablaze, and is itself set ablaze by hell. ⁷Every species of beast and bird, of reptile and sea creature, you see, can be tamed, and has been tamed, by humans. ⁸But no single human is able to tame the tongue. It is an irrepressible evil, full of deadly poison. ⁹By it we bless the Lord and father; and by it we curse humans who are made in God's likeness! ¹⁰Blessing and curses come out of the same mouth! My dear family, it isn't right that it should be like that. ¹¹Does a spring put out both sweet and bitter water from the same source? ¹²Dear friends, can a fig tree bear olives, or a vine bear figs? Nor can salt water yield fresh.

Some while ago I was asked to give a talk about my early life and why I had chosen the path I did. I was surprised, when preparing the talk, to discover how many of the key moments in my first fifteen years were to do with my teachers. Like many others, I suppose, I had some good teachers and some bad ones; but among the good ones there were two or three who took the trouble to get to know me, to find out what made me tick, and to give me friendly words of encouragement and advice. Often that's all it takes. Someone you trust says one or two sentences, and a door opens into a whole new world.

That, no doubt, is why James says that teachers will be judged with greater strictness. One hint in the wrong direction, and someone else's life – perhaps a whole classroom full of other lives – can be sent down a wrong path. Now there are, of course, different kinds of wrong paths. Many people will realize something is amiss and find their way back. But in other cases the damage will be done.

How much more is this the case in the church! One sermon pushing a line, pouring scorn on a cherished doctrine or advocating something that's not quite right, and a whole churchful of people may set off in the wrong direction. One word out of place in a pastoral conversation, and the listener, at a vulnerable and impressionable moment, can be encouraged to make a false move. Teachers, beware! is the lesson here. Perhaps that's why many vocational advisors tell prospective ministerial candidates that if they can find anything else to do, they should do it.

From that rather sombre beginning, James proceeds to develop his theme. Having begun by warning about how difficult it is to come up to the mark as a teacher, he expands the point: taming the tongue in general, for anyone, is so difficult as to be almost impossible. Get that right and you've obviously got your entire self under control. The tongue, it seems, is the last bit of a human being to learn its lesson.

But how important it is! It may be small, but like a horse's bit or a ship's rudder it can determine the way the whole person is going. Let slip the wrong word at the wrong moment and a precious relationship can be spoilt for ever. A promise can be broken. A bad impression can be given which can never be repaired. No wonder the psalmist prayed that God would place a sentry in front of his mouth, to check on everything that was coming out (Psalm 141.3). As he said before, any pretence of being devout that doesn't result in a serious working-over of speech habits is a sham. This is a central and vital part of what it means to be truly human.

But it is more serious even than that. The tongue, declares James, is a fire, ready to set things ablaze. We know only too well, from the way the media eagerly trip up politicians and other public figures, that one word out of place can ruin a career or bring down a government. One unwise remark, reported and circulated on the internet, can cause riots on the other side of the world. So, says James, the tongue is like a little world all of its own, a country within a country: the larger area, the person as a whole, may be well governed, but in this smaller region corruption and wickedness reign unchecked.

This brings home the real underlying point. Why is the tongue like this? Jesus had pointed out that what comes out of the mouth is a sign of what is really there, deep in the heart (Matthew 12.34; Luke 6.43). James echoes this passage when he speaks of the fig tree bearing olives or the vine bearing figs. Things just aren't like that! If someone turns out to be pouring out curses – cursing other humans who are made in God's likeness – then one must at least question whether their heart has been properly cleansed, rinsed by God's powerful **spirit**. And if that isn't the case, it turns out that the tongue isn't simply a private world of injustice. It is getting its real inspiration from **hell** itself (verse 6).

What James is after, then, is consistency. He wants people to follow Jesus through and through, to be blessing-only people rather than blessing-and-cursing people. It's a high standard, but we should expect no less if the **gospel** is indeed the **message** of **salvation**. The danger, as always, is that people will take the bits of the message they want, and quietly leave the real challenges to one side. But it can't be done. The spring must be cleansed so that only fresh, sweet water comes out. For this we need help. That, fortunately, is what the gospel offers.

JAMES 3.13–18

True and False Wisdom

[13]Who is wise and discerning among you? Such a person should, by their upright behaviour, display their works in the humility of wisdom. [14]But if you have bitter jealousy and contention in your hearts, don't boast, and tell lies against the truth. [15]This isn't the wisdom that comes from above. It is earthly, merely human, coming from the world of demons. [16]For where there is jealousy and contention, there you will get unruly behaviour and every kind of evil practice. [17]But the wisdom that comes from above is first holy, then peaceful, gentle, compliant, filled with mercy and good fruits, unbiased, sincere. [18]And the fruit of righteousness is sown in peace by those who make peace.

It all began with a wrong diagnosis. I came upon the obituary of a famous actress in the newspaper just the other day. She wasn't particularly old – in her early 70s, quite young these days. Her doctor hadn't seen the early warning signs. By the time she complained of a pain it was too late. The disease had spread, and she had only months to live.

It's a sad story, repeated of course countless times, even with all the medical advances we now have. It is possible for someone to imagine they are perfectly healthy when they are walking around with something unpleasant eating away at them inside.

That is what James is talking about here. He isn't, of course, referring here to physical illness – though the sickness in question can sometimes go with actual physical ill-health. It may sometimes be difficult to say which causes which. What he is talking about is 'bitter jealousy and contention', a spirit which is always carping and criticizing, which cannot let a nice word go by without adding a nasty one, to take the taste away (as it were). And when someone with that kind of spirit claims to be healthy – claims, for instance, to be a practising Christian – James has a sharp response. Such a person, he says, is boasting. They are telling lies against the truth (verse 14).

The diagnosis goes deeper still. He has already said that the tongue is a fire set aflame by **hell**; now (verse 15) he says that a mindset like that comes from the world of **demons**. It may give some appearance of wisdom. Cynicism often does. Well, you wouldn't expect a demonic mindset to identify itself too obviously, would you?

We are faced, then, with two kinds of wisdom. This may well be a word for our day, when so many people across the world are fed up with the way their country is run, with the way their police force behaves, with the way the global economy functions, and so on. Often these criticisms are fully justified, as they certainly would have been in James's own day. But the challenge then for God's people is to be able to tell the truth about the way the world is, and about the way wicked people are behaving, without turning into a perpetual grumble, and in particular without becoming someone whose appearance of 'wisdom' consists in being able to find a cutting word to say about everyone and everything. There is still, after all, a vast amount of beauty, love, generosity and sheer goodness in the world. Those who follow Jesus ought not only to be celebrating it but contributing to it. It's better, as the saying goes, to light a candle than to curse the darkness.

Jesus himself had declared a special blessing on 'peacemakers', and James picks that up here (verse 18), pointing forward to the challenge about war and desire in the next chapter. Allowing a jealous spirit to spill out into fault-finding and backbiting is not only not making peace. It is allowing the build-up of a climate of fear, anger and suspicion in which wars and fightings can all too easily occur.

So what's the answer? In the middle of these warnings, James offers in verse 17 a lovely, though compact, description of 'the wisdom that comes from above'.

He has already told us, right at the start of the letter, that God will give this wisdom to anyone who asks in **faith**. Now he tells us what it will look like when that happens. It's clear that this 'wisdom' isn't a matter of knowing a large number of facts. Nor is it a particular skill in negotiating, or managing, or leadership, or academic scholarship.

It is much deeper than any of these. It is 'holy, then peaceful, gentle, compliant, filled with mercy and good fruits, unbiased, sincere'. It might be easy for those James has described already, those filled with jealousy and contention, to pour scorn on these characteristics. In our cynical age people might look on someone who is gentle and compliant as a wimp, perhaps a bit naive, not really aware of how nasty the world is.

But these characteristics have nothing to do with naivety. They are hard to acquire and hard to maintain. They can only be sustained at great personal cost. They only appear where there has been a steady habit of prayer and self-discipline; even then they may take a while to show themselves. It would be worth spending the time to work through the words in this list one by one. Do it slowly. Review your life in the light of them. You might want to make a note of the times, the places, and particularly the people, that make it hard for you to live in this way – and then to pray for strength, and for this wisdom from above, to hold firm when the challenge comes round once more.

Think of it like this. Suppose you lived in a village, or worked in a college, or a factory, or a farm. Suppose some of the people you met every day were like the people in verse 16, and others like the people in verse 17. Which one would you rather see coming towards you down the street? Which one would you rather have as a neighbour? The question answers itself. The challenge is how to become that neighbour yourself. And once more the answer is this: Wisdom comes 'from above'. Pray for it. Persevere.

JAMES 4.1–10

Humility and Faith

¹Where do wars come from? Why do people among you fight? It all comes from within, doesn't it – from your desires for pleasure which make war in your members. ²You want something and you haven't got it, so you murder someone. You long to possess something, but you can't get it, so you fight and wage war. The reason you don't have it is because you don't ask for it! ³And when you do ask, you don't get it, because you ask wrongly, intending to spend it on your pleasures. ⁴Adulterers! Don't you know that to be friends with the world means being enemies with God? So anyone who wants to be friends with the world is setting themselves up as God's enemy. ⁵Or do you suppose that when the Bible says, 'He yearns jealously over the spirit he has made to dwell in us', it doesn't mean what it says?

⁶But God gives more grace; so it says, 'God opposes the proud, but gives grace to the humble.' ⁷Submit to God, then; resist the devil and

he will run away from you. ⁸Draw near to God, and he will draw near to you. Make your hands clean, you sinners; and make your hearts pure, you double-minded lot. ⁹Make yourselves wretched; mourn and weep. Let your laughter turn to mourning, and your joy to sorrow. ¹⁰Humble yourselves before the Lord, and he will exalt you.

Schoolchildren of a certain age form exclusive friendships. Great human dramas are played out on a small scale when your daughter comes home in tears because her 'best friend' has declared she isn't her best friend any more, but has taken up with someone else. It seems for a moment like the end of the world. Such crises are often short-lived, not least because children grow out of that phase of life and learn to make friends more widely, and on a variety of levels.

But in other respects exclusivity is the very essence of a relationship. The obvious example is marriage. Various societies have experimented with polygamy, and even polyamory, but something deep in the human psyche seeks to bond with one person above all others. The temptation to stray is of course notorious and sometimes powerful, but it usually leads, if anywhere, not to multiple simultaneous relationships (or, if it does, the people concerned find themselves torn apart inside), but to a new exclusive bond.

In the Bible, the exclusive partnership of marriage is often used as an image of the exclusive claims of God on the human **life**, and so it is here. James uses the accusation 'adulterers!' (verse 4), not to accuse his readers of actual adultery, but to warn them that 'being friends with the world means being enemies with God'. It's such an important principle that he repeats it, almost word for word.

But what does he mean by 'the world' here, and how does 'friendship' with the world in that sense relate to what he's been saying about war, fighting and asking for things in the wrong way? By 'the world' he seems to mean, as often in scripture, 'the way the world behaves', the pattern of life, the underlying implicit story, the things people want, expect, long for and dream of that drive them to think and behave the way they do. If you go with the drift, if you don't reflect on what you're doing but just pick up habits of mind and body from all around you, the chances are you will become 'friends' with 'the world' in this sense. You will be 'normal'. It takes guts to stand out and be different. It also takes thought, decision and determination.

So why is 'friendship with the world' at the root of war and fighting? Because in 'the world' in this sense, the ultimate argument is a fist. Or a boot. Or a gun. Or a bomb. Violence, force, power – that's what counts. People may smile and appear friendly and civilized; society may appear open and generous; but if you go against them, if you challenge cherished assumptions, there are ways of making you feel their displeasure. Only today a friend told me that, after he had witnessed a robbery taking place and was called to give evidence, he had a brick thrown through his window. Violence, and the threat of more of it, is the way the world ultimately works, whether it's with small-town criminals or large-scale dictatorships.

So what would it mean to be a friend of God instead? It would mean, for a start, taming the desires that are agitating inside you for things you can't get, the desires that push you to fight, and even to kill to make war. The desires, too, that lead you to pray for something (verse 3), but to pray simply for your own pleasures to be satisfied rather than for God's glory. And yet, James says, you claim to be God's people! That is spiritual adultery. Married to God, but having a long-running affair with 'the world'. God longs for exclusive friendship with all those who are made in his image.

In particular, James highlights a major lack in the world of his day: humility. Its opposite is arrogance: the arrogance that says that *my* desires come first, that *my* cause is so important it's worth fighting and killing for. The cure, of course, is to submit to God and resist the devil (verse 7) – rather than the other way around!

This may well mean a time of serious self-examination. Where are all these impulses coming from, these desires that are pulling me away from the God who truly longs to be my friend? Verses 8–10 (drawing near to God; cleansing hands and hearts; mourning and humility) sound to me like an agenda for at least six months of spiritual direction, or perhaps for an extended silent retreat. 'The world' will do its best to encourage you to play at doing these things. Five minutes of drawing near to God, and then quickly back to two hours of television. A brief cleansing of the hands and then back to the mud and the muck. A short, painful glance at the depths of the heart, and then we'll decide that that had better wait for another occasion. After all, we don't want to be gloomy, do we? Doesn't God want us to be joyful?

Well, yes, he does, but the road to joy is not the same as the road to self-satisfied 'happiness'. Being double-minded – a quick nod to God to keep him happy, and then linking arms with 'the world' once more – simply won't do. It may take time and effort to look God in the face and admit just how far we've been going wrong.

At the heart of this challenge there lies a double promise so stupendous that I suspect most of us never really take it seriously. To begin with, 'resist the devil and he will run away from you'. The devil is a coward; when he is resisted, with the prayer that claims the victory of Jesus on the cross, he knows he is beaten. His trick is to whisper that we know we can't resist; he's got us before and he'll get us again, so why not just give in straight away and save all that bother? It's a lie. Resist him and he will run.

Second, though, 'draw near to God and he will draw near to you'. That is astonishing! God is ready and waiting. He longs to establish a friendship with you, a friendship deeper, stronger and more satisfying than you can ever imagine. This, too, will take time, as any friendship worthy of the name will do. But what could be more worthwhile? If even a few more people were prepared to take these promises seriously, think what a difference it would make to the world, never mind the church.

JAMES 4.11-17

Living by Trust in God

¹¹Do not speak evil against one another, my dear family. Anyone who speaks evil against another family member, or passes judgment against them, speaks evil against the law and judges the law. But if you judge the law, you are not a doer of the law but a judge! ¹²There is one lawgiver, one judge who can rescue or destroy. But who are you to judge your neighbour?

¹³Now look here, you people who say, 'Today, or tomorrow, we will go to such-and-such a town and spend a year there, and trade, and make some money.' ¹⁴You have no idea what the next day will bring. What is your life? You are a mist which appears for a little while and then disappears again. ¹⁵Instead, you ought to say, 'If the Lord wills, we shall live, and we shall do this, or that.' ¹⁶But, as it is, you boast in your pride. All such boasting is evil. ¹⁷So then, if anyone knows the right thing to do, but doesn't do it, it becomes sin for them.

One of the most memorable minor characters in C. S. Lewis's famous 'Narnia' stories is the strange and increasingly sinister 'Uncle Andrew' in *The Magician's Nephew*. Uncle Andrew is, in fact, the 'magician' of the title, and his nephew Digory is the male hero of the story. To begin with, Uncle Andrew appears merely a bit odd. He is quirky, idiosyncratic, unpredictable, but no more than that. But gradually it becomes clear that he has planned a sinister plot – to get Digory and his sister Polly to try out what he believes to be magic rings. He is, it appears, too scared to try them for himself.

Well, they do try them out, and that sets the whole adventure in motion. But the truly sinister moment in the story, as Lewis must have intended, comes towards the end, when Uncle Andrew is explaining that while it might have been wrong for someone else to do what he had done, he lived in a world where a different set of rules applied. 'Men like me, who possess hidden wisdom', he says, 'are freed from common rules just as we are cut off from common pleasures. Ours, my boy, is a high and lonely destiny.' Lewis, as so often, had his finger on a key moral point. The moment when someone says – to themselves, never mind to anyone else – that an action which would be wrong for 'ordinary mortals' is all right for them, because they are somehow set apart and different, that person has puffed themselves up with a gross form of pride, and is heading for disaster as a result.

James uses more or less exactly this argument in issuing another warning against speaking evil of a fellow Christian. He seems to have in mind the kind of slander or gossip which eats its way like a cancer in a Christian **fellowship**, and requires urgent treatment if it is not to prove fatal. His point is this: anyone who does such a thing is thereby implying, like Uncle Andrew, that the ordinary '**law**' which applies to Christians – that they should love their neighbour as they love themselves – does not apply to them. They are above it! They can look down on such petty standards from a great height! They are, says James, 'judging the law', instead of trying to do what the law says. But to take such a stand is not just foolish and arrogant. It is to usurp the very role of God himself (verse 12). There is only one lawgiver, only one judge; and he can either rescue or destroy.

That last line may be a way of saying that only God is in a position to pass the kind of judgment that a Christian is making when he or she speaks evil of another Christian. But it may also be a warning. The lawgiver and judge can indeed rescue and destroy – and, if you have set yourself above his holy and royal law of freedom (see 1.25; 2.8, 12), you may find that you yourself are judged by that law.

The two halves of this passage are both, therefore, warning against the temptation to put yourself in the place of God. Verses 13–16 highlight this danger in relation to one's future plans. Here is a Christian who is running a small business. All right, he thinks to himself (and perhaps says to a friend), we shall go off to a different town and ply our trade there and make some money. He (or indeed she; there were independent businesswomen in the ancient world, as we know from Acts and elsewhere) thinks that the future can be planned like that, all laid out. Perhaps there is even a suggestion that, since we are now the people of the **Messiah**, our plans can be made more securely, because God is on our side!

Whatever the case on that point, James again has stern words in store. Don't you realize, he says, what your life is like? Think of the mist you see out of the window on an autumn morning. It hangs there in the valley, above the little stream. It is beautiful, evocative, mysterious; yes, just like a human being can be. Then the sun comes up a bit further, and . . . the mist simply disappears. That's what your life is like. You have no idea what today will bring, let alone tomorrow.

The lesson, once more, is humility, applying what had been said in verses 6 and 10. Learn to take each day as a gift from God, and to do such planning as is necessary in the light of that. This, indeed, has been built into Christian understanding to this day, so that many people will say 'God willing' or 'if the Lord wills', to make it clear that in their proposals for the future they are taking care not to usurp God's sovereignty. Sometimes this is even shortened to the Latin abbreviation 'DV', standing for *Deo volente*, 'God willing'. That too, of course, can just become a slogan which people say without thinking, and perhaps without really meaning it. But at least it serves as a sign that this particular lesson of James (unlike some others, sadly) has been taken into the bloodstream of Christian understanding.

The chapter then ends with a warning which is far more general, and indeed far more worrying, than what has gone before. Not to do what you know you should do is actually to sin! It isn't enough to avoid the obvious acts of sin. Once you learn the humility to accept God's royal law and to live by it, to accept God's sovereign ordering of all life and to live within that, then you will see more clearly the positive things to which you are being called. This may be a major life-decision, a question of your whole vocation and path of life. Or it may be the small **spirit**-given nudge to do a small act of kindness for a neighbour or stranger. But once you have had that nudge, that call, then to ignore it, to pretend you hadn't heard, is a further act of pride, setting yourself up in the place of God.

This closing verse has sometimes produced, in sensitive souls, a continual anguish of heart-searching: am I being disloyal or disobedient? Can I be sure I've done what I ought to do? The best thing to say about that is that if you're worried on that score – and frankly I wish a few more Christians would search their hearts in that way – then the chances are you are doing fine. To worry obsessively about it may in itself be a way of putting yourself in the middle of the picture, focusing all the attention on 'me and my state of mind and heart' rather than on God and on your neighbour. Of course, some people do suffer from pathological or paranoid heart-searching, and that requires more careful pastoral help. But for most of us, there's nothing like helping someone else in their troubles for putting our own internal worries into perspective.

JAMES 5.1–6
Warnings to the Rich

[1]Now look here, you rich! Weep and wail for the horrible things that are going to happen to you! [2]Your riches have rotted, and your clothes have become moth-eaten, [3]your gold and your silver have rusted, and their rust will bear witness against you and will eat up your flesh like fire. You have stored up riches in the last days! [4]Look: you cheated the workers who mowed your fields by keeping back their wages, and those wages are crying out! The cries of the farm workers have reached the ears of the Lord of hosts. [5]You have lived off the fat of the land, in the lap of luxury. You have fattened your own hearts on a day of slaughter. [6]You have condemned the Righteous One and killed him, and he doesn't resist you.

Suddenly we find ourselves in two quite different worlds – and we realize that James has been thinking this way all along. Reading through the book casually to this point, we might suppose it was a ragbag collection of different moral commands: a general guide to life, what to do and what not to do. Now we discover that there are two other elements, two further dimensions, to all of this. We might want to go back and reread the letter to this point in the light of them.

The first of these two worlds opens up in front of us as a great, dark pit when we get to verse 6. The final condemnation of 'the rich' is not that they are oppressive, living in luxury and denying the workers their wages. The worst thing they have done is that *they have condemned the Righteous One and killed him*. They are responsible for the death of Jesus.

Suddenly we realize who 'the rich' really are – and, almost certainly, where and when James is writing this letter. 'The rich' are the Jerusalem elite – the **Sadducees** and the **chief priests** – who live in their fine houses and grow fat on the proceeds of pilgrimages and **sacrifices** brought by faithful Jews, but whose attitude to God and his **law** is purely pragmatic. Doing what's required in the **Temple**, running the liturgy and the festivals the way the people expect, is simply their way of staying in power. Their job is to keep the peace for the Romans, by force if necessary; and that means keeping a tight hold on what happens in Judaea, and in particular in Jerusalem and the Temple itself.

So when Jesus arrived in Jerusalem, and famously 'cleansed' the Temple, most likely as a prophetic act which, like those of Jeremiah or Ezekiel, was meant to symbolize the Temple's imminent downfall, he was treading right on their toes. They reacted the way rich elites always react to such provocation. He must be eliminated.

But you can't eliminate Jesus, as countless tyrants have discovered down the years. God raised him from the dead, and that meant that not only his first followers, but family members like James himself who had not to that point believed that he was the **Messiah**, realized that he was 'the righteous one'. God had declared him to be 'in the right' by his **resurrection**, and hence 'in the right' all along.

And it was 'the rich' who had killed him. Like Jesus himself, James points the finger at the economic oppression which had become rife throughout Judaean society, for which the official rulers bore most responsibility. They set the tone, and others (tax-collectors and the rest) followed suit. Jesus had shown a different way: he had announced the **jubilee**, the great release from debt, for which God's people had longed. As we know in our own day, anyone who suggests forgiving poor people their debts will be laughed at – by the rich! (However, when the great credit crisis of 2008 struck the Western world, the rich themselves lined up to have their debts forgiven, at the cost of the tax-payer; and several governments meekly did what they were asked. One law for the rich, another for the poor. It was ever thus.)

In particular, 'the rich' have committed the most basic social sin of holding back the wages of day-labourers. No doubt they realized that they might be able to make a little interest on the money if they hung on to it for a day or two . . . and no doubt their mansions were well protected against the shouts of the workers who had families to feed and nothing to feed them on. All right, James declares: the wages themselves, which you have kept back, are shouting out, and God is listening!

And now we come to the second fresh perspective on the whole let-ter, here unveiled in verse 3. 'You have stored up riches', warns James, '*in the **last days***'. This, too, is based on what James believed about Jesus. With Jesus, God's new world had begun! He had launched God's **king-dom**, on earth as in **heaven**: this is 'the **age to come**' for which Israel had longed and prayed! These are, in that sense, 'the last days', the great new time in which everything would be set right at last.

And in this new age one of the most inappropriate things you could do was – to store up riches. God is turning everything upside down, exalting the poor and humble and bringing the powerful and rich crashing down – and yet you are trying to make yourself richer! You are riding, says James, for an even bigger fall than you might have imagined. James looks with the eye of the prophet, and he sees the fine houses filled with silver, gold and lovely clothes, with larders full of food and cellars full of wine. And he sees them as God sees them: full of rust and moth (another echo of Jesus: compare Matthew 6.19–20), and with all that food simply fattening them up, like turkeys before Christmas, for the day of slaughter (verse 5). This is one of the sharpest warnings against careless luxury anywhere in the Bible.

It resonates, of course, with many parts of today's world. We may be weary of saying it and hearing it, but the way the global economy is set up is designed to produce more or less the same effect as the ancient Judaean economy, with most of the money flowing steadily in one direction. This is reproduced again and again more locally, as small groups of powerful people make sure they possess not just 'enough', but more than enough – and then more again; while others starve and beg, within sight of them.

No doubt, like the Jerusalem elite, the rich will then pour scorn on the poor: they deserve it, they're lazy, they don't know what life is all about. But the church must keep James 5.1–6 at its elbow, and must continue to speak out against the wickedness, not only individual but also systemic, that colludes with such a situation. It was behaviour like that which hardened the hearts of the leaders, and made the killing of Jesus seem not only right but easy and natural. It is behaviour like that which will be shown up for what it is as the day dawns and God's new age is complete, filling the hungry with good things and sending the rich away empty.

JAMES 5.7–12

Patience and Trust

> [7]So be patient, my brothers and sisters, for the appearing of the Lord. You know how the farmer waits for the valuable crop to come up from the ground. He is patient over it, waiting for it to receive the early rain and then the late rain. [8]In the same way, you must be patient, and make your hearts strong, because the appearing of the Lord is near at hand. [9]Don't grumble against one another, my brothers and sisters, so that you may not be judged. Look – the judge is standing at the gates! [10]Consider the prophets, my brothers and sisters, who spoke in the name of the Lord. Take them as an example of longsuffering and patience. [11]When people endure, we call them 'blessed by God'. Well, you have heard of the endurance of Job; and you saw the Lord's ultimate purpose. The Lord is deeply compassionate and kindly.
>
> [12]Above all, my brothers and sisters, do not swear. Don't swear by heaven; don't swear by earth; don't use any other oaths. Let your 'Yes' be 'Yes' and your 'No' be 'No'. That way, you will not fall under judgment.

When my sister and I were reckoned to be old enough not to need a babysitter any more, my parents occasionally went out for the evening, leaving us on our own. Normally this worked fine. We could see to ourselves, the front door was locked, and in any case the world seemed a safer place in those days. But one evening, for some reason, I began to worry. I have no idea why, but instead of going to sleep as usual I stayed awake and fretted. Surely they would come soon! I guessed their likely time of return; it came and went, and still no sign of them. I could hear cars on the main road, and I listened eagerly for one to turn up our street. Occasionally one did – but then it drove on by. After a while all sorts of thoughts crept over me. Supposing something had happened to them? What if there had been an accident? Perhaps they wouldn't come, not that night, not ever? I think my sister must have been asleep by then, because she would have told me not to be silly, but I ended up sitting by the window, cold with fear, hardly able to believe it when eventually the car turned up our road, stopped, and there were my parents safe and sound after a good evening, and puzzled that I would have been anxious.

I suspect that when Jesus finally appears many of us will have the same sense as I did then: how could we have been so foolish as to doubt it? How could we think that, just because it was later than we had wanted and hoped, it might mean he would never come at all? Every generation of Christians has prayed that he would come, as he promised, and so far every generation has had to learn the lesson of patience. Indeed, the command to be patient, and the fact that patience is one of the key aspects of the **spirit**'s work in our lives, might in itself tell us that such a precious gift is going to be needed. We shouldn't be surprised at the delay. The Jewish people, after all, had lived with exactly that problem through the long centuries when they had wanted their **Messiah** to come and sort everything out, and some of them had begun to believe that the promises hadn't after all meant what they said.

Once again it's a matter of humility – one of James's primary lessons, as we are realizing. Don't imagine that our timescale corresponds to God's timescale. Think of it like a farmer. Some weeks ago I watched a local farmer ploughing his field and sowing his crop. I can see the field as I write this: nothing seems to have changed (except for the fact that the seagulls that followed the plough are no longer there). The soil looks just as bare as it did when he went to work. So was he wasting his time? Has the crop failed? Of course not. It just takes time, more time than we might like. Farmers learn to live with the rhythm of the seasons. Our frantic modern society, which wants to have every vegetable in the shops all year round and so brings them in by plane from far away, has done its best to obliterate the need for patience. It's all the more important that we who follow Jesus should learn it and practise it.

The way to do this is, as usual in James, to focus our attention on God himself. 'The Lord', he says, 'is deeply compassionate and kindly.'

How hard it is to believe that – but how vital. How easy it is, by contrast, to think of God as remote, uncaring, unfeeling – or, if he feels anything, perhaps (we think) he's annoyed or cross with us about this or that. Well, there may be things to sort out, but as James already said (2.13), God's mercy is sovereign. That is the deepest truth about him.

That was the truth glimpsed by the great prophets of old. Through long acquaintance with God himself, they had learned to see the truth behind the way things seemed, to see the heavenly dimension of ordinary earthly reality, to see the heavenly timescale intersecting with the earthly one. Job is a supreme example, but there were many others who, as the letter to the Hebrews insists, went on faithfully even though they had not themselves received the things which had been promised. A hasty, impatient spirit is another form of pride, of the human arrogance that imagines it knows better than God.

And, once more, this patience and trust must issue in appropriate speech. Again, there is a warning about grumbling against one another (verse 9): clearly this was quite a problem in James's church. Sad though this is, we shouldn't be surprised. The early Christians in Jerusalem and the surrounding area had suffered persecution ever since the death of Stephen (Acts 7). When groups and **fellowships** find themselves under threat from the outside, the fear and anxiety can easily breed quarrels and grumbles on the inside as well. Patience with one another is a further aspect of humility.

The repeated warnings about the coming judgment have now developed from the general truth stated in the early chapters (e.g. 2.8–13) into a more specific warning about the coming day of the Lord. 'The judge is standing at the gates!' (verse 9). It is possible, James insists again, to incur that judgment by the wrong kind of speech. How easy it is to add a few words to a statement, as though to strengthen it. To add an oath would mean, if taken literally, that we were invoking some supernatural power in support of what we were saying ('I swear by God', and so forth). This remains a solemn matter in a court of law, and the crime of perjury is still regarded as extremely serious, even in a secular world where most people don't actually believe in the 'God' by whom, officially, they are swearing. But James, once more following the teaching of his older brother (Matthew 5.34–37), insists that saying 'yes' and 'no' is quite enough. Anything more risks invoking not divine support, but divine judgment.

This has, of course, been controversial, because many countries still use an oath in a court of law as a way of guaranteeing truthful testimony. Many Christians believe that that is a 'special case' in which the normal rule, as here, doesn't apply. But that controversy shouldn't blind us to the very interesting point that lies behind the teaching of both James and Jesus here. Following Jesus is supposed to be the path to a genuine human existence; and genuine human life should issue in clear, straight, honest speaking. To add oaths or other similar embellishments to what we are saying has the effect of debasing the coinage. It makes it look as though a plain statement isn't enough. The one time we are told in the Bible that someone began to curse and swear was when Peter was insisting that he didn't know Jesus. That should give us pause for thought.

JAMES 5.13–20

Praying in Faith

[13]Are any among you suffering? Let them pray. Are any cheerful? Let them sing psalms. [14]Are any among you sick? They should call for the elders of the church, and they should pray over the sick person, anointing them with oil in the name of the Lord. [15]Faithful prayer will rescue the sick person, and the Lord will raise them up. If they have committed any sin, it will be forgiven them. [16]So confess your sins to one another, and pray for one another, that you may be healed.

When a righteous person prays, that prayer carries great power. [17]Elijah was a man with passions like ours, and he prayed and prayed that it might not rain – and it did not rain on the earth for three years and six months. [18]Then he prayed again, the sky gave rain, and the earth produced its fruit.

[19]My dear family, if someone in your company has wandered from the truth, and someone turns them back, [20]know this: the one who turns back a sinner from wandering off into error will rescue that person's life from death, and cover a multitude of sins.

There are many things in life which look extremely odd to someone who doesn't know what's going on. Imagine watching someone making a musical instrument if you'd never heard music in your life. What, you might think, can such an object possibly be for? Why waste such time and effort on it? Or imagine a child, who has no idea about babies and where they come from, or of the fact that his mother is expecting one soon, watching her get the room ready for the new arrival. It makes no sense. Why this little cot? Why these new decorations?

Of course, when the moment comes all is explained. But sometimes you have to wait; to be patient (that theme again); to trust that things will come clear. James has used other examples, too, the farmer and the harvest being the obvious one. This theme of patience, which has run through the whole letter, marks his thinking out from the ordinary moralism of his day. James is constantly aware of living within a story – living, in fact, within God's story; and of the fact that this story has already reached its climax in his brother Jesus and will one day complete what he had so solidly begun.

This is the setting within which prayer, that most incomprehensible of activities, makes sense. To someone with no idea of God, of there being a world other than what we can touch and see, prayer looks at best like an odd superstition and at worst like serious self-deception. Fancy just talking to yourself and thinking it will make a difference to anything! But almost all human traditions, right across history and culture, have been aware of other dimensions which seem mysteriously to intersect with our own. The ancient Jewish tradition, which comes to fresh and vital expression in Jesus himself and in his early followers and family, sharpens up this general vague awareness of Something Else into not only Someone Else but a named Someone: the God we know in, through and as Jesus himself. Then, suddenly, prayer, and the patience which it involves, make all the sense in the world.

To finish this letter, then, with a call to prayer, though perhaps unexpected, is quite appropriate. Prayer must surround everything else that we do, whether sad or happy, suffering or cheerful. The Psalms are there, to this day, as the natural prayer book of Jesus' followers (verse 13), even though many Christians today seem to ignore them altogether. Anointing with oil is there, to this day, as a very simple yet profound and effective sign of God's longing to heal people. Like prayer itself, such an act is mysterious; yet, for those who take what James says seriously, it is full of meaning and power. And **forgiveness** is there, to this day, as the great open door, the fresh possibility, the chance of a new start, for all who will confess the sin which is dragging them down, and will join in prayer for healing.

James seems, again like Jesus himself, to have seen a connection between sin and ill-health. Jesus warned (in John 9) against making too close a link, but at other times, for instance in Mark 2.1–12, it seems that forgiveness and healing went hand in hand. Maybe these are the two things which push to the fore when we take our stand in the place where prayer makes sense, at the place where **heaven** and earth overlap, and at the place where our own present time and God's future time overlap.

That is, after all, what Christian prayer, and for that matter Christian sacraments, are all about. Prayer isn't just me calling out in the dark to a distant or unknown God. It means what it means and does what it does because God is, as James promised, very near to those who draw near to him. Heaven and earth meet when, in the **spirit**, someone calls on the name of the Lord. And it means what it means and does what it does because God's new time has broken into the continuing time of this sad old world, so that the person praying stands with one foot in the place of trouble, sickness and sin and with the other foot in the place of healing, forgiveness and hope. Prayer then brings the latter to bear on the former.

To understand all this may require some effort of the imagination. But once you've grasped it, prayer, like that puzzling musical instrument, can begin to play the tune it was designed to play. Suddenly it all makes sense.

That is why James alerts us to the great example of prayer, the archetypal prophet Elijah. There are many lessons one might draw from the story in 1 Kings chapters 17 and 18, but we might not have grasped the point that James is making: that the drought which came as judgment on the people of Israel, and the rain which came when they returned to the Lord and abandoned their idols, all happened in the context of Elijah's prayer. And prayer, of course, is not only a task for the 'professionals', the clergy and Christian leaders. Every Christian has not only the right but the vocation to engage in prayer like that, prayer for one another, prayer for the sick, prayer for the sinners, prayer for the nation and the world. If everyone who reads these words were to determine to devote half an hour every day to this task, the effect could be incalculable.

As ever, James brings things right down to the practical level as he finishes. Once the lesson has been grasped, that in prayer the Christian stands at the overlap point of heaven and earth, of the present and the future, there is pastoral work to be done. To see someone wandering off in a dangerous direction and do nothing about it is a tragic dereliction of duty. It may be hard to turn them back – they may insist that they are right and we are wrong! – but the effort must be made, precisely in the humility and patience which James has been urging all through. When that is done, a bit of heaven arrives on earth; a bit of God's future becomes real in the present. New **life** and forgiveness are there in person.

We shouldn't be surprised at this. James knew that his older brother, Jesus himself, had embodied new life and forgiveness. He had hung at the place where new life and forgiveness came bursting through from God's world to ours. Everything James has been saying flows from that astonishing fact. To learn, with James, to understand and obey 'the royal **law**' of love is to get to know Jesus himself. And as that happens, so the patience and humility, the love and the prayer, the wisdom and the true speech on which he has been insisting will become part of our lives. These are the 'works' which will demonstrate our **faith**.

1 PETER

1 PETER 1.1–9

Genuine Faith and Sure Hope (See map, page xiii.)

[1]Peter, an apostle of Jesus the Messiah, to God's chosen ones who live as foreigners among the Dispersion in Pontus, Galatia, Cappadocia, Asia and Bithynia, [2]who have been set aside in advance by God the father, through the sanctification of the spirit, for obedience and for sprinkling with the blood of Jesus the Messiah. May grace and peace be poured out lavishly on you!

[3]May God be blessed, God the father of our Lord Jesus the Messiah! His mercy is abundant, and so he has become our father in a second birth into a living hope through the resurrection from the dead of Jesus the Messiah. [4]This has brought us into an incorruptible inheritance, which nothing can stain or diminish. At the moment it is kept safe for you in the heavens, [5]while you are being kept safe by God's power, through faith, for a rescue that is all ready and waiting to be revealed in the final time.

[6]That is why you celebrate! Yes, it may well be necessary that, for a while, you may have to suffer trials and tests of all sorts. [7]But this is so that the true value of your faith may be discovered. It is worth more than gold, which is tested by fire even though it can be destroyed. The result will be praise, glory and honour when Jesus the Messiah is revealed. [8]You love him, even though you've never seen him. And even though you don't see him, you believe in him, and celebrate with a glorified joy that goes beyond anything words can say, [9]since you are receiving the proper goal of your faith, namely, the rescue of your lives.

I am sitting in a newly built room. It was, before, simply a garage, without even a door: almost an open shed. But we needed to transform it into a place where I could work. So, for the first time in my life, I had to deal with architects and builders, carpenters and electricians, and to understand something of the challenges they face every day.

Let's stick with the architect who designed the room. To begin with, we needed a floor plan, and that meant deciding how wide the room was to be, how much of the existing frontage we would use. Then there was the question of the height: granted the existing roof, how high could the ceiling be once we had added insulation and lighting? Then, finally, we had to consider how far back we would extend, allowing for the width of bookcases in particular.

Once those decisions were made, we had the basic shape of the room. Now the real work could begin, designing and creating everything from windows to wall fittings, from colour to carpets. At last, the room has emerged, in the space we had mapped out all those months earlier. And here I am sitting in it.

And I have before me this wonderful letter, written by the **apostle** Peter himself to Christians scattered over the country we know today as Turkey. The opening three paragraphs, which we take here all together, set out the width, the height and the depth within which everything that follows will take its place. These first nine verses are quite a mouthful – and a mindful! – but it's worth seeing them all together as the framework for the more specific things Peter has in mind to say as the letter develops.

To begin with, the width of the building (verses 1–2). This is what Christians are: chosen; set aside; sanctified for obedience; sprinkled with the **Messiah**'s blood! Already we have much to ponder. Peter doesn't address these people in terms of their ancestry, their moral background, their social status, their wealth or poverty. All those things are part of the old building, and he is sketching out the new one. It is easy to forget our basic identity as Christians, and it is therefore important to be reminded of it on a regular basis. If we are wise, we regularly take a car to be serviced, so that anything which is starting to go wrong can be put right. In the same way, we need to remind ourselves frequently, seriously and thoroughly who we really are. Unless we do that, the insidious messages we get from the world around (that we are who we are because of who our parents were, where we live or how much we earn) will eat away at us like rust into a car.

So who are we? What is the first basic dimension of the room into which Peter is inviting us? We are people who, by the mercy of God, have been chosen for a particular purpose. All Christians live a strange double life: Peter addresses his audience as 'foreigners', not because they have emigrated to where they now live but because they now have a dual citizenship. They are, simultaneously, inhabitants of this or that actual country or district (Pontus, Galatia, or wherever), and citizens of God's new world which, as he will shortly say, is waiting to be unveiled.

This is God's purpose: to set people aside from other uses so that they can be signposts to this new reality, this new world. The new world has in fact already come into being through the life, death and **resurrection** of Jesus the Messiah. Through that sacrificial death on the one hand and the indwelling of God's **spirit** on the other hand, God has set people apart to be living signals of this new world. They are therefore to be 'holy', both in the technical sense that God has set them apart for this purpose and in the practical sense that their actual lives have been transformed. The way they behave now reflects God's desire for his human creatures. That – however daunting and unlikely it seems – is who we are as Christians.

But what about the vertical dimension of this room into which we are invited (verses 3–5)? The best way of talking specifically about God and what he's done is by praise, not simply description; and praise is what Peter now offers. May God be blessed, he says, because of his mercy. The height of this room is the mercy of God; that's the highest ceiling you can get. We can see what that mercy means because, no matter who our actual parents were, God himself has become our father. We have become new people – a theme that Peter will shortly explore quite a bit further. A new **life** has come to birth within us, because a new life has come to birth in the world in the resurrection from the dead of Jesus the Messiah (verse 3). Becoming a Christian means that what God did for Jesus at Easter he does for you, in the very depth of your being. (That's why, by the way, Christians often celebrate this new life by holding **baptisms** on Easter morning.)

What's more, the new life which God created at Easter isn't just about individuals being transformed. God has, through that great action, created a whole new world. At the moment it is being kept safe, out of sight, behind the thin invisible curtain which separates our world (earth) from God's world (**heaven**). But one day the curtain will be drawn back; and then the 'incorruptible inheritance', at present being kept safe in heaven, will be merged with our earthly reality, transforming it and soaking it through with God's presence, love and mercy (verse 4). And if that new world is kept safe for us, Peter assures us that we are being kept safe for it. **Faith** itself is the anchor which holds us firm in that hope (verse 5).

Finally, the depth of the room (verses 6–9), and what it is going to contain. Quite a bit of this letter is concerned with the suffering of the early Christians. Here Peter states the theme which he will develop: that this suffering is the means by which the quality of the Christians' faith can shine out all the more, and when Jesus is finally revealed this will result in an explosion of praise. Meanwhile, they are to live their lives, to inhabit this great room of the **gospel**, with love for Jesus in their hearts and 'a glorified joy' (verse 8) welling up within them. This is the beginning of the 'rescue' which God has accomplished for them.

As we begin to walk into the room and look around us, there is much to see. But already we know its breadth, its height and its depth. There are difficult things here which must be faced. But with this new identity, and with the powerful mercy of God keeping us safe, we can go ahead and make the room – this remarkable letter, and its meaning for our lives today – a place where we feel thoroughly at home.

1 PETER 1.10–21

Ransomed by Grace

¹⁰The prophets who prophesied about the grace that was to be given to you searched and enquired about this rescue. ¹¹They asked what sort of time it would be, the time that the Messiah's spirit within them was indicating when speaking of the Messiah's sufferings and subsequent glory. ¹²It was revealed to them that they were not serving themselves, but you, when they were ministering these things – things which have now been announced to you by the holy spirit who was sent from heaven, through those who preached the good news to you. The angels long to gaze on these things!

¹³So fasten your belts – the belts of your minds! Keep yourselves under control. Set your hope completely on the grace that will be given you when Jesus the Messiah is revealed. ¹⁴As children of obedience, don't be squashed into the shape of the passions you used to indulge when you were still in ignorance. ¹⁵Rather, just as the one who called you is holy, so be holy yourselves, in every aspect of behaviour. ¹⁶It is written, you see, 'Be holy, for I am holy.' ¹⁷If you call on God as 'father' – the God, that is, who judges everyone impartially according to their work – behave with holy fear throughout the time in which you are resident here.

¹⁸You know, after all, that you were ransomed from the futile practices inherited from your ancestors, and that this ransom came not through perishable things like gold or silver, ¹⁹but through the precious blood of the Messiah, like a lamb without spot or blemish. ²⁰He was destined for this from before the foundation of the world, and appeared at the end of the times for your sake, ²¹for you (that is) who through him believe in the God who raised him from the dead and gave him glory, so that your faith and hope are in God.

John went into a junk shop the other day, in a little town not far from here. He was looking for something in particular, and after wandering around for a while he thought he saw just the thing. It was a bowl, about eight inches across. Someone had obviously used it for flowers at some stage, and it was still dirty with soil and the remains of a few leaves. It looked, too, as though it had a crack running through one side. The owner of the shop had probably not bothered about it, since it was almost entirely covered up with a pile of other old stuff, books, bottles, and goodness knows what else.

John carefully fished the bowl out and, disguising his pleasure, went and bought it at the till. Then, taking it home, he set about cleaning it. He took care. He had spotted (as the shop owner obviously hadn't) that it was in fact a fine piece of porcelain. He could repair the crack, but equally importantly he could gradually get the dirt and soil out of its pattern and bring it up as good as new. Then, when it was done, he put it in a place of honour, where it was to hold three gorgeous ornamental eggs and show them off to perfect effect. Just what he had wanted.

Now supposing the original owner of the bowl had turned up the next day at the junk shop and had asked for his bowl back, since he wanted to use it again to hold flowers. The shop owner might direct him to John; but John, perfectly properly, would say that the bowl was no longer available. Not only had he bought it, but he had cleaned it inside and out and given it a whole new use, for which it was really suited. It would be an insult to it, as well as an injustice, to use it simply to hold a few flowers.

The **good news** is that we are like that bowl. The key word in this passage is 'ransomed' (verse 18). It means that we have been 'bought back', like a dirty object in a junk shop. We had, all of us, been used for all kinds of purposes other than those for which we were made. 'Futile practices', says Peter. God had come into the junk shop, and had paid the ultimate price for us: the precious blood of the **Messiah**, God's own son. Peter is thinking here, as he makes clear, of the sacrificial lamb in the Bible, particularly perhaps of the lamb that was **sacrifice**d at the Jewish festival of Passover, marking the moment when God 'bought back' his people Israel from their abusive slavery in Egypt. Now, declares Peter, the sacrificial death of Jesus has 'ransomed' us, too. That is why Jesus was sent in the first place. That was God's intention from the very beginning.

That explains (working back to the middle paragraph, verses 13–17) why it is that Peter can call his readers, ourselves included, to a life that is so radically different from the way people normally behave. And the way it works is through straight *thinking*. You are the bowl, bought in the shop, and now cleaned up and put to quite a new use, with far greater honour than sitting in a corner filled with soil and a few dusty plants. Remind yourself of that, and don't let any previous owners come up and try to force you back into the use you once had (verse 14). Think it through. Peter describes the previous state as 'ignorance'; you didn't know what you were made for! But now you do. Now you've been cleaned up for a much finer use. So be sure you live up to it.

That means 'holiness': being set apart for God in every part and at every level. This vocation will be reinforced as you look to the future, both to the glorious hope of what will happen when Jesus is personally revealed at last (verse 13) and to the coming judgment in which God will be the impartial judge of what everyone has done (verse 17).

All this is based, as much of the letter is going to be, on Peter's awareness that the sudden dramatic events of the previous few decades – the life, death and **resurrection** of Jesus, the giving of the **spirit**, and the rise and spread of the early Christian movement – has not been a totally new idea, starting from scratch. On the contrary. It is the fulfilment, admittedly in very surprising ways, of the age-old divine plan which the ancient prophets had glimpsed. As we saw earlier, the prophets were people who stood on the borders between **heaven** and earth, between our present time and God's future time. They came to know God so well (a very painful experience, as some of them discovered) that they could discern the shape of his plan: to rescue the world through the sufferings of his chosen one, his anointed, the Messiah, and then to establish the Messiah in 'glory', that is, as the sovereign over the world.

Peter is going to draw on several prophets in the coming passages, notably Isaiah and Zechariah. And he looks back to their days, realizing what it must have meant for them. They knew that God had more grace coming – grace that would rescue people from where and what they had been, and would give them a wonderful, glorious new destiny and hope. They saw, in a measure, something of how that would happen. But when? That was the question. Like prayer, prophecy was never and is never automatic, saying something one day and having it happen the next. It might be tomorrow, or it might be in a thousand years. What matters is that, with God, the matter is certain. It's fixed and won't change. God promised to give this grace, this generous favour, to you, and he has done it (verse 10). He has promised to complete this work with a further wonderful gift of grace when the thin curtain is drawn back and Jesus is revealed (verse 13).

The prophets knew this much (verse 12). They knew that there was coming a time when folk of all sorts, spreading across the world from Judaea, would have people announce the good news to them, and when God's **holy spirit** would be sent from heaven to make that good news do its powerful work in their lives. Since that has now happened, the next stage is all the more certain, as is the 'ransom' that has already happened. What matters now is to keep our eyes fixed on the one who has 'bought us back', has cleaned us up, and has already begun to put us to new use. That's what it means, as Peter says at the end, for us to believe in 'the God who raised Jesus from the dead and gave him glory', placing him in authority over all things. That's what it means, in the present time, to have 'faith and hope in God' (verse 21).

1 PETER 1.22—2.3

Newborn Babies

²²Once your lives have been purified by obeying the truth, resulting in a sincere love for all your fellow believers, love one another eagerly, from a pure heart. ²³You have been born again, not from seed which decays but from seed which does not – through the living and abiding word of God. ²⁴Because, you see –

All flesh is like grass
and all its glory is like the flower of the field.
The grass withers, and the flower falls
²⁵but the word of the Lord lasts for ever.

That is the word that was announced to you.
²·¹So put away all evil, all deceitful, hateful malice, and all ill-speaking. ²As newborn babies, long for the spiritual milk, the real stuff, not watered down. That is what will make you grow up to salvation – ³if indeed you have tasted that the Lord is gracious.

I was in the car the other day when a programme came on the radio which won my admiration – for sheer daring. An interviewer had gone to a farm where they were raising different kinds of deer, whose meat they were selling as venison to smart restaurants right across Europe. Apparently there is a new fashion for venison, and they are doing their best to cash in.

Now some of my readers may well disapprove of eating meat in general, or of eating deer in particular. That's not the point. The point is that the interviewer went to the restaurant which was part of the farm, and sampled the different meat. And here's the thing. This was a radio programme, and we heard him nibbling and chewing and describing the different tastes of the various types of venison and the different cuts of meat. You might think it's almost impossible to do such a thing on radio. How can you convey the finer points of taste? But he had a good go at it. Whatever anyone's views on it, he made me feel hungry, which is quite an achievement for a radio broadcast.

Peter uses the idea of 'taste' as a key signal, at the end of this passage, that one of the central things in all Christian **life** is to 'taste' that the Lord is gracious. It's hard to describe – perhaps almost as hard as describing the taste of a particular meat on the radio! – but he challenges his readers. Have you had that taste? he asks. Do you know what I'm talking about?

As so often, he is quoting scripture – in this case, Psalm 34 verse 8. 'Taste and see', says the psalmist, 'that the Lord is gracious.' Then, like a newborn baby who has tasted his mother's milk, you will want more. And more.

That is the controlling image of this section: the baby that has recently been born and now needs to feed, to grow and to learn to live within the family. Becoming a Christian is about the new life within us first coming to birth, then being nourished and sustained, then growing to maturity. That last stage is marked, as it should be for a growing child, with the discovery that there are good ways and bad ways of relating to those around you. You have to learn to choose the first and renounce the second.

In this case – here Peter is saying exactly the same, of course, as all other early Christian teachers we know – the good way is the way of eager, pure, sincere love (1.22), and the bad way is that of deceit, hatred, malice and evil-speaking (2.1). That wasn't hard to figure out, was it? But it is, of course, hard to do. And that's why we need the 'spiritual milk', the real stuff. All too often it gets watered down, perhaps by preachers thinking to be 'kind' and not wanting to make too many demands all at once. Then the spiritual baby fails to grow properly, and, like a malnourished child, may become spiritually listless and helpless. A true, strong, vital relationship with the Lord is the key: taste that he is gracious, and go on thirsting for that taste and refusing, like a sensible baby, to be satisfied with anything less.

Inside the image of the tasting, and the controlling image of the baby, Peter has placed another picture: that of the farmer sowing seed. But this is no ordinary seed. In fact, as he draws on one of his favourite books, the prophet Isaiah, Peter distinguishes between the ordinary seed which produces mere grass, and flowers that fade, and the kind of seed which matters. The picture of a sower sowing seed was, of course, popular in early Christianity, not least because Jesus himself used it in some of his key **parables**.

It was, in any case, a popular picture in ancient Israel when people were thinking about the way in which (they hoped) their God would rescue and restore them after all the awful things that had happened to them. God would go out like a farmer, to sow seed once again in his field; and his true people, his real Israel, would spring up as a great crop, ready for harvest. Peter is picking this up when he quotes from Isaiah 40.6–8. What matters is 'the **word** of the Lord' (verse 25), 'the living and abiding word of God' (verse 23), 'the word that was announced to you' (verse 25). So what is this 'word', and how does it do its work?

Many Christians, hearing about 'the word of God', assume that it simply means 'the Bible'. The phrase is indeed often used in that sense. But when Peter was writing, the New Testament as we know it didn't exist, except for a few bits and pieces circulating here and there. For him, 'the Bible' would have meant the ancient Israelite scriptures, the

'Old Testament'. But he seems to mean more than that. When he speaks of 'the word that was announced to you', he seems to mean the **message** about Jesus the **Messiah**, about God sending him so that through his sacrificial death and his outpoured **spirit** people from every nation might be ransomed, as we saw, from their previous life, and given a whole new life and purpose in God's service.

But the message about Jesus only means what it means because, as Peter has already said, it is the fulfilment of what the ancient prophets had said. Perhaps we could put it like this: 'the word of God' means 'the message about Jesus, and about what God has done through him, seen as the fulfilment of the ancient scriptures'. That is the key. That is the thing which causes people to be 'born again' (verse 23).

How does this work? It seems to be something like this – drawing on verse 1, in our previous passage, as well as ideas from elsewhere in early Christianity. The followers of Jesus seem to have discovered, as early as the **day of Pentecost**, that when they spoke to people about Jesus something happened. It wasn't just that people were interested, or that they decided either to go along with the message or to reject it. It was that the 'word' seemed to carry an energy, a power, beyond the mere 'words', remarkable though they were in themselves. It was as though, when the 'word' was spoken, something like a blood transfusion was taking place in some at least of the hearers. They found themselves gripped by it, transformed by it, rinsed out by it, given a new sense of the presence of God. Yes: hearing 'the word', they 'tasted that the Lord is gracious'. They had been born again.

Isaiah's image about the word abiding for ever is worth studying for its own sake. You will find it particularly in the passage Peter quotes here (40.6–8) and then again in 55.10–13. These vital passages come at either end of the great central section of the book (chapters 40—55). In that central section the figure that gradually emerges is the 'suffering servant', the one seen by the early church as a direct prophecy of Jesus and his sacrificial death. Peter is going to draw on just that passage in the next chapter. It looks as though he is already pondering this whole section of Isaiah. Perhaps we should do so too if we want to understand what he is saying.

1 PETER 2.4-10

The Living Stone

⁴Come to him, to that living stone. Humans rejected him, but God chose him and values him very highly! ⁵Like living stones yourselves, you are being built up into a spiritual house, to be a holy priesthood,

to offer spiritual sacrifices that will be well pleasing to God through Jesus the Messiah.

⁶That's why it stands in scripture:

Look! I'm setting up in Zion
a chosen, precious cornerstone;
believe in him! You'll not be ashamed.

⁷He is indeed precious for you believers. But when people don't believe, 'the stone which the builders rejected has become the head cornerstone', ⁸and 'a stone of stumbling and a rock of offence'. They stumble as they disobey the word, which indeed was their destiny. ⁹But you are a 'chosen race; a royal priesthood'; a holy nation; a people for God's possession. Your purpose is to announce the virtuous deeds of the one who called you out of darkness into his amazing light. ¹⁰Once you were 'no people'; now you are 'God's people'. Once you had not received mercy; now you have received mercy.

I have never been a great gardener. Among many other reasons – lack of patience, moving house too often – I would name the problem I met the very first time I tried to take control of the small garden outside our first house. It was overgrown and needed tidying up. As I set to work, it seemed that my spade was forever hitting something hard. The more I went at it, the more frustrating it became. The earth was simply full of stones, large, small and everything in between. After half an hour or so I realized that if I was going to get all the stones out so I could put some plants in, it would not only take me a long time, I would have a large pile of stones to deal with at the end.

That, indeed, may be one reason why in some countries – Ireland comes to mind – there are so many small fields surrounded by dry stone walls. The point may not have been so much to keep the sheep in the field as to get the stones out of it.

That's part of the problem, for us, about reading this splendid passage in which the word 'stone' occurs six times in five verses, with a 'rock' thrown in for good measure. For us, stones are simply a nuisance. They get in the way.

But for a first-century Jew who knew the scriptures, the very word 'stone' carried a double promise. First, the great hope of Israel was that the true God, YHWH, would return to Zion (Jerusalem) at last, coming back to live for ever in the **Temple** – once, that is, it had been properly rebuilt so as to be a suitable residence for him. What's that got to do with a 'stone' or a 'rock'? Well, there was a long tradition of speaking about the Temple being built on the 'rock', on the 'cornerstone'. Find the right 'stone', and you may be on the way to building the new Temple, ready for God to return.

Second, the word 'stone' in ancient Hebrew is very like the word for 'son'. In fact, just as our word 'son' has three out of the five letters of 'stone', so the Hebrew word for 'son', *ben*, has three out of the four letters of the word for 'stone', *eben*. Jesus himself seems to have used this play on words at the end of one of his most famous stories (Mark 12.1–12: the story is about the 'son', but Jesus' punchline is about the 'stone', quoting Psalm 118.22 and thereby alluding to the same passage of Isaiah that Peter quotes here in verse 7).

How do the 'stone' and the 'son' join up? Well, in another famous biblical promise, much quoted in Jesus' day, God promised David that his son would build the Temple in Jerusalem, and that this **son of David** would actually be the **son of God** himself (2 Samuel 7.12–14). The royal son (*ben*) of God will build the Temple, says this prophecy. Yes, continues Isaiah: and he will do so on the proper stone (*eben*). Indeed, the way some people, including the early Christians, were reading the passage in Isaiah, it seems that the 'chosen, precious cornerstone' is no longer a physical stone itself, but a human being, the coming king, upon whom Israel's God will build something quite new. Certainly that's how Peter seems to understand it in verse 6. Believe in *him*, he says.

If this seems complicated, it's because it is. But once you get the picture firmly in mind – God's promise to send his son, and his promise to build a house where he will come to live for ever, with the two stitched together in these various ways – the rest of the passage is plain sailing.

For Peter, obviously, Jesus himself is the 'stone', and the new Temple is already being built up on him. He is the 'living stone' (verse 4), and already Peter is thinking within the Temple-building picture, not now of Isaiah but of Psalm 118.22. In that passage, the builders discard one particular stone because it doesn't seem to fit, only to find that when they get to the very top of the wall, right in the corner, they need a stone of exactly that shape. Jesus was rejected by his own people, Peter is indicating, because he didn't fit with the plans they had at the time, but God has shown him to be the most important stone in the whole building, the one who wouldn't fit anywhere else because only the most exalted place would do.

If you're going to suggest such an extraordinary scenario, where the very people you might think would get the point were the ones who missed it, it helps to be able to find in scripture a passage or two which say exactly that. Peter, like Paul, uses these texts from Isaiah and the Psalms to this effect.

The point is vital. What he says about Jesus is crucial for all Christian **life** and devotion (think about the people you would describe as 'precious' to you; would you use that word about Jesus?). But it is even more important that the scattered communities to which he is writing get it firmly in their minds that they, too, are part of this new Temple. God is no longer to live in a Temple in Jerusalem, but in the 'spiritual house' which, made up of 'living stones', is being 'built' all over the world. God wants, after all, to fill the whole world with his glory (see Numbers 14.21; Psalm 72.19; and other similar passages). To establish a people around the world who already make up a 'house' for him to live in is an important development in that overall project.

But this all means that Peter can address this scattered group of Jesus-followers in terms which, in scripture, belong to the nation of Israel itself. The early church was, of course, solidly Jewish. But Peter, like Paul, saw that God had brought non-Jews into this family, to share Israel's destiny with those Jews who, like Peter and the other **apostles**, had believed in Jesus despite the enormous shock to the system of having a crucified **Messiah**. They were the 'holy priesthood' offering 'spiritual **sacrifices**'. They were the 'chosen race, the royal priesthood' spoken of in Exodus 19.3–6. They were to show the world what the true God had done.

To stress the point, Peter picks up in verse 10 a famous passage from Hosea 2.23. The people who before were 'not a people' are now 'God's people'. The people who had not received mercy now have received mercy.

All these things were spoken before of ethnic Israel. Peter believed that all God's promises to Israel had been fulfilled in the Messiah, Jesus himself, and that therefore all who belonged to Jesus had now been brought into that 'people of God', that true Temple. The one true God was now living in them! The 'Temple' had been rebuilt – not in Jerusalem but all round the world! That is the great truth on which everything else in the letter will depend.

If we find it hard to keep up with the bewildering range of scriptural references which Peter is pouring into the letter at this point, think what it was like for ex-pagan converts in rural Turkey in the first century, without many books or other aids to understanding. And think what a responsibility we have, privileged as we are, to stretch our minds to understand these enormous truths, and to teach tomorrow's church to do so too. Only by being firmly anchored in the truth of who Jesus is, and who we ourselves are as his followers, will we be able to live in the way the rest of this letter urges us to.

1 PETER 2.11–17

Living in a Pagan World

[11]My beloved ones, I beg you – strangers and resident aliens as you are – to hold back from the fleshly desires that wage war against your true lives. [12]Keep up good conduct among the pagans, so that when

they speak against you as evildoers they will observe your good deeds and praise God on the day of his royal arrival.

[13]Be subject to every human institution, for the sake of the Lord: whether to the emperor as supreme, [14]or to governors as sent by him to punish evildoers and praise those who do good. [15]This, you see, is God's will. He wants you to behave well and so to silence foolish and ignorant people. [16]Live as free people (though don't use your freedom as a veil to hide evil!), but as slaves of God. [17]Do honour to all people; love the family; reverence God; honour the emperor.

I woke up gradually that morning. I had been tired out by the events of the previous day, and I had been sleeping so deeply that I seemed to be emerging slowly from a warm, dark tunnel. It's not an unpleasant feeling, but when eventually I opened my eyes I wondered, for a few moments, where on earth I was. Nothing seemed familiar. I wasn't at home, clearly. Nor was I with my grandparents, or in any other house I knew well.

Then it all came flooding back. The long car journey. The suitcases and boxes. Up and down three flights of stairs. Sorting out the room. Meeting a couple of old friends and lots of new faces. A meal, a drink, then collapsing into bed. I had at last arrived in college. I was an undergraduate student. This was one of the biggest steps of my whole life.

I lay there for a while, trying to take in the fact of who I now was and where I now was. I had thought about this step often enough, but now that it had happened it seemed, and indeed it was, truly enormous. I was about to learn a new language. I was about to study new subjects and texts. I was in the process of becoming someone different. I had to discover how the whole system worked, how to live within this new world. The new identity offered so much, but also posed major challenges.

After the breathtaking vision of the opening verses of chapter 2, which we looked at last time, this passage has something of that feeling of blinking, rubbing our eyes, and saying, in effect: All right, this is who we now are, so what are the priorities? How are we now going to behave? How do we live within this new world? Right away Peter gets to business. Once you've understood who you really are within God's great, world-changing purposes, it is vital that you learn to live appropriately.

For centuries the people of Israel had had to learn to live out their **faith**, hope and communal life while being ruled over by non-Jews ('pagans' as they would later be called). The pagans cared nothing for the Jews' faith, they certainly didn't share their hope, and they either mocked their communal life or tried actively to disrupt it. This experience of the Jewish people in 'dispersion' – the very term which Peter has used for these scattered Christian communities in 1.1 – gives him the shape for what he must now say. The position he takes is subtle, and delicately balanced, and it's important to ponder it carefully.

To begin with, he seems to be simply a stern moralist: hold back from fleshly desires! The ancient world, like many parts of today's world, tended to assume that the more one could gratify fleshly desires, the better. The only thing holding you back was money (could you really afford all the food and drink you might like?) and fear (if you indulged in as much sexual activity as you might like, would you have to face a few jealous spouses, including your own?). Like the other early Christians, Peter is emphatically not saying there is anything wrong with food, drink or sex in themselves. Everything in its proper time and place: but we humans seem to have desires that, left to themselves, would lead us into all sorts of stupid and dehumanizing places. Think of the people who, today, eat and drink themselves into an early grave. Self-control is vital.

For Peter, there is something more at stake as well. You have a 'true life', the hidden life of your real self, the new self as described in 1.1–5 and 2.4–10. These bodily desires, if given their head, will conduct a military campaign against that true life. Remember, he says, that though you are indeed God's new **Temple**, you are dispersed among the nations. You must not behave as they do, otherwise your real purpose – to reveal to them who God is and what he's done (2.9) – will be squashed flat before it's even begun. That, of course, is what the surrounding world would prefer: 'Oh, a new religion, is it? I bet you're like all the rest underneath.' But the Christians weren't. One of the reasons the faith spread, despite persecution, is that people gradually saw that this really was a new way of life, a way which nobody had ever imagined could really happen.

At the same time, however, it is important that the watching pagan world, sneering and criticizing as folk always do when other people do things they don't understand, will see that the Christians are observing the moral standards which were and are widely acknowledged (even if many people don't live up to them). The fact that you are different, in other words, doesn't mean you can ignore the basic principles of right and wrong. Some Christians were indeed tempted to go that route, imagining themselves to be so utterly removed from ordinary life, so super-spiritual, that they were above 'right and wrong' altogether. Not so, says Peter. The world needs to see that your conduct is honourable. Though they don't know it, there is coming a day when God will come back in person, in the person of his royal son, and at that moment of his arrival the pagans who have watched you ought to be saying 'Wow!

Those Christians were right all along!', not 'Well, those Christians certainly made a mess of what they were supposed to do!'

This theme, of letting the watching pagans see a genuine way of being human, continues in verses 13–17. We today, after a century of horrible tyrannies in Europe and Russia (and with more emerging in other parts of the world), are very used to thinking of 'emperors', and indeed any heavy-handed authorities, as obviously in the wrong, obviously corrupt, obviously not what a good God would want. And there is indeed, throughout scripture, a powerful and sustained attack on all abuse of power by human rulers.

But it remains the case, as Jews throughout the world of the day knew well, that though tyrants can behave abominably, not least towards God's faithful people, it is part of God's will that his created earth should be ruled and governed by human authorities. Order is better than chaos, even though 'order' can turn into tyranny, and frequently does. And though our hatred of tyranny might lead us into the normal kind of revolutionary politics (which hasn't changed much from the first century to our own day), Peter advocates a different way. Be subject to the ruling authorities, but make sure at the same time that, by your good behaviour, you shame those who, out of folly and ignorance, want to criticize you. That is how God is establishing his presence and his rule on earth as in **heaven**. Oppressive tyranny and violent revolution are not the only options. Serving the true God by living a peaceful, wise, visibly good life is, in the end, far more revolutionary than simply overthrowing one corrupt regime and replacing it by . . . well, most likely by another, as history shows.

As the letter goes on, we realize that Peter is not imagining for a moment that this will be easy, or that the authorities will always and instantly respect the followers of Jesus. Far from it. The Christians will be called to suffer, to suffer greatly, to suffer unjustly – after the pattern of Jesus himself. But all that happens within this solid advice, to which the moral and social compass must swing back after whatever interruptions may occur. Christians are to respect all people. They are to love the family – in other words, to share with other Christians anything that is needed. They must always put God himself first in everything. And – they must pay respect to the emperor.

'Respect' does not mean, of course, that you agree with everything the emperor says and does. But God has appointed him as ruler, for the moment, as Jesus himself said to Pontius Pilate (John 19.11).

How easy it is for us, in a very different climate of political thought, first to misunderstand what Peter is saying here (to imagine he is advocating an easy-going collusion with tyrants), and then to mock him for his naivety. The passages that are now coming up will show how wrong that attitude would be. When we wake up to who we now are, we will find all kinds of new challenges awaiting us, including the challenge to think right outside our usual boxes of social and political ideologies.

1 PETER 2.18–25

Suffering as the Messiah Did

[18]Let slaves obey their masters with all respect, not only the good and kind ones but also the unkind ones. [19]It is to your credit, you see, if because of a godly conscience you put up with unjust and painful suffering. [20]After all, what credit is it if you do something wrong, are beaten for it, and take it patiently? But if you do what is right, suffer for it, and bear it patiently, this is to your credit before God.
    [21]This, after all, is what came with the terms of your call, because

the Messiah, too, suffered on your behalf,
leaving behind a pattern for you
so that you should follow the way he walked.
[22]He committed no sin,
nor was there any deceit in his mouth.
[23]When he was insulted, he didn't insult in return,
when he suffered, he didn't threaten,
but he gave himself up to the one who judges justly.
[24]He himself bore our sins
in his body on the cross,
so that we might be free from sins
and live for righteousness.
It is by his wound that you are healed.
[25]For you were going astray like sheep,
but now you have returned to the shepherd
and guardian of your true lives.

Not long ago, at the height of a snowstorm, our house, and two nearby villages as well, were without electric power for fourteen hours. Our heating system is controlled by electricity, so the house became very cold. We could burn logs in a stove, but though that could keep us warm it wouldn't be easy to cook on it. The telephones didn't work. The computers, of course, didn't work either. It reminded me once more not only what it's like for many people today in parts of the world where electric power is only intermittent, but what it was like for everyone until extremely recently within human history.

    Now imagine, as well, that there was a fuel shortage, so that nobody could use their cars. No trains running, either; no planes flying. Suddenly life is a lot more basic. And a lot more time-consuming. I doubt if I'd be sitting here writing a book if I lived in a world without electric power or motorized transport. I'd probably be out chopping wood, or walking to the nearest town to pick up vegetables. And if I wanted to make the time to do anything more creative, I would have to find someone to do all those things for me. In a world of scarce resources, there might be plenty of people willing to work in return for their keep.

In the ancient world, more or less everything that today is done by electricity, gas and motorized engines was done by slaves. That is not, of course, a defence of the system of slavery. Slavery was a form of systematic, legalized dehumanization. A slave was the 'property' of his or her owner, who would provide enough board and lodging to enable the slave to work the next day, and the one after that. But, as 'property', the slave could be ill-treated, physically and sexually abused, exploited in a thousand different ways.

We look down our noses at such a world – without realizing that in many parts of today's supposedly 'free' Western society there are many people in virtually the same position. Often hidden from view, they work long hours for minimal wages. They cannot take time off, or look for another job. They may have families to support, and to lose even a single day's wages, and perhaps their 'job' as well, could be disastrous. They are stuck. They are slaves in all but name. If we want to sneer at ancient societies for being so barbaric, we should be careful. They might just sneer back.

Peter does something far more creative than sneering. Quite a few Christians were slaves, as you might expect granted that the **gospel** of Jesus gives dignity and self-worth to all those who believe it. Peter addresses these Christian slaves. Instead of telling them (as we might prefer) that they should rise up in revolt against their masters, he tells them to obey, and to show respect. And he stresses this, not only when the masters in question are kindly and fair-minded, but also when they are unjust.

Here, from our point of view, he sails very close to the wind. Putting up with unjust suffering looks, to us, very much like colluding with wickedness. Many a violent household, many an abusive workplace, has been able to continue acting wickedly because people have been afraid to speak out, and have kept their heads down and put up with the abuse. Blowing the whistle on such behaviour can cost you your job, your home or even, in extreme cases, your life.

Peter would tell us, I think, to stay with him while he explains. He has glimpsed a deeper truth, behind the moral quagmire which is so obvious to us when we think of people putting up with unjust and painful treatment. He has reflected long and hard on the extraordinary events to do with Jesus. He has thought and prayed through them in the light of the strange and dark scriptures which came to fulfilment in those **messianic** moments. And he invites followers of Jesus to inhabit his extraordinary story: to embrace it as their own, and, being healed and rescued by those events, to make them the pattern of their lives as well.

The key to it all, of course, is that the crucifixion of the **Messiah** was the most unjust and wicked act the world had ever seen. Here was the one man who deserved nothing but praise and gratitude, and they rejected him, beat him up and killed him. To understand this, Peter goes back, as many early Christians did, to Isaiah, this time to the famous chapter 53, where the royal figure of the 'servant', called to carry out God's worldwide saving purposes (42.1–9; 49.1–7; 51.4–9), does so precisely by being unjustly treated, being insulted but not replying in kind, suffering without throwing back curses at his torturers. 'He himself bore our sins in his body on the cross,' says Peter, picking up Isaiah 53.4. We were going astray like lost sheep, but the wound which he suffered gave us healing (Isaiah 53.5, 6). This is one of the clearest statements in the whole New Testament of the fact that Jesus, the Messiah, took upon himself the punishment that his people deserved. As Israel's Messiah, and hence the world's true Lord, he alone could represent all the others. He alone could, completely appropriately, stand in for them.

Now we see how important it is for Peter to say what he does about slaves and masters – and about other situations later in the letter. He isn't simply recommending that people remain passive while suffering violence. He is urging them to realize that somehow, strangely, the sufferings of the Messiah are not only the means by which we ourselves are rescued from our own sin. They are the means, when extended through the **life** of his people, by which the world itself may be brought to a new place.

This is hard to believe. It looks, to many, as though it's just a clever way of not confronting the real issue. But Peter believes that the death and **resurrection** of Jesus was and is the point around which everything else in the world revolves. Somehow, he is saying, we must see all the unjust suffering of God's people as caught up within the suffering of his son.

As I was writing this, an email arrived from a Christian friend who lives in a country where the Christian **faith** is barely tolerated and often persecuted. Things have become very bad, he says. His livelihood has been taken away. The authorities are closing in. Receiving such a message, I feel helpless. Somehow, in prayer, and in such campaigning as we can do, those of us who read 1 Peter in comfortable freedom have a deep responsibility to help our brothers and sisters for whom the persecution of which Peter speaks is a daily reality.

1 PETER 3.1–7

Marriage and Its Challenges

¹In the same way, let me say a word to the women. You should be subject to your husbands, so that if there should be some who disobey the word, they may be won, without a word, through the behaviour of their wives, ²as they notice you conducting yourselves with reverence and purity. ³The beauty you should strive for ought not to be the external sort – elaborate hairdressing, gold trinkets, fine clothes! ⁴Rather, true beauty is the secret beauty of the heart, of a sincere, gentle and quiet spirit. That is very precious to God. ⁵That is how the holy women of old, who hoped in God, used to make themselves beautiful in submission to their husbands. ⁶Take Sarah, for instance, who obeyed Abraham and called him 'Master'. You are her children if you do good and have no fear of intimidation.

⁷You men, in the same way, think out how to live with your wives. Yes, they are physically weaker than you, but they deserve full respect. They are heirs of the grace of life, just the same as you. That way nothing will obstruct your prayers.

I remember a wise preacher pointing out that even when people are free to make up their own minds and form their own decisions, most of them quickly find a framework to fit into. They adopt a stereotype; they fit into a pattern; they behave in an utterly predictable way. Perhaps we're not so free after all.

He gave two examples. Watch people coming into a church. They are free to sit wherever they like. But most people, left to their own devices, will go halfway up one side. It's usually the same side, too. Only when those seats are all occupied will people gravitate elsewhere. I suppose he could have said similar things about the psychology that drives supermarket shopping. People have studied which colours sell best at which height, no matter what the product.

The other example he gave was that of teenagers. They are free to wear whatever they want. But they all instinctively go for the same things – the jeans, the trainers, perhaps the earrings – so that when you see several of them together they look as though they are in uniform. In a sense they are. It seems safer that way. Easier, too.

This passage slices through the stereotypes into which women and men easily fell in the ancient world as in the modern. Look at the 'women's magazines' to this day. Hairdressing, jewellery, clothes – those are part of the staple diet. It seems from verse 3 as though they were the regular things for women to think about in the ancient world as well. And look at the men's magazines (at least, the ones you aren't ashamed to be seen with). Bodybuilding, strength, fast cars, high technology. Perhaps even golf. Symbols of power, skill, control and show.

Now watch what Peter does. Try it a different way round, he says! Suppose the real womanly beauty comes from the heart! Supposing what really gives a married woman her full stature as a human being is something that affects her whole character, rather than something merely stuck on to the outside! Now there's a radical idea.

And supposing the way a married man can find true fulfilment is not by bullying his wife into submission, forcing her to do what he wants. Supposing the way to fulfilment is through treating the wife as an equal, even though she will, in the normal run of things, be less physically strong? Supposing, in religious terms as well as other ways, she stands on level ground with you? Now there's a radical idea.

We should allow these radical ideas – radical then, radical now – to sink into our imagination. What would it be like if the magazines reflected a quite different idea about what it means to be a woman, or a man? What would it be like if Christians were to start cheerfully behaving in that different way, whether or not the magazine trade caught up with the idea? The fact that this still sounds quite drastic indicates that this is a lesson each generation has to learn. Left to ourselves, even (alas) in the church, we gravitate towards what women and men have always done, allowing social stereotypes and natural hormonal instinct to dictate to us. We don't find it easy to go by the hard road of rethinking roles in the light (not of 'liberation' of this or that kind, but) of the **gospel** of Jesus the **Messiah**.

Of course people will be suspicious. Many men, down the years, have emphasized verses 1–6 and quietly forgotten verse 7. Many women have gone along with this. The line between a cheerful and creative radicalism and a falsely 'meek' subservience is no doubt a fine one. But, just because that false 'meekness' remains a temptation ('keep your head down, do as you're told, and you won't get hurt!'), that doesn't mean we shouldn't think through the cheerful radicalism.

The aim, after all, is not simply that husband and wife should be able to get along happily, though that is central and important. There are two other aims, larger and quite different.

The first, larger aim is that non-Christian husbands be won for the **faith** (verse 1). As historical studies have shown, this is in fact one of the primary ways in which the Christian faith spread during the first two or three centuries, despite the fact that the authorities were doing their best to stamp it out. In fact, there were many more Christian women around than non-Christian ones, since in pagan households it was common to 'expose' a second or subsequent girl child – in other words, to throw her away to starve or be eaten by wild animals, or perhaps picked up and reared into slavery, probably prostitution. Girls were considered an expensive and difficult nuisance. Christians, like Jews, refused to do this, so there were far more marriageable Christian women available. They took advice such as this chapter to heart. And Christian families grew and spread.

The second larger aim is that Christian couples should be able to pray together and to do so effectively (verse 7). If one is domineering or bullying, shared prayer will be an imposition rather than a natural and delightful joint project. Of course, a couple may well find that, temperamentally, they like to pray in quite different ways. But when they do come together to pray, for instance when they attend church together, there should be no resentment between them, in particular no resentment because of the man forcing his wife into compliance or treating her as a lesser being. Only when we have considered the ways in which women were regarded in the ancient world – as a secondary form of human being, according to Aristotle! – will we realize just how revolutionary Peter's message (like that of other early Christians, and following the actual practice of Jesus himself) actually was. And is.

1 PETER 3.8–16

The New Way of Life

⁸The aim of this is for you all to be like-minded, sympathetic and loving to one another, tender-hearted and humble. ⁹Don't repay evil for evil, or slander for slander, but rather say a blessing. This is what you were called to, so that you may inherit a blessing.

¹⁰For the one who wants to love life and see good days
should guard the tongue from evil, and the lips from speaking deceit;
¹¹should turn away from evil and do good;
should seek peace, and follow after it.
¹²For the Lord's eyes are upon the righteous, and his ears are open to their prayer,
but the face of the Lord is against those who do evil.

¹³Who is there, then, to harm you if you are eager to do what is right? ¹⁴But if you do suffer because of your righteous behaviour, God's blessing is upon you! 'Don't fear what they fear; don't be disturbed.' ¹⁵Sanctify the Messiah as Lord in your hearts, and always be ready to make a reply to anyone who asks you to explain the hope that is in you. ¹⁶Do it, though, with gentleness and respect. Hold on to a good conscience, so that when people revile your good behaviour in the Messiah they may be ashamed.

Most of us know the feeling of getting into a car we haven't driven before. You have a look round, see where the switch for the lights is, check the angle of the mirrors, and so on. It may take a moment to figure out, with some of today's cars, how to start the engine. But then, as you drive off, you revert to instinct. You think you're putting the lights on, and the windscreen wipers start up. Or the other way around. It's harder to change these little habits than we might think.

The same is true in relationships. A child, growing up, learns how to be a friend with the two or three children closest at hand. But then, perhaps when they move to a different school, there are different challenges. People don't respond in the same way. For a week or two the child may feel like a fish out of water. It may take an effort to work at doing things differently.

And so on through life. The point doesn't need to be stressed.

But it does need to be stressed when it's a matter of Christians learning to navigate in the dangerous new world they find themselves in. This was so in the first century, and it's increasingly so in the twenty-first. In what used to be thought of as the 'Christian' West, particularly Europe and North America, it used to be taken for granted that we lived in a 'Christian' country. In fact, unless people were obviously Jews, Muslims or some other definite religion, it was assumed that everyone was, more or less, 'Christian'. Now all that has been swept away, and anyone who really is 'Christian' may well stand out. In some quarters – politics, art, the media and particularly journalism – anyone known as a Christian may well attract scorn, criticism or even discrimination. In other words, Christians in the Western world are in a process of rejoining the mainstream. This is what it was like from the beginning. This is what it's like for probably a majority of Christians in the world today – in China, in many officially Muslim countries, and so on.

But it's not easy for Western Christians, faced with this shift, to unlearn old habits and learn the necessary new ones. We are not as used, as many Christians have had to be, to treading the fine line between sinking without trace into the surrounding culture, on the one hand, and adopting a stand-offish, holier-than-thou approach on the other. High-profile cases in the media, like an airline worker who was sacked for refusing to remove the cross she was wearing, have drawn our attention to this quite new set of circumstances. How does a Christian behave when surrounded by a world that doesn't understand what we think we're about, and is potentially hostile?

The answer comes in Peter's quotation from Psalm 34. *Seek peace, and follow after it.* It may be hard to find, this 'peace' which we're supposed to be looking for, but we should hunt it down as you would with a favourite book that you can't put your hand on around the house.

You should follow after it in the way you would with a dog that has panicked and run off in a busy town. Don't expect 'peace' to come to you when you whistle. You have to do the work. You have to learn the new habit.

You have to learn it because it will be all too easy to lapse into the way many people behave. Here is the irony: Christians are supposed to stand out as distinctive, but when we do, and are mocked or criticized for it, we are tempted to mock and criticize right back – and then we are no longer distinctive, because we are behaving just like everyone else! Another victory for the hostile world: when Christians 'give as good as they get', repaying slander with slander, they are colluding with the surrounding world, just as surely as if they went along with immorality or financial corruption.

The new habits of heart and **life** are, then, to be learned in the comparatively safe environment of the church itself (verse 8), so that they can then be practised and applied in the wider world (verses 9 and 12–16). Sadly, it's all too easy to get this badly wrong, even in the church. But Peter, like Paul in one passage after another, insists on this as a basic rule of life: like-minded, sympathetic, loving, tender-hearted and humble. We may think of some people as naturally tender-hearted, and others as naturally a bit rough and cross-grained. But the early Christians assumed that they were all called to become tender-hearted, however difficult that might be. That's why we are given the **holy spirit**, to enable us to work at the new habits of heart and life.

I mentioned cars before, purely as an illustration. But of course the way we drive, and (not least) the things we think and say about other drivers, are major challenges for many of us. Here is that person dawdling along when we, stuck behind, are nearly late for an appointment! How dare they get in our way? And as we finally overtake, we are strongly tempted to look round at the person, sum up their character in a glance, and think ourselves vastly superior. We get away with it in the privacy of a car (as people do when contributing anonymously to blog sites), but the corrosive effect on our character, our habits of mind and heart, is disastrous. It will emerge, if we're not very careful, in more public and shaming places.

The wisdom of Psalm 34, then, is all the more needed today: guard the tongue the way you would fence in an unbroken horse. Stop it doing damage. Then, and perhaps only then, you will be ready to face the hostile world, which may well attack even when you are doing right, let alone when you are letting yourself down ('You Christians! You think you're so holy but actually you're no better than the rest of us – in fact, probably a lot worse.') Then and only then will you be able to 'make a reply to anyone who asks you to explain the hope that is in you' (verse 15). It must be done, as everything must be done, with gentleness and respect, not implying that we are terribly clever or superior because we've got this new religion all figured out.

And, in particular, hold on to a good conscience. This is vital. Day by day, hour by hour, we need to keep a watch over our inner moral monitoring system. Don't let it get rusty. Don't start ignoring it or telling it to be quiet. And this is not for your own sake merely (though you are yourself at risk if you try to silence your conscience). It is outward-looking. A good Christian conscience means a good witness in a puzzled and suspicious world. It may take time to have its effect, but that's a lot better than a single moment of stupidity which gives the watching world the perfect excuse to ignore the **gospel** ever afterward.

1 PETER 3.17–22

Suffering for Doing Right

[17]It's better to suffer for good conduct (if God so wills it) than for bad. [18]For the Messiah, too, suffered once for sins, the just for the unjust, so that he might bring you to God. He was put to death in the flesh, but made alive by the spirit. [19]In the spirit, too, he went and made the proclamation to the spirits in prison [20]who had earlier on been disobedient during the days of Noah, when God waited in patience. Noah built the ark, in which a few people, eight in fact, were rescued through water. [21]That functions as a signpost for you, pointing to baptism, which now rescues you – not by washing away fleshly pollution, but by the appeal to God of a good conscience, through the resurrection of Jesus the Messiah. [22]He has gone into heaven and is at God's right hand, with angels, authorities and powers subject to him.

The older I get, the more I dislike things which need to be put together, after you buy them, by following complicated instructions and diagrams. Part of my dislike is my sense that I will probably get it wrong, force something where it wasn't meant to go, and ruin the whole thing. Behind that is a lack of trust: sometimes the instructions and diagrams are not only unclear but actually inaccurate. Sometimes they describe another item, similar but not identical to the one we are trying to assemble.

The classic dilemma, when putting together something complicated out of many parts, is to finish the whole thing and then find that an important-looking part is still in the box. Morale sinks. Where should it go? What is it supposed to do? Why didn't we notice it before? We thought we were getting along quite nicely, but what shall we do now?

Many people have exactly that reaction when, after reading 1 Peter to this point, they suddenly stumble over chapter 3 verses 19, 20 and 21. We have become used to Peter warning his readers to expect suffering. He has already said that this may be inflicted by the authorities, even if in fact the Christians have done nothing to deserve it. He has already pointed out that this innocent suffering puts the **Messiah**'s people in the place where the Messiah himself had been, the victim of the worst injustice of all. But now, quite suddenly, he tells us four new things. First, after his death Jesus made a 'proclamation' to 'the spirits in prison'. Second, these spirits had been disobedient in the days of Noah. Third, Noah's building of an ark to rescue his family points forward to **baptism**. Fourth, baptism is less about washing clean and more about 'the appeal to God of a good conscience'. Here are not just one, but four elements which many readers might have preferred to leave in the box as they were mentally 'assembling' 1 Peter. What job are these pieces doing? What do they *mean*? How do they fit?

We should remind ourselves of what the passage is basically all about. It is an encouragement to people who are likely to suffer unjust treatment from the human authorities – not just, in other words, from a random act of mob violence or casual brutality, but an official, legal, persecution. And the point that Peter is making is not only that this brings them into line with the Messiah himself, who suffered in the same way. The point is that after his suffering *he announced God's victory over all 'authorities', particularly the ones in the heavenly places.* In other words, the point of these four elements, which may seem strange to us, is to add further dimensions to what he's already said about the new authorities. The human authorities embody 'spiritual' authorities which stand behind them in the shadowy, unseen realm. And Peter's point is that these complex authorities have received notice that Jesus has overthrown their power. He is now sovereign over the whole world, all other authorities included. That is why the passage ends with the emphatic claim that Jesus, through his **ascension** into **heaven**, now has 'angels, authorities and powers subject to him' (verse 22).

So how do these four apparently peculiar elements add up to this conclusion? Here there is a bit of local colour which will help. One of the better-known books in first-century Judaism, much treasured by many who were hoping for God to do some great act of liberation, was the one we know as *1 Enoch*. It wasn't actually written by the Enoch we find in Genesis 5.18–24, but it was written to look as though it was. This book traces the woes and problems of the world right back, in particular, to the wicked angels of Genesis 6, spiritual beings who, in the time of Noah, rebelled against God their creator. The book *1 Enoch* celebrates, in particular, the victory that God has won, or will win, over these spiritual beings. What Peter is saying here is that the victory over these dark forces of evil has in fact been won – through the Messiah; and that, after his **resurrection** (after he had been 'made alive by the **spirit**', as in verse 18), he, the Messiah, made this definitive announcement to the 'spirits': they had indeed been judged. Their power, such as it was, had been broken. This ought then to function as a considerable encouragement to the little groups of Christians who face persecution from their own local authorities, and from the shadowy spiritual 'forces' that seemed to give them their power. Ever since their original rebellion these 'forces' had been wielding usurped power. Now the Messiah has triumphed over them, and deep down they know it.

Noah's ark, then, comes into the frame. There was a widespread belief among not only Jews but also pagans in ancient Turkey that Noah and his ark had come to rest on a mountain in their region. Peter is appealing to a story that was well known in the wider culture. Since that story involved people being rescued through the great flood, it is a fairly obvious picture of **baptism**, which in Romans 6 is seen as the means of dying and rising with the Messiah. But baptism, the thing which marks out the Christian publicly from the world around, isn't just a matter of being made clean from one's former life, though it can be seen that way as well. Precisely because it functions as the boundary marker for the Christian community, it shapes the confrontation that must then take place between that community and the watching world. As Peter has already said in verse 16, this means that baptism provides the ground (through the **forgiveness** of our sins through Jesus' death) for that 'good conscience' which means that when the confrontation happens the Christian need not be ashamed.

The passage then really does fit together. These pieces, strange to us at first sight, really do belong where they are, and they mean what the opening and closing verses say they mean. What we need to know, when facing trouble or persecution, is this. Jesus the Messiah has fulfilled the hope of Israel by defeating all the spiritual powers in the world, the ones who were responsible for wickedness and corruption from ancient times. It may not look like it to the little Christian communities facing the possibility of suffering, but their baptism places them alongside the Messiah in his victory. They must hold their heads up, keep their consciences clear, and trust that his victory will be played out in the world to which they are bearing witness. There are many Christians today who need precisely this message. And those of us who don't think we do should learn it, partly to pray for our brothers and sisters who are being persecuted and partly against the day when we might well suddenly need it ourselves.

1 PETER 4.1-11

Transformed Living

¹So, then, just as the Messiah suffered in the flesh, you too must equip yourselves with the same mental armour. Someone who suffers in the flesh has ceased from sin, ²so as to live the rest of their mortal life no longer according to human desires but according to God's will. ³Pagan ways of life have had quite enough of your time already, and you should put all that behind you for good – all that uncleanness, passion, drunkenness, excessive feasting, drinking-parties and lawless idolatry. ⁴People are shocked that you don't now join in with the same wild and reckless behaviour, and so they call down curses on you. ⁵But they will have to account for it before the one who is ready to judge the living and the dead. ⁶That is why, you see, the gospel was preached even to the dead, so that, being judged in human fashion, in the flesh, they might live in God's fashion, in the spirit.

⁷The end of all things is upon us. You must keep sober, then, and self-disciplined for your prayers. ⁸Above all, keep absolutely firm in your love for one another, because 'love covers a multitude of sins'. ⁹Be hospitable to one another without complaining. ¹⁰Just as each of you has received a gift, so you should use it for ministry one to another, as good stewards of God's many-sided grace. ¹¹If anyone speaks, they should do so as speaking God's oracles. If anyone ministers, they should do it as in the strength which God grants, so that God may be glorified in all things through Jesus the Messiah, to whom be glory and power for ever and ever. Amen.

My dental hygienist was enthusing the other day about a new kind of electric toothbrush. Only two minutes, she said, morning and night; that's all it will take. Just what you need.

I lay there in the chair, my mouth full of dentistry, and did the maths. Two minutes twice a day is roughly two hours a month, which means twenty-four hours every year! Fancy spending *a whole day* every year cleaning my teeth! When you look at it in little bits it doesn't seem so much, but add it up and you realize just what an investment of time you are being asked to make. (And yes, I don't want my teeth to fall out in my old age, so I have bought the machine, and intend to use it.)

It is easy, almost fatally easy, to spend a lot of time on various pursuits far less worthwhile than cleaning our teeth. Add up the number of hours per week you watch television, or read in the newspaper about trivial events that amount to no more than gossip. Add up, if you dare, the time you not only fritter away but positively throw in the fire, doing things which you didn't need to do and didn't even particularly want to do, but into which you just drifted for want of anything better.

Now we begin to get the force of what Peter says in verse 3. 'Pagan ways of life have had quite enough of your time already!' Why should they have it any more? Nothing is to be gained from licentious and lawless behaviour. It merely wastes the time you could have been growing as a human being, discovering more about how God's love can transform your **life** and that of those around you. That, after all, is what you are here for (verses 8–11): there is plenty to occupy any Christian in reflecting God's love to others, in using to his glory the gifts we have been given. In particular, the positive, outgoing act of love is the most creative thing in the world. When Peter quotes (from Proverbs 10.12) the famous saying that 'love covers a multitude of sins', he doesn't mean, and Proverbs doesn't mean, that love is what we call a 'cover-up' operation, hiding things we'd rather not face. Rather, the gift of love we are invited to offer one another minute by minute, day by day throughout our lives actually *transforms* situations, so that the 'multitude of sins' which were there before are taken out of the equation. They are forgiven! We can be reconciled! Instead of squabbling and fighting, we can now live together and work together! All sorts of things will no doubt go wrong in human relations. That is how things are. But there is no need to despair. Abandon the old pagan ways, and learn the new habit of love. That will provide the answer.

So far, so good. But, as with the previous section, in the middle of this quite clear line of thought we have a genuinely puzzling passage. In fact, it appears at first sight to be saying something rather similar to what we found in 3.19–20. Perhaps, many have thought, Peter is talking about the same thing? When he here (verse 6) says that 'the **gospel** was preached even to the dead', are these the 'spirits in prison' of 3.19?

The best answer is, 'No, they are not.' Here, as there, the overall context is the vital thing. Peter, as ever, is encouraging those who have to face downright hostility because of their following of the **Messiah**, and because they refuse to go along with the wild and dehumanizing behaviour of those around (verses 3–4). But this will all be sorted out at the judgment. When that time comes, the wicked will have to give account of themselves. The pagan world can look on when a Christian dies and say, 'There you are! Now what's happened to your splendid "hope"?' It may even look, to the pagan, as though the Christians have lost the struggle. But these Christians, now dead, had already received the powerful **word** of the gospel which was preached to them during their lifetime (1.23–25). Thus, even though bodily death has come to them as a form of 'judgment' (compare Romans 8.10), their believing in the gospel during their lifetime means that now, by God's **spirit**, they are alive in God's presence, awaiting the **resurrection** which is yet to come.

For Peter, then, as for the whole of early Christianity, what had happened in Jesus' death and resurrection was the ushering in of a whole new world. 'The end of all things is upon us' (verse 7): this doesn't mean that the space-time universe is about to come to a shuddering halt (that would hardly be a vindication of the God who made it and loved it!), but that God has already begun, in Jesus, the process of cosmic renewal, the renewal whose sign and foretaste is the renewal of human lives through sharing Jesus' death and resurrection.

All this comes together in the opening command of chapter 4. Like the Messiah, we must put on the mental armour that will make us strong to face the suffering which we may have to face. And here suffering is given yet another meaning. Suffering, it seems, brings about a particular transformation of character. It makes you re-evaluate your whole life. Sometimes it happens that someone who has had a potentially fatal stroke or heart attack makes a remarkable recovery; in such cases people often say that they have rethought their whole lives, and now realize much more clearly what matters and what doesn't. In the same way, someone who has suffered for the gospel may attain a new kind of clarity. They see more sharply the kind of world that sin produces, and they know that they are done with it. And they see, far more gloriously, that God's will is the only thing worth following (verse 2).

Once again, Peter is treading a fine line. He is not glorifying suffering for its own sake. He is not saying you should go looking for it. But, just as the crucifixion of the Messiah was at the same time the most wicked thing humans ever did and the most powerfully loving thing God ever did, so the wickedness of those who persecute God's people forms the strange frame within which the power of God's transforming love can shine through all the more strongly.

1 PETER 4.12–19

Sharing the Messiah's Sufferings

[12]Beloved, don't be surprised at the fiery ordeal which is coming upon you to test you, as though this were some strange thing that was happening to you. [13]Rather, celebrate! You are sharing the sufferings of the Messiah. Then, when his glory is revealed, you will celebrate with real, exuberant joy. [14]If you are abused because of the name of the Messiah, you are blessed by God, because the spirit of glory and of God is resting upon you. [15]None of you, of course, should suffer as a murderer or thief or evildoer, or even as a busybody. [16]But if you suffer as a Christian, don't be ashamed; rather, give God the glory for that name! [17]The time has come, you see, for judgment to begin at God's own household. And if it begins with us, what will be the end of those

who do not obey the gospel? [18]And if the righteous person is scarcely saved, where will the ungodly and the sinner appear? [19]So also those who suffer according to God's will should entrust their whole lives to the faithful creator by doing what is good.

When the early English reformer William Tyndale was translating the New Testament into English, he was living in hiding, in exile in northern Europe. Translating the Bible into the vernacular language was strictly forbidden; the official clergy were worried that it would bring heresy into the church. Tyndale was short of funds for the project, and anxious to sell copies of the first edition of his translation so that he could fund further work and the revisions he knew were needed. But would people in England be prepared to buy his work, knowing they might get into trouble if they were found with it in their possession?

Then it happened. The Bishop of London got wind of the project and was furious. He was determined to stamp this nonsense out once and for all. So he commissioned his agents *to buy up all the copies they could find* and bring them together – to be burned! Little did he realize that he was feeding the problem he was trying to prevent. He got the books all right, and destroyed them. But the money he paid enabled Tyndale to move to the all-important second phase of the project. And it is his translation, though not always acknowledged, that forms the basis and the backbone for the world-famous King James Bible of 1611.

The argument of this passage of 1 Peter turns on a point like that, when something the opponent does actually serves to advance the cause. The heart of the passage is in verse 14: 'If you are abused because of the name of the **Messiah**, you are blessed by God, because the **spirit** of glory and of God is resting upon you.' The persecutors will lay a charge against you, in other words, that you belong to Jesus, known as Messiah. But the very naming of Jesus, and giving him his royal title, invokes Jesus himself in all his majesty and glory, and the curses the persecutor wants to call down on you turn into blessings instead.

As the **apostles** in Acts discovered, it is an enormous privilege to be labelled with the name of the Messiah (Acts 5.41). It means you are known as part of the royal family. But, more than that, the name itself carries power, and the Messiah as the chief **Temple**-builder (2.4–5) will come in his glorious spirit and dwell in your midst. Give God the glory for that splendid name, says Peter (verse 16)! That is the promise, however galling it would be to the persecutors if they did but know what they were doing.

The problem Peter is facing here is not simply that, by definition, nobody likes to be persecuted and ill-treated. That is a given. The underlying problem is that this must have come as a great surprise to the early Christians – to discover that even though the Messiah had been raised from the dead there was still a period of time, the time they themselves were living through, in which intense suffering would occur to his people. Had he not defeated all the powers of sin and death? Why should this still be happening?

In answer, Peter once more invokes memories of Israel's scriptures. This time he is thinking particularly of the (to us) quite difficult book of Zechariah. There, in a passage which Jesus himself quoted on the night he was betrayed (Mark 14.27), the prophet speaks of the 'shepherd' who is to be struck and killed, with the sheep being scattered (Zechariah 13.7). Jesus himself seems to have seen that as a prophecy of his own death. But, immediately after that, those who remain of his followers are to be put into the fire to be refined like silver or gold (Zechariah 13.9). The effect of the 'shepherd's' death is not in question. Jesus has rescued his people from the power of evil. But they are still to expect this time of 'fiery ordeal' (verse 12). It isn't something strange. It's what the scriptures had foretold. It is not pleasant to be persecuted. But if, when it happens, you can see it as a road sign, telling you that you are on the right path, that may make all the difference.

Once again Peter reminds his readers that they must see everything that is happening in the light of the final judgment which is yet to occur. The outcome is not in doubt: Jesus will vindicate his faithful people. But even for them the thought ought to be sobering. Judgment will begin – not with the obviously wicked, but with God's own household (verse 17).

The fact that God's faithful people are assured of ultimate **salvation** does not make this any less serious. As Paul insisted in 1 Corinthians 3.12–15, there will be a judgment for Christians too, and though genuine Christians will be saved, some will be saved 'only as through fire'. Peter puts it even more strongly here in verse 18: the righteous person is scarcely saved! From God's perspective, the holiest, most loving person is still someone who needs to be rescued, and is still so weighed down with sin that without the grace and mercy shown through Jesus that rescue would not happen.

This alarming reflection is not meant to produce panic, but rather gratitude. Those who are at present persecuting the church will meet their own judgment in due course, and God's people are called in the meantime to **faith** and patience. In particular, they should 'entrust their whole lives' to God, their faithful creator. We might expect this to mean that they should pray, day by day, giving over their lives to God; and no doubt this will be true as well. But Peter says something a bit different. They are to entrust their lives to God *by doing what is good*. This doesn't just mean rule-keeping, keeping your nose clean, not getting into trouble. 'Doing good' is much more positive than that. It means bringing fresh goodness, fresh love, fresh kindness, fresh wisdom into the community, into the family, to the people we meet on the street. When we do this, we are not saying 'Look at me, aren't I being good?' We are saying, to God, 'I trust you; this is what you have called me to do; this is what I am doing with the **life** you've given me; even though I am facing suffering, I will continue to be this sort of a person, to your glory'. Part of Christian faith is the settled belief that God is faithful, and that we can rely on him utterly at this point as at all others, and get on with the task of bringing his light and love into the world.

1 PETER 5.1–7

Humble Shepherds

¹So, then, I appeal to the elders among you, as a fellow-elder and a witness of the sufferings of the Messiah, and as one who will share in the glory that is to be revealed. ²Do the proper work of a shepherd as you look after God's flock which has been entrusted to you, not under compulsion, but gladly, as in God's presence, not for shameful profit but eagerly. ³You should not lord it over those for whom you are responsible, but rather be an example to the flock. ⁴And when the chief shepherd appears, you will receive the crown of glory that won't wither away. ⁵In the same way, too, the younger men should submit to the elders. But let all of you clothe yourselves with humility towards one another. You see, 'God resists the proud, but gives grace to the lowly'. ⁶Humble yourselves, then, under God's powerful hand, so that he may lift you up at the right time. ⁷Throw all your care upon him, because he cares about you.

From time to time the television or the newspapers tell us that there is a crisis of 'leadership'. What that means, often enough, is that the media disapprove of the actual political leaders we happen to have at the moment, but even without that rather cynical observation I find myself anxious about discussion of 'leadership' in a vacuum. Sometimes, when I have been asked to give talks on the subject, I have begun by saying either that I don't really believe in 'leadership', or that I don't think it's the most important category – certainly not in the way it is often talked about today.

What I find is that anything worth calling 'leadership' happens, often without people thinking about it as such, when someone is so energetically and productively involved in whatever it is, whether making music or running a business, whether organizing a market stall or heading up a government department, that they communicate that energy and productivity, that enthusiasm and effectiveness, to those around them. Leadership, in other words, is a bit like friendship: it's something that happens best when you're not thinking about leadership (or friendship, as it might be), but about whatever it is that you're actually doing together.

Come to think of it, 'happiness' falls into the same category. If you start the day thinking, 'Now: what will make me happy today?' you are less likely to be happy than if you think, 'Now, the sooner I can start painting that picture/going for that walk/playing with the grandchildren the better!' I would rather belong to a group or a **fellowship** where the 'leader' had no idea about 'leadership', but was out-and-out committed to God and the **gospel**, than one where the person in charge had done three or four courses on 'leadership' but had found it left little time for studying scripture or for praying.

Now I know there's more to it than that. Any 'leadership' experts reading this will no doubt shake their heads at me as another hopeless case who just doesn't get it. But I have to say that today, whether in church or in society, what we need is people who care deeply about the state of the community and the wider society; people who have studied the relevant issues with professional attention; people who listen to what all sorts of other people have to say; and people who can articulate and communicate the vision to which they have come in such a way as to help others to share it as well. Now of course the 'experts' might say, 'But that's what we mean by "leadership".' If it is, well and good. But let's study and practise the thing itself, not some abstract category removed from reality.

What Peter is describing here is not 'leaders' but shepherds. And the point about 'shepherds' is that the best of them aren't thinking, 'How can I be a shepherd?', but, 'How can I best look after these sheep?' The focus of the good shepherd is not only on his or her own qualities but on the needs of, and potential dangers for, those they are looking after. That, of course, is the first main point Peter makes here (verse 2): don't think about your own profit, but rather about the needs of the flock. Peter appeals as himself an 'elder' – the word means 'senior', both in the sense of status within the community and in the sense of older in years, and the two of course often go together – who has responsibilities like this and hence knows what he's talking about.

In particular, Peter has learnt well from Jesus himself the central thing about being God's under-shepherds: don't lord it over them, but be an example (verse 3). I was recently visiting a large college which trains army officers, and to my surprise and delight met, at almost every turn, the college's motto: 'Serve to Lead'. This isn't an empty slogan: they mean it, model it and teach it. Unless an officer is *serving* the soldiers in the unit – thinking about them as people, getting to know who they are, what they are afraid of, what makes them give of their best, and looking after them in those and all other ways – they will simply not be able to *lead* them in any difficult or dangerous situations. Thus, whether we are talking about the 'younger men' (verse 5) or the 'elders', all should clothe themselves 'with humility'. We hear so much of humility within early Christian writing that it's easy to forget that, until this strange movement of Jesus and his followers, nobody outside a narrow strand within the Jewish tradition had regarded it as a virtue. Something has happened to generate an entirely different way of going about things.

No prize for guessing what it is that 'has happened'. *Jesus* 'has happened', has announced God's **kingdom**, has died and been raised and enthroned. He is 'the chief shepherd' (verse 4), who will reappear when **heaven** and earth are brought together at last. He will be the model, the standard by which all other 'shepherds' are to be judged. Jesus himself drew heavily on the biblical traditions about God's desire to 'shepherd' his people Israel. In a rural economy, it's hardly surprising that this is one of the standard images for the way in which either God himself, or the anointed king, are to look after the 'sheep', to make sure they are fed, and to protect them from predators. A glance at Psalm 23 or Ezekiel 34 will show where some of this comes from. A further glance at Luke 15.3–7 and John 10.1–16 will show you what Jesus himself made of it. And a further glance at John 21.15–19 gives us a sharp and intimate glimpse of Peter himself being recommissioned as a 'shepherd' of Jesus' followers after the disaster of his earlier denials.

The normal 'worldly' way of 'leadership', of course, is to boss and nag, to threaten and punish. You may be able to get sheep to do what you want that way, but they will be neither happy nor healthy. Such an approach may look 'strong', but it is in fact weak. The call to be a humble shepherd is the call to the true strength in which one doesn't have to shout or bully, because the work of humble service has forged such a strong bond between shepherd and sheep that the shepherd only needs to walk towards the pasture and the sheep will follow.

Of course, it frequently doesn't seem as easy as that. A shepherd's task remains challenging. Perhaps that is why Peter finishes this exhortation with the remarkable invitation to throw all our cares on God himself. The verb is a strong one: pick up everything that is bothering you, everything that is weighing you down, and fling them on God's back. He will carry them. He will be delighted to do so. He loves you, after all.

1 PETER 5.8-14

Standing Firm by God's Power

⁸Stay in control of yourselves; stay awake. Your enemy, the devil, is stalking around like a roaring lion, looking for someone to devour. ⁹Resist him, staying resolute in your faith, and knowing that other family members in the rest of the world are facing identical sufferings. ¹⁰Then, after you have suffered a little while, the God of all grace, who called you in Messiah Jesus to the glory of his new age, will himself put you in good order, and will establish and strengthen you and set you on firm foundations. ¹¹To him be the power for ever. Amen.

¹²I have written this briefly, and am sending it to you with Silvanus, whom I regard as a faithful brother. My main point is to urge and bear witness to you that you are indeed standing in the true grace of God. ¹³Your chosen sister in Babylon sends you greetings; so does my son Mark. ¹⁴Greet one another with a holy kiss.

Peace to you all in the Messiah.

One of the great advances in tropical medicine came when researchers discovered how malaria was spread. They had been trying to treat the disease for a long time, but it seemed hopeless. As fast as you helped one patient, three more were contracting the disease. Then, one day, someone realized that it was the mosquito, of which there were millions, especially in low-lying and damp tropical regions, that was carrying the illness this way and that. Once they realized what the real enemy was, new steps could be taken, such as draining the swamps where mosquitoes had been breeding near human habitations, and inventing new kinds of netting so that people could sleep without being attacked by the nasty little insects. Malaria is still very unpleasant, but it is far less of a problem now that we know what's causing it.

For most of the time in this letter we have been aware of persecution coming from the surrounding non-Christian culture. Part of it will have been unofficial, simply involving ordinary people sneering, criticizing, ostracizing or using occasional violence. Some of it, though, will have been official, as the local authorities took a hand and made life difficult for the Christians. How easy it will have been, as it still is, for the Christians then to demonize their visible, human opponents, to regard them as the real source of the problem. Now at last we see that this isn't the case. There is a real enemy. Like the mosquito, this enemy is seriously dangerous, particularly when ignored.

Peter, however, uses a more obvious animal as the image to describe the enemy. The enemy is like a roaring lion, looking for someone to swallow up. The word Peter uses is far more than simply 'eat'; it implies that the lion will simply gulp you down in a single mouthful. No time to protest or struggle. You'll be gone.

It's a terrifying image, and one which alerts us at once to the serious nature of the Christian life. Too many Christians soft-pedal the idea of actual spiritual warfare, of a real confrontation with a real devil. As C. S. Lewis said when writing about his world-famous book *The Screwtape Letters*, consisting of letters from a senior devil to a junior one on how to tempt people, some people dismiss the idea of a devil by thinking of a ridiculous little person with horns and hooves wearing red tights. They can't believe in a creature like that, so they decide they can't believe in the devil. Other people become so fascinated with the devil that they can think of little else, and suppose that every ordinary problem in life, or difficulty in someone else's personality, is due to direct devilish intervention. Lewis steers a wise path between these two extremes, and so should we. But perhaps, for many of my readers, the danger may be more in ignoring the tempter than in overdramatising him.

The thing about recognizing the existence and power of the devil, and learning to see him behind not only temptations to sin but also persecution and suffering, is that this enables you to take the position which the rest of the letter has been advocating. When, two hundred years ago, many Western countries took a decisive move towards democracy, this was sometimes (not always) accompanied by a resolute dismissal of God, or public religion, from the civic and social stage. We were the masters now! But the danger with that, as has been apparent throughout the last two centuries, is that once you get rid of God you get rid, too, of the devil; and then you yourself, and your friends, or your party, or your country, take the role of God, *while your enemies take the role of the devil.* And that leads to disaster.

The whole letter has been insisting, on the contrary, that the way to respond to attacks of whatever sort is with a firm but gentle **faith**, treating non-Christians with respect, living within the law (except, as in Acts, when it tries to force you into denying Jesus), behaving with humility and patience in all circumstances. The point is this. The actual, human opponents, even your fiercest persecutors, are not in fact the real enemy. There is a real enemy, and he will be using them. But if you resist him, staying resolute in faith and remembering that you are holding your bit of the line while your Christian brothers and sisters across the world are holding theirs, you will find that courteous and civil behaviour, acting with respect and gentleness, will again and again win an answering respect from outsiders, even if they still don't understand what makes you tick.

The picture then falls into place. The devil will try to swallow you whole with persecution and other attacks. If that isn't working, he will try to tempt you to live in ways that are destructive of your faith and, ultimately, of your entire humanity (see 1.14; 2.11; and so on). That will go on for a while, and it may well (to put it mildly) be most unpleasant. But, as Peter explained in the previous chapter, this 'fiery trial' is there to do for us what the fire will do for silver and gold: to consume the imperfections and make the true metal shine the more brightly. That bright shining will consist of God's setting right of all things – eventually, as we know, and perhaps in various ways even in the present time. He will 'establish and strengthen you', and 'set you on firm foundations'. Many Christians, much of the time, feel insecure and wobbly in their faith. The promise of firm foundations is one to which we should cling with delight – especially as it is backed up by the promise that all power belongs to God (verse 11).

As so often with ancient letters (and early Christian letters are no exception), we find, at the end, just a flicker of a hint about the actual circumstances of writing. We don't know whether 'Silvanus', who is taking this letter to the churches in Turkey, is the same person who is called 'Silas', one of Paul's companions in Acts ('Silas' and 'Silvanus' being variant forms of the same name), or indeed the 'Silvanus' mentioned by Paul as being with him when he was writing 1 and 2 Thessalonians. It may have been quite a common name. Nor can we be absolutely sure that when Peter says 'Babylon' in verse 13 this is really code for 'Rome', as in the book of Revelation. Mark, mentioned as 'my son', is almost certainly the John Mark we meet in Acts, and again at the end of Colossians, Philemon and 2 Timothy.

But the real point of interest in the closing verses is the one Peter highlights at the end of verse 12: 'this grace, in which you stand, is the true grace of God'. Using the letter as an angled mirror in which to glimpse what was going on in the churches to which it was addressed, it's safe to say that the small groups of believers in ancient Turkey must have been very concerned that the persecution which was now increasing meant that they were on the wrong road; that they had taken a false turning; that they had given their allegiance to Jesus as a false **Messiah**. Otherwise why would these things still be happening? Peter's solid reassurance has been based on scripture, based on his sense of how God's purpose was always going to work out, and based above all on Jesus himself. Hold on to his death and **resurrection**, he says. That's the sheet anchor. He is the true Messiah, and one day he will be publicly revealed as such. This is the true grace of God; stand firm in it. And – the note that we all need, especially when the going is tough: peace. Peace to you from God. Peace to you in the Messiah.

2 PETER

2 PETER 1.1-11

Confirm Your Call!

[1]Simon Peter, a slave and apostle of Jesus the Messiah, to those who have obtained a share of faith equal to ours in the righteousness of our God and saviour Jesus the Messiah: [2]may grace and peace be multiplied to you, in the knowledge of God and of Jesus our Lord.

[3]God has bestowed upon us, through his divine power, everything that we need for life and godliness, through the knowledge of him who called us by his own glory and virtue. [4]The result is that he has given us, through these things, his precious and wonderful promises; and the purpose of all this is so that you may run away from the corruption of lust that is in the world, and may become partakers of the divine nature. [5]So, because of this, you should strain every nerve to supplement your faith with virtue, and your virtue with knowledge, [6]and your knowledge with self-control, and your self-control with patience, and your patience with piety, [7]and your piety with family affection, and your family affection with love. [8]If you have these things in plentiful supply, you see, you will not be wasting your time, or failing to bear fruit, in relation to your knowledge of our Lord Jesus the Messiah. [9]Someone who doesn't have these things, in fact, is so shortsighted as to be actually blind, and has forgotten what it means to be cleansed from earlier sins. [10]So, my dear family, you must make the effort all the more to confirm that God has called you and chosen you. If you do this, you will never trip up. [11]That is how you will have, richly laid out before you, an entrance into the kingdom of God's coming age, the kingdom of our Lord and saviour Jesus the Messiah.

My grandson, aged one and a half, was taken the other day into a big toyshop. It was a riot of exciting things, all in bright colours. From floor to ceiling, from one end of the shop to the other, and all over the tables and stands in the middle, there were so many exciting things to see that he didn't know where to start. He looked quickly this way and that, then round, then up and down. He was in happy shock at this overload of delight. All he could say – one of his few words, but most expressive – was, 'WOW'.

That's a bit how I feel on reading quickly through the beginning of the letter we call 2 Peter. (Some people doubt that it was written by Peter himself, but several parts of it indicate that it is indeed supposed to come from him in some sense, even if he didn't physically write it himself.) Every sentence, every word almost, glitters and flashes. Every idea beckons and says, 'Look at me! This is fascinating!' And it is. But if we are to make a start it will be good to see the big picture within which all this cluster of exciting and challenging ideas means what it means.

The big picture is *what God wants for his people*. All too often, people think that 'religion', or even 'Christian **faith**', is about what God wants *from* us – good behaviour, renunciation of things we like, a gritted-teeth morality of forcing ourselves to behave unnaturally. This is a total caricature. Here, in this breathtaking paragraph from verses 3 to 11, we see the truth.

First, God has already given us everything we need: a starter kit, if you like, for all that we need to become (verse 3). There is indeed quite a lot in this letter about the moral effort we have to make. But Peter is quite clear. It all comes from God in the first place.

Second, he wants nothing less for us than that we should come to share his own very nature (verse 4). Some Christians have felt uneasy about this idea, as though the humility to which we are so often exhorted ought to stop us short from thinking of actually sharing God's very being or nature. Others, though (particularly in the Eastern Christian traditions), have seen this as central to what it means to be a Christian. After all, if we say that the **holy spirit** is fully divine, and if we say that the holy spirit comes to live within us and transform us from within, what is that but to say that the divine nature is already dwelling within us, leading us forward until we are suffused with God's own presence and power? Obviously for most of us, most of the time, it won't feel like that. But that may be because we are not yet adept at recognizing what actually happens when God takes up residence in someone's life. More of that as the letter progresses.

Third, God has indeed called and chosen those who find themselves following Jesus (verse 10). In this verse Peter urges his readers to 'confirm' this call and choice. He doesn't mean that they can make *God* more sure of it; rather, they can make themselves more sure. This leads directly to the fourth point: God has already set up his '**kingdom**', his sovereign rule over earth as well as **heaven** (verse 11). When 'the **age to come**' has fully and finally arrived (again, there will be more on this in due course) those who in the present time follow Jesus will find that they are welcomed into that ultimate heaven-and-earth reality.

All this is just the outer framework for this remarkable passage, but it is all the more important because it shows that whatever *we* do by way of obedience and allegiance to God and the **gospel**, it all takes place within the grace of God, by means of the promise of God, through the power of God, and leading to the kingdom of God. That's a great place to start.

But it's not a good place to stop, because, as you will have noticed, the passage has plenty more besides. Central to it all is the idea that, by God's grace and power in our lives, we are to learn the discipline of Christian moral development. This has sometimes been frowned upon, as though it was, after all, 'me making myself good enough for God', and leading to pride or arrogance ('See what a fine Christian I've become!'). The framework I've just sketched should make it clear that nothing could be farther from the truth. But once this point is grasped, there are two basic things which must happen.

The first is that we must 'run away from the corruption of lust', in order to become partakers of God's own nature. Interesting, isn't it, that we are told to resist the devil (1 Peter 5.9), but, both here and in 2 Timothy 2.22, to run away from the lust which drags us down to the subhuman level. The word for 'run away from' is sometimes translated as 'shun', as though merely pushing these things away, like someone refusing a second helping of food, were enough, but neither Paul nor Peter is satisfied with that. Think of Joseph when Potiphar's wife tried to seduce him (Genesis 39). She made a grab at him, but he ran away. That isn't cowardice. A coward, as a wise old writer once put it, saves his prospects at the cost of his honour; Joseph did the opposite. Both Paul and Peter want us to do the same.

This running away from the lusts of the flesh isn't a negative thing, despite what people will rather frantically tell you today. Lust is a drug. Like all drugs it demands more and more but gives less and less. It turns people into shadows of real human beings. Like shady financial dealings, it 'corrupts': it does to the moral fibre what cancer does to physical cells.

Peter is urging his readers to go in the opposite direction. Become more fully human, he says, by building one aspect of Christian character on top of another: faith, virtue, knowledge, self-control, patience, piety, family affection, and finally love. All these take thought; all these take effort. They don't happen by accident. You have to want to do them; you have to choose to do them. But when you do, and pray for God's grace, promises and power to help, you will be coming to know Jesus the **Messiah**. And in that knowledge you won't just be a Christian for your own sake, as it were. You will become fruitful in God's service (verse 8).

2 PETER 1.12–21

Prophecy Made Sure

¹²So I intend to go on and on reminding you about all this – even though you know it, and have been firmly established in the truth which has come to you. ¹³But it seems right to me, as long as I am living in this present tent, to stir you up with a reminder, ¹⁴since I know that I shall shortly be putting off this tent, as our Lord Jesus the Messiah showed me. ¹⁵So I shall also be making every effort to ensure

that, once I am gone, you may be able to call these things to mind at any time.

¹⁶You see, when we made known to you the power and appearing of our Lord Jesus the Messiah, we were not following cleverly devised myths. Rather, we were eyewitnesses of his grandeur. ¹⁷For when he received honour and glory from God the father, a voice spoke to him from the Wonderful Glory, 'This is my son, my beloved one, in whom I am well pleased.' ¹⁸We heard this voice, spoken from heaven, when we were with him on the holy mountain. ¹⁹And we have the prophetic word made more certain. You will do well to hold on to this, as to a lamp shining in a dark place, until the day dawns and the morning star shines in your hearts. ²⁰You must know this first of all, that no scriptural prophecy is a matter of one's own interpretation. ²¹No prophecy, you see, ever came by human will. Rather, people were moved by the holy spirit, and spoke from God.

I am writing this in the middle of winter. First thing in the morning, when I get up, there is no sunlight visible at all. The sky is dark. But, if the clouds are not too thick, there is a light which from ancient times has been seen as an early herald of dawn: 'the morning star', though actually it's a planet, Venus. It isn't always, of course, in that place in the sky. But very often it is, and functions as a sign that morning is on the way. So it was this morning.

For Peter, 'the morning star' which 'shines in your hearts' (verse 19) is the promise of Jesus himself, returning at last to signal that God's great coming day is about to dawn. Everything the early Christians believed had this as its further horizon: that the time would surely come when what had begun with Jesus would be completed at his return, his reappearance.

That helps us to understand why Peter says what he does in verses 12–15. He knows his own time to die is drawing near. Jesus had warned him of this (John 21.18–19), and verse 14 may refer to a later word which Peter had received. But it was important to be sure that his readers would be able to hold on to the truths which he had taught. The death of an **apostle** must not mean the decline of the apostolic **faith**.

But we don't simply have to wait in darkness for the morning star to appear. Jesus has already been revealed, to Peter, James and John, as they stood with him on the mount of transfiguration (Mark 9.2–8). This is the only time outside the first three **gospels** that anyone refers to the 'transfiguration', the time when Jesus was suddenly radiant with light, talking with Moses and Elijah, and when a voice from **heaven** proclaimed that he was indeed God's son. This story, Peter insists, is not a 'cleverly devised myth'. Presumably by this stage in the early church some of the opponents of the faith were scoffing at the extraordinary tales that were going around about Jesus. Peter insists that it was the truth.

The result of this eyewitness testimony is that the apostles could look back on the entire world of biblical prophecy – that great, untidy, all-over-the-place story which functioned all through as a set of signposts pointing forward to what was to come – and could see that in retrospect it all made sense. Among the great prophecies, indeed, was that of the 'star' that would arise from Jacob (Numbers 24.17). This was widely understood at the time as a prophecy of the **Messiah**, and it may well have supplied Peter with the inspiration for the idea of Jesus as 'the morning star' in verse 19. What Peter is saying, then, is that the stories of Jesus, reaching something of a climax in the extraordinary revelation of glory at the transfiguration, mean that one can now read the entire ancient Jewish scriptures knowing the end from the beginning, and can see with God-given hindsight how everything came rushing together at the point where the Messiah himself emerged. The revelation of God's glory in him, indeed, goes closely with the promise that we, too, will come to 'share in the divine nature'. This letter is unique in bringing these two together.

Peter is thus addressing the new situation that had emerged, for which no ancient Jew had, as it were, a road map. Everything had been straining forward to the day when God's glory would be revealed, the **Temple** would be rebuilt, and the Messiah would appear to save his people. Well, that had happened, so the early Christians believed, even though it didn't look like they had thought it would: the coming of Jesus simply *was* the fulfilment of all those aspirations. His **resurrection** – and, indeed, his transfiguration – proved it. But nobody had ever imagined that there would then be a further time lag *between* the time of the Messiah's appearance and the time of the final end, the final dawning of the great day. There were no speculations about what such an interim period might be like, or even why such a period should exist.

So Peter, like the other apostles, went to work to explain, from the scriptures, why such a delay was happening and what one should be doing in the meantime. Christians from that day to this are in the position he outlines in verse 19: Jesus, his coming, transfiguration, death and resurrection has confirmed the prophetic words of scripture, and we hold on to these, like people clinging to a bright lamp through the darkest time of the night, until the day when Jesus reappears at last as the morning star, ready to usher in God's final great day.

But now another possible objection rears its head. Supposing this way of reading scripture is all a Christian invention? Supposing the Bible never meant all that in the first place? Peter has a firm word for such suggestions (verses 20 and 21). It isn't a matter of private interpretation. It isn't up to us – because scripture itself didn't come about in the first place by individuals simply deciding to write this or that. Yes, the Bible contains a remarkably wide range of material, from poetry and history to prophecy and strange symbolic revelations. But behind the different genres, and the different authors, was the divine inspiration, not bypassing the human minds, personalities and situations in question but working through them to breathe God's **word** through human words. 'People were moved by the **holy spirit**, and spoke from God.' Sometimes, we may suppose, they were aware of it (Amos? Jeremiah?) and sometimes they probably weren't (Ecclesiastes?). That's not the point. The point is that, for us looking back, Jesus himself stands there as the fulfilment of it all. Like all other early Christians, Peter holds firm to two things: the ancient scriptures, and the newly revealed **son of God**. Until we see him, we don't understand where they were going. Until we understand *them*, we don't see the point of who *he* was and what he did. We need the scriptures and the son, prophecy made sure. And we need to hold on to both until the morning star shines in our hearts, and then, through us, shines out into the world.

2 PETER 2.1–10a

False Prophets

> ¹There were, however, false prophets among the people, just as there will be false teachers among yourselves, who will sneak in with their destructive false teachings, even denying the master who paid the price for them. They will earn swift destruction for themselves, ²and many will follow after their disgusting practices. The way of truth will be blasphemed because of them, ³and in their greed they will exploit you with fake prophecies. For a long time now, their condemnation has not been idle, and their destruction has not fallen asleep.
>
> ⁴God didn't spare the angels who sinned, you see, but he threw them into the pit, into dark caverns, handing them over to be guarded until the time of judgment. ⁵Similarly, he didn't spare the ancient world, but brought a flood on the world of the ungodly and rescued Noah, a herald of righteousness, with seven others. ⁶Similarly, he condemned the cities of Sodom and Gomorrah, reducing them to ashes and ruin, thus setting up an example of what would happen to the ungodly. ⁷He snatched righteous Lot out of the disaster, a man who had been deeply troubled by their shameful and unprincipled behaviour. ⁸That righteous man, you see, living in their midst, could see and hear day after day lawless deeds which tortured his righteous soul. ⁹The Lord knows how to rescue the godly from testing, and also how

to keep the unrighteous ready for the day of judgment and punishment, [10a]especially those who follow after the pollution of fleshly lust and despise authority.

'I told you it was easy to get lost.'

Our host stood on the doorstep with a wry smile on his face. We had assumed we more or less knew the way. We have a good sense of direction. We had even been there before; surely we would remember the route once we saw the landmarks? But no: we had taken at least one wrong turning, and there wasn't an obvious way to cut across country and get back on track. So we had driven round back streets in small towns, trying to find a road that would put things right, and all the time worrying they would think we weren't coming (this was in the days before mobile phones).

No harm was done, except to our pride. But the lesson is obvious. Don't just assume, because you're a cheerful sort of person and don't like to think about possible problems, that the way will be clear and simple. It very often won't be. And this applies especially in that long, twisting, complicated journey called Christian discipleship.

How we wish things weren't like this. We would like, of course, a nice straight path, a smooth and easy road, so that we could follow Jesus cheerfully and without the worry that we might at any minute take a wrong turning. But, as Jesus himself warned us, things are not like that. Even among his own followers there was one whom he once called 'satan', and another one who did eventually do the satan's work for him.

And now Peter, remembering perhaps how easily he himself had been led astray, utters a stern warning against false teachers and prophets. How we wish this sort of thing wasn't necessary! Wouldn't it be kinder, gentler, more . . . well, more *Christian*, to assume that people who claim to be speaking the truth, to be teaching the Christian way, are doing so in fact? Surely we shouldn't have such suspicious minds?

Well, the same early Christians who tell us to be kind and gentle also tell us to be on our guard against being deceived. Jesus himself told us to be not only innocent as doves but also wise as serpents. It's a difficult combination. But we won't get very far in the right direction unless we work hard on both sides of our character.

Here, obviously, Peter is going for the wisdom of the serpent. There are false prophets and false teachers; the problem is that they don't wear a label round their necks giving the game away. The devastating thing about such prophets and teachers *is that they sound all too plausible*. When you listen to them, your first impression is, 'Yes: this is good; this is what we need to hear. It may not be quite what I expected, but I like the sound of it.' Sometimes, of course, that is the sign that the teaching is genuine and true. There are indeed times when what we've heard before needs to be expanded, or seen in a different light. But sometimes this is a sign that all is not well. There is such a thing as paranoia, jumping straight to accusations of wicked heresy when in fact what is on offer is freshly glimpsed truth. But there is also, alas, such a thing as deliberately shutting your eyes to things, assuming or pretending that something is all right when in fact it's all wrong. A church, or an individual Christian, that cannot tell the difference, or that assumes everything is always going to be more or less 'all right', is in deep danger.

So Peter is putting up a sign which says, 'Danger this way!' Right off the top he is offering danger signs. False teaching will regularly 'deny the Master', saying that Jesus is only one among many teachers, or that perhaps his death didn't really 'pay the price' (verse 1). False teaching will encourage 'disgusting practices' – Peter isn't more specific at this point, but even the general warning ought to put us on the alert (verse 2). Is this teaching telling people that behaviour which most Christians have found abhorrent is all right after all? Then he warns that 'the way of truth will be blasphemed': outsiders will look at such would-be Christian teachers and find them a soft target at which to fire their blasphemous barbs. Finally (verse 3) they may use their fake prophecies as a way of boosting income. Nothing like some strange ideas to get people buying books or signing on for lecture courses. There are always plenty of people who want to be told that proper full-blooded Christian **faith** and **life** is a mistake and that there's an easier way.

Before he goes into any more detail, Peter sends his readers back to stories they might be more familiar with than we are. These stories are all drawn from the early chapters of Genesis, and they reflect subsequent Jewish traditions in which the plots, and the characters, are developed a bit further. Peter isn't simply highlighting the dangers of false teaching and behaviour, and the fact that God will bring judgment upon such things. He is more encouraging than that. He is stressing that God will rescue his people out of the mess. Judgment and mercy: those are the solid promises upon which you can rely.

The first example refers back to the famous story of the wicked angels in Genesis 6. God has kept them guarded until the day of judgment. But judgment was swifter in the second case, that of the world at the time of Noah; and also in the third case, the destruction of Sodom and Gomorrah and the rescue of Lot. In each case, we should note, the wickedness to be judged, from which God rescues people, is not so much fancy or off-beam teaching about theoretical matters, but the practices which give the game away: sin, ungodliness and shameful and unprincipled behaviour.

Again, Peter isn't very specific, but the general sense is clear. When teachers emerge who remove the normal restraint that Christian faith, like Judaism, had imposed on human desires, we should beware. The deadly combination at which he points in verse 10a has a sharper focus: 'those who follow after the pollution of fleshly lust and despise authority'. It would be a bold person who claimed that no such problems existed in today's church. It is easy to get on the wrong road – easier than you might think.

The underlying point, though, is the positive one, and Peter states it clearly in verse 9. You are not left to your own devices. Yes, you will be tested, and yes, wicked and unscrupulous people will appear to flourish. But God is not mocked. He knows how to rescue his people from the test. And he knows how to keep the wicked ready for the day of judgment. God's judgment and mercy are, if you like, the twin characteristics which correspond to the command that we should be wise as serpents and innocent as doves. Life would be very pleasant if it was all mercy and innocence. But it isn't. It's easy to get lost.

2 PETER 2.10b–22

From Bad to Worse

¹⁰ᵇSuch people are arrogant and self-willed! They are not afraid to blaspheme the glorious ones, ¹¹whereas the angels, stronger and more powerful though they are, do not bring a charge of blasphemy against them before the Lord.

¹²These people are like unreasoning beasts, by nature born to be caught and destroyed. They curse at things of which they have no knowledge; they are destroyed by their own self-destructive tendencies. ¹³They commit injustice, and receive injustice as their reward. They count it pleasure to hold wild revels in the daytime. If they join you for a meal, they pollute and stain the whole thing as they wallow in their disgusting pleasures. ¹⁴Their eyes are full of adultery; they can't get enough of sin; when they find unsteady souls, they lead them astray; their hearts have been trained in greed; they are children of the curse. ¹⁵They have left the straight path and have wandered off in pursuit of Balaam son of Bosor, who loved the reward of unrighteousness, ¹⁶and was rebuked for his disobedience when a normally speechless donkey spoke in a human voice to stop the prophet's madness in its tracks.

¹⁷These people are springs without water. They are patches of fog driven along by a storm. The depth of darkness has been reserved for them! ¹⁸They utter bombastic words of folly as they entice, with licentious fleshly desires, those who have only just escaped from the company of people who behave improperly. ¹⁹They promise them freedom,

but they themselves are slaves to corruption. (A person who is defeated by something, you see, is enslaved to it.) [20]For if they have fled the pollutions of the world through the knowledge of our Lord and saviour Jesus the Messiah, but again become entangled in them and are defeated, they have ended up in a worse state than they were before. [21]It would have been better for them never to have known the way of righteousness than, having known it, to turn away from the holy commandment which had been given to them. [22]There is a true proverb which now applies to them: the dog returns to its own vomit, and the sow gets washed only to wallow once more in the mud.

A year or two ago I was invited to dinner with some friends, who had also invited a judge. I don't often meet senior members of the legal profession, and I was intrigued to hear what he might say about his work.

My anticipation turned to shock when he told me what he'd been doing that day . . . and the day before, and the day before that and so on. His world, he explained, was very far from the glamorous vision you see in the TV dramas (though now, of course, some countries allow actual trials to be broadcast, so the harsh reality is all too apparent). Most of what a judge has to deal with, in his part of the profession at least, is a sad and sordid procession of people whose lives have become hopelessly murky and muddled – in and out of different relationships, in and out of debt and financial problems, in and out of jail. Everyone who goes that route drags other people down with them. That brings its own trail of personal bitterness, mutual accusations, fault-finding, self-justifying – and sometimes then self-hatred, self-harm and even suicide. It's a horrible, dark world, said the judge; and now, since he was off duty, could we please talk about something more pleasant? Had I listened to any good music recently?

For most of us, most of the time, the dark reality is hidden. It goes on in back streets and back rooms, and in the twisted and self-deceived minds – not only, I should say, of the poor and ill-educated, but also of apparently 'nice' and civilized professional people: teachers, doctors, even clergy. Even judges. But if we imagined it wasn't there we would be living in a fool's paradise.

Our present passage from 2 Peter is a bit like that judge's catalogue of sad and sordid behaviour. Peter is doing his best to warn his readers, who might well be in a moral muddle as they tried to navigate their way as Christians in a swirling world of competing ideas and ideals, about the real dangers they face. It isn't simply a matter of people who are basically all right but get one or two points wrong. There are seriously dangerous people out there, and you have to learn to recognize them.

His first charge against the dangerous teachers – that they are arrogant and self-willed – is backed up by what, to us, seems strange and remote. They blaspheme angels, 'the glorious ones'. (The angels, by contrast, do not stoop to counter-accusations; here Peter is again drawing on various Jewish traditions and interpretations.) The point seems to be that at the fountainhead of all rebellion against God there is a rejection of appropriate authority, which in Peter's day emerges as blasphemy against angels.

It's a pity we today don't reflect more on angels, on what they are and what they do. They turn up all over the place, of course – on calendars, on Christmas trees, on greetings cards and so on. We rather like the idea of angels, but we have made them cosy and domestic. They are safe like that. We don't need to take them seriously. But in fact God's creation is peopled with all kinds of beings, and it seems that the angels have a hand in running the world; so that people who want to cast off authority begin by rubbishing the God-given invisible powers that stand behind human authorities.

With that, we are into a world every bit as murky as that of my new friend the judge. We ought to read this list, not with a self-righteous pride ('Oh, yes, look at those wicked people! Not at all like us!'), but with appropriate sorrow and fear. These tendencies are present in all of us; the point of self-control is to keep them back, to crucify wrong desires and grow right ones in their place. Injustice; wild orgies; grossly enlarged sexual appetites: these are people who leave their stain, like a bad smell in the air, in any company they join (verse 13).

Once more Peter invokes scriptural parallels (verse 15–16). It's like the time when the strange prophet Balaam was doing his best to earn money by cursing Israel, until his own donkey spoke up and rebuked him (Numbers 22). There is a sense about such people that they are indeed plugged into a kind of spiritual power, but that they are using it for their own gain. And, notoriously, when Balaam found he couldn't curse the Israelites to earn his money from the pagan king, he advised him to try a different tack. Send in seductive women, who will lead God's people into immorality and from there into idolatry (Numbers 31.15). That will do the trick. It still works today.

Out of the last paragraph of denunciation (verses 17–22), two things stand out in particular. First, in verse 19, such people promise 'freedom', but they are themselevs enslaved to corruption.

The cry of 'freedom' is heard on all sides today, but the question of what counts as freedom is more complicated than one might think. I may be 'free' to eat all the wrong kinds of food, and drink everything I fancy. Nobody will stop me; no police will come and arrest me; no preacher will tell me how wicked I am. But I will not, then, be 'free' to live a genuinely healthy, fully human **life**. I may well die young, having miserably failed to be the person I could have been. I may be 'free' to gamble away all the money I earn. But the habit will grip me, and I will fail in all my responsibilities. Is that 'freedom'? Peter seems to have sexual licence particularly in mind: that, too, is dangerously habit-forming, and produces a life where sexuality, sexual behaviour and sexual practices become the main topic of thought and discussion. Is that 'freedom'? Sex is like fire. Fire is good: it gives you the freedom to be warm and to cook food. But if you so enjoy it that you decide to light a fire in the middle of the room instead of in the fireplace, don't be surprised if you burn the house down. Sadly, 'freedom' can turn into 'freedom to destroy yourself'.

Second, there is a particular sorrow, a kind of ironic horror, about people who have come close enough to Christian **faith** and life to discover the way of genuine holiness, but who then decide it's too hard and head off in the opposite direction. They run away from moral danger one minute, then the next minute they creep up to it again. It is, after all, rather exciting. It has the tang of new experience. Maybe it's all right after all . . . and for such people Peter chooses a harsh old proverb. Call a spade a spade. Don't disguise the nasty reality with fine words. What's going on here is like a dog being sick in the street and then coming back to eat it all up again. Disgusting? Yes, precisely. That's why Peter says it. Time for a reality check.

2 PETER 3.1–10

The Day of the Lord

[1]My dear family, this is now the second time I am writing you a letter. Your motives are pure, and what I'm trying to do in reminding you is to stir them into action, [2]so that you'll remember the words spoken earlier by the holy prophets, and by the command of the Lord and saviour which you received from your apostles. [3]But you must first know this. Deceivers will come in the last days, with deceitful ways, behaving according to their own desires. [4]This is what they will say: 'Where is the promise of his royal arrival? Ever since the previous generation died, everything has continued just as it has from the beginning of creation.' [5]They willingly overlook this one thing, you see: the ancient heavens and earth were formed out of water and through water, by God's word – [6]and it was destroyed by flooding the world of that time with water. [7]The heavens and earth that we now have are being preserved for fire by the same word, being kept for the day of judgment and the destruction of the wicked. [8]So, beloved, don't forget this one thing, that a single day with the Lord is like a thousand

years, and a thousand years like a single day. [9]The Lord is not delaying his promise, in the way that some think of delay, but he is very patient towards you. He does not want anyone to be destroyed. Rather, he wants everyone to arrive at repentance.

[10]But the Lord's day will come like a thief. On that day the heavens will pass away with a great rushing sound, the elements will be dissolved in fire, and the earth and all the works on it will be disclosed.

The late Bishop Stephen Neill spent some time, early in his life, as a missionary teacher in India. Once he suspected that the class he was teaching had been cheating. The boys who were not so good at the subject had been copying from the work of those who were better, and one or two very able pupils had had their work used, directly or indirectly, by almost the whole class.

Neill's solution was to study the scripts carefully. Nobody had got all the answers right, and in the process of copying from one another some of the boys had introduced new mistakes of their own, which were then copied by other pupils further down the chain. Neill was able, by studying where these mistakes occurred, to draw a chart on the blackboard of exactly who had copied from whom. The class was dumbfounded, and accused him of witchcraft. It was as though he had been secretly present when they were all doing their homework! But he hadn't. He had worked it out purely logically.

Neill himself used that illustration to explain how it was that, in the early church, mistakes were introduced into the text of the New Testament. Even in printed books, mistakes creep in. In the days before printing, books were copied out by hand: a long, tedious task. Even copy-typing is boring; using handwriting is even more so. How easy it is for the eye to slip from one word to a similar one in the next line – or to go back and repeat a line, or a word. And how easy it is, when the text says something that seems very strange, to 'correct' it, either deliberately ('Surely', thinks the copyist, 'they can't have meant *that*! There must be a mistake! I'd better put it right') or purely accidentally, producing a smoother sentence or – dangerous, this – a smoother idea.

The trouble is, of course, that the New Testament regularly says things which don't fit neatly into the world-view of the day, and which don't always read easily either. For this reason, students of the text are alert to the possibility that there might have been corruption or distortion. Because we have so many manuscripts of the New Testament, dating from the early second century onwards – far, far more manuscripts than for any other ancient book – we can usually tell when this has happened, because like the schoolboys copying from one another we can track variations across different 'families' of manuscripts. In almost every case we can be reasonably certain that we know what the author wrote. In almost all cases the variations are so small that the sense of the passage is not seriously altered. (If, for instance, the words for 'and' or 'but' or 'the' were to drop out, or be wrongly included, it normally wouldn't make much difference.)

But just once or twice – and you will have guessed that this is one of those times – it really makes an enormous difference. Here, at the end of this passage, we have a statement which in older translations of the Bible came out one way, but which, with all the biblical manuscripts we now have, almost certainly needs to be changed. In the older versions, this passage ends with the warning that 'the earth and all the works on it *will be burned up*'. A cosmic destruction: the end of the physical world! Is that really what Peter wrote? If so, it's the only place in the whole of early Christian literature where such an idea is found.

But in some manuscripts of the New Testament, including two of the very best, the word for 'will be burned up' isn't there. Instead, there is a word which means 'will be found', or 'will be discovered', or 'will be disclosed'. Perhaps 'will be found out' would be another way of getting at the meaning. What I believe has happened is this. Several early **scribes**, faced with 'will be found', thought to themselves, 'That can't be right! It makes no sense! Surely he meant "will be burnt up".' And so the change was made. (You can see that there was confusion, because there are several other manuscripts which try out other options as well.)

And look at the difference it makes! As with the rest of the New Testament, Peter is not saying that the present world of space, time and matter is going to be burnt up and destroyed. That is more like the view of ancient Stoicism – and of some modern ideas, too. What will happen, as many early Christian teachers said, is that some sort of 'fire', literal or metaphorical, will come upon the whole earth, not to destroy, but to test everything out, and to purify it by burning up everything that doesn't meet the test. The 'elements' that will be 'dissolved' are probably the parts of creation that are needed at the moment for light and heat, that is, the sun and the moon: according to Revelation 21 they will not be needed in the new creation. But Peter's concern throughout the letter is with the judgment of humans for what they have done, not with the non-human parts of the cosmos for their own sake.

The day will come, then, and all will be revealed. All will be judged with fire. That is the promise which Peter re-emphasizes here over against those who said, at or soon after the end of the first Christian generation, that the whole thing must be a mistake since Jesus had not, after all, returned. Many in our own day have added their voices to those of the 'deceivers' of verse 3, saying that the early Christians all expected Jesus to return at once, and that since he didn't we must set aside significant parts of their teaching because, being based on a mistake, they have come out wrong. But this merely repeats the mistake against which Peter is warning – and, in fact, this is the *only* passage in all first-century Christian literature which addresses directly the question of a 'delay'. It doesn't seem to have bothered Christian writers in the second century or thereafter. They continued to teach that the Lord would return, and that this might happen at any time (hence: 'like a thief', in verse 10, picking up an image from Jesus himself).

The misunderstanding, both ancient and modern, seems to have come about partly because 'at any time' could of course mean 'therefore perhaps today or tomorrow', and partly because there really were some things which Jesus did say (in Mark 13 and elsewhere) would happen within a generation. But those events concerned the destruction of Jerusalem and the **Temple**, which did indeed happen within a generation of Jesus' day (AD 70, to be precise). But Peter warns, as Jewish teachers had done before him and would do again, that God doesn't work on our timescales. Psalm 90.4 put it well: a thousand years in God's sight are like a single day, and vice versa. We can't box God in to our chronology.

The point here, which will be developed in the final section of the letter, is about patience. This virtue, as we have often seen, was emphasized by many early Christian writers, partly because it is always necessary in ordinary human relationships and partly because it was, for most of them, quite a new idea. Patience wasn't seen as a virtue in the ancient pagan world. But here it's elevated to a new level. The patience we practise in day-to-day relations with one another must be translated up to the cosmic scale. God will indeed bring upon the whole world 'the day of the Lord', the day when all will be judged, all will be revealed. But he will do that in his own time. And that doesn't mean that we simply have to sit around and twiddle our thumbs. What appears to us (in our impatient moments) as God's delay is in fact God's moment of fresh vocation. There are tasks to do in the meantime. But that takes us into the next, and final, section of the letter.

2 PETER 3.11–18

God's Patience

¹¹Since everything is going to dissolve in this way, what sort of people should you be? You should live lives that are holy and godly, ¹²as you look for God's day to appear, and indeed hurry it on its way – the day because of which the heavens will be set on fire and dissolved, and the elements will melt with heat. ¹³But we are waiting for new heavens and a new earth, in which justice will be at home. That is what he has promised.

> [14]So, my dear family, as you wait for these things, be eager to be found without spot or blemish before him, in peace. [15]And when our Lord waits patiently to act, see that for what it is – salvation! Our beloved brother Paul has written to you about all this, according to the wisdom that has been given him, [16]speaking about these things as he does in all his letters. There are some things in them which are difficult to understand. Untaught and unstable people twist his words to their own destruction, as they do with the other scriptures.
>
> [17]But as for you, my dear family, be on your guard, since you have been warned in advance. That way you won't be led astray through the error of lawless people and fall away from your own solid grounding. [18]Instead, grow in grace and in the knowledge of our Lord and saviour Jesus the Messiah. To him be glory both now and in the day when God's new age dawns. Amen.

We were looking through an old photograph album one evening, identifying family members as they were fifty years ago. Can he really have had a moustache like that? Was she really wearing that kind of dress? Yes: he did, and she was. It's fascinating, especially when you pick out resemblances with the next generation and the one after that.

But in one picture there was a different sort of surprise. There was someone we all recognized – but he wasn't part of the family at all! He didn't live anywhere near them. We knew of him because, by a much later marriage, he had come into the family as a kind of honorary uncle. But what was he doing there back then?

The answer was quite mundane; he was staying with a friend nearby, and together they had come over for a quick visit. Just a coincidence. But I thought of this sudden surprising appearance as I was pondering Peter's sudden reference to someone we haven't been thinking about at all: St Paul! What is *he* doing here in verse 15, making as it were a guest appearance on someone else's show?

The answer is that, by the time this letter was written, Paul's letters had already been circulating for some while in many of the churches, both in Turkey and Greece (where all of Paul's letters except Romans were addressed), and possibly further afield as well. Many early Christians were energetic travellers, and there is every indication that texts – letters, gospels and so on – were copied, taken from place to place, and studied. And what Peter is saying here fits closely with a theme which, though not all readers of Paul now realize it, is in fact very important in his writings as well. We have already spoken of the patience to which we are called: patience in our dealings with one another, patience with God as we wait for the day of the Lord. Now we must consider God's own patience.

This is, after all, the right way round. We might present a some-what comical sight, stamping our little feet with impatience while the creator and ruler of the universe calmly goes about his own business, knowing infinitely more than we do about how to run his world. No: the proper perspective is to regard anything that looks to us like 'delay' as an indication not that we have to be patient with God, but that God is having to be patient with us.

Which is just as well. If God were to foreclose on the world, and on ourselves, straight away, what would happen? This was already a theme which Jews before the time of Jesus were pondering, as they agonized over the apparently endless delay in waiting for God's prom-ises to be fulfilled. God, they concluded, was holding back the great day, leaving a space for more people to repent, for lives to be trans-formed, for the world to come to its senses. One should be grateful for this 'patience', not angry with God for failing to hurry up when we wanted him to.

This is very much what Paul has in mind in a passage like Romans 2.1–11. It might be worth looking that up and pondering it; perhaps this is the sort of passage Peter has in mind. For Paul, 'God's kindness is meant to bring you to **repentance**' (Romans 2.4). But if you don't avail yourself of that opportunity, the result will be the opposite: what you do instead with that time, with that interval before final judgment, will just make matters worse when the day finally arrives (Romans 2.5–11).

This seems to be what Peter is saying, too. 'When our Lord waits patiently to act, see that for what it is – **salvation**!' (verse 15). God's patience is our opportunity. It is our chance to work on the holy, godly lives we ought to be living. It is our chance, too, to spread the **gos-pel** in the world. Since we know that the day is coming, the day when new heavens and new earth will emerge, filled to the brim with God's wonderful justice, his glorious setting-right of all things, we should be working towards that already, here and now.

This is the point where a wrong view of what God intends to do will really damage both our understanding and our behaviour. If we imagine that God wants simply to burn up the present world entirely, leaving us as disembodied **souls** in some kind of timeless 'eternity', then why should we worry about what we do here and now? What does it matter? Why not just enjoy life as best we can and wait for whatever is coming next – which is of course the answer that many philosophies have given, in the first century as well as today. But if God intends to *renew* the heavens and the earth – as Isaiah had promised all those years before (Isaiah 65.17; 66.22), then what we do in the pres-ent time matters. It matters for us that we are 'without spot or blemish' (verse 14). It matters for God's world as a whole.

All this comes together in the closing paragraph of the letter, which sums up well the two main things Peter has been saying all through. First, be on your guard! This doesn't mean adopting a fault-finding, mean-spirited approach, ready to criticize anybody and everybody in case some of them turn out to be heretics. It means, once more, the wisdom of the serpent. Don't imagine that there are not lawless people out there, ready to lead you astray with smooth talk. Don't imagine there won't be times when it feels the natural and right thing to go along with them. If that wasn't a real danger, we wouldn't need the warnings. And that real danger is that we might fall away from the solid grounding we have received in the **faith**.

But, second, the message isn't all negative. There is such a thing as sustained and lasting growth in Christian character, faith and **life**. It is your privilege and birthright, as a follower of Jesus, that you should 'grow in grace and in the knowledge of our Lord and saviour Jesus the **Messiah**'. This looks right back to the opening section, in which Peter urged his readers to add one thing to another: faith, virtue, knowledge, self-control, patience, piety, family affection and love. Some of these, such as self-control and patience, he has expounded at some length. Others he has left for his readers to work out for themselves.

I have a sense that this letter might be a word for our times. If our desire is to bring God glory both now and in the day when his new age dawns we could do a lot worse than study it carefully, pray it in, take it to heart and put it into practice.

1 JOHN

1 JOHN 1.1-4

The Word of Life

¹That which was from the beginning, which we have heard, which we have seen with our eyes, which we have gazed at, and our hands have handled – concerning the Word of Life! ²That life was displayed, and we have seen it, and bear witness, and we announce to you the life of God's coming age, which was with the father and was displayed to us. ³That which we have seen and heard, we announce to you too, so that you also may have fellowship with us. And our fellowship is with the father, and with his son Jesus the Messiah. ⁴We are writing these things so that our joy may be complete.

'I have seen the future; and it works.' That notorious statement was made by an American journalist, Lincoln Steffens, in 1919. He had just returned from a visit to the recently established 'Soviet Union', formed on Marxist principles after the Russian Revolution had swept away the old aristocracy and its method of government. Steffens was echoing the hopes of millions in Europe and America. Perhaps this entirely new ideal, this new way of ordering human society, was the answer to all the old problems of tyranny and oppression. Perhaps this was indeed 'the future', the thing that would come to the rest of humanity as a great revelation, a great display of enlightened progress. We would all catch up one day; but for the moment Steffens, at least, had had a glimpse into that future, and declared that it worked.

Subsequent history has revealed, of course, that it only 'worked' in the sense of achieving certain ends at the most enormous cost of human lives. The Soviet system, like other revolutionary regimes, found it necessary to imprison or kill millions of its own subjects, never mind enslaving several adjacent nations. When it finally came crashing down under its own dead weight in the late 1980s, it became apparent that it had been rotten and hollow inside for many years, perhaps for many decades, perhaps all along. The problems it caused are with us still.

But that sense of a glimpse of the future, of an advance display of the new world waiting to be born, however tragically mistaken in that case, is exactly the picture John is offering at the start of this short but glowing letter. The ancient Jews believed that world history was divided into two periods, or 'ages'. There was 'the **present age**', which was full of misery and suffering, injustice and oppression; and there was 'the **age to come**', the time when God would sort it all out, would put everything right, and would in particular rescue his people from the evil they had suffered.

Unfortunately, the word for 'age' has often been translated as 'eternal' or 'eternity', which has given modern readers the idea that John, and other early Christian writers who refer to God's new age, were thinking of something 'eternal' in the sense of 'purely spiritual', something that had nothing to do with the world of space, time and matter. That's what people often hear when they read the phrase 'eternal life', which is what most translations have at verse 2. But this is mistaken. John, like Paul, and indeed like Jesus himself, is thinking of the new age, the age to come, which God has promised. This is the future, and it really does work.

And God has provided an advance display of this future! God has kept the age to come under wraps, as it were, waiting to reveal it at the right time. But the secret at the heart of the early Christian movement was that the age to come had already been revealed. The future had burst into the present, even though the present time wasn't ready for it. The word for that future was **Life**, life as it was meant to be, life in its full, vibrant meaning, a life which death tried to corrupt, thwart and kill but a life which had overcome death itself and was now on offer to anyone who wanted to come and take it. Life itself had come to life, had taken the form of a human being, coming into the present from God's future, coming to display God's coming age. And the name of that life-in-person is of course Jesus. That is the very heart of what John wants to say.

Of course, the very idea of God's new life becoming a person and stepping forward out of the future into the present is so enormous, so breathtaking, that a tone of wonder, of hushed awe and reverence, becomes appropriate. That is what we find in these opening verses. *That which was from the beginning ...* pause and think about that for a moment ... *which we have heard, which we have seen with our eyes, which we have gazed at ...* pause again: your own eyes? You didn't just glimpse it, you gazed at it? Yes, says John, and what's more *our hands have handled ...* you touched it, this Life? You touched *him*? You *handled* him? Yes, repeats John: we heard, saw and touched this from-the-beginning Life. We knew him. We were his friends.

And we still *are* his friends. Once the future has come into the present, the present is transformed for ever. The life has been 'displayed', has been put on show for all to see (though some still prefer not to look). And we who saw it, who knew it, who knew *him*, are now like witnesses in a lawcourt, speaking to a surprised jury about the strange things which we have encountered. Oh, we can talk about Jesus and what he did and said. As John says at the end of his **gospel**, if you tried to write it all down the world would explode with the books that would be written. But when you reflect on what it means, then you have to say this: we have seen the future, and it is full of light and life and joy and hope.

The rest of the letter will explore all this. For the moment, John explains his purpose in writing. Those who have seen this life, and have been captured by its beauty and promise, find that they have come to belong to a new kind of family, a **'fellowship'** as we sometimes say. The word he uses at this point is sometimes used of a business partnership, but he means much more than that. It can also refer to the 'sharing' of particular goods or benefits between people; that comes into it, as we shall see, but John means much more than that, too. He seems to mean (stretching the word to fit the new reality, as the early Christians often had to do), that there is a kind of life, a quality of life, which is God's very own life, and which God himself is now sharing with the people who have heard and seen the life-come-to-life called Jesus.

Indeed, John sees God's own life as already a shared fellowship: the fellowship between father and son. Jesus, as **Messiah**, has been marked out as **'son of God'**, both in the sense that this was his rightful royal title as Israel's true king, and in a deeper, richer sense previously hardly suspected or imagined, but now celebrated by his followers as the only possible way to explain the extraordinary things that they had seen, heard and even handled. As his life, death and **resurrection** demonstrated, Jesus was clearly the life-in-person of God's coming age. He was, in fact, God's own new life, both the life of God himself and the gift of life from God to the world. The earliest Christians quickly seized upon the words 'father' and 'son' as the simplest and clearest way of saying the unsayable at this point: that there was a common life, a deep sharing of inner reality, between God and Jesus, enough to take your breath away at the thought of such a human being. And, indeed, of such a God.

But it doesn't stop there. It gets even more breathtaking. This deep sharing of inner reality, this 'fellowship' between father and son, has been extended. It extends to all those who came to know, love and trust Jesus while he was alive, while he was, so to speak, on display as God's public unveiling of the coming life. And now (this, it seems, is the point of the letter) this sharing, this 'fellowship', is open to others too, to others who didn't have the chance to meet Jesus during his period of public display. This 'sharing' can be, and is being, extended to anyone and everyone who hears the announcement about Jesus. They can come into 'fellowship' with those who *did* see, hear and handle him. And they, in turn, are in 'fellowship' with the father and the son, with the two who are themselves the very bedrock and model for what 'fellowship', in this fullest sense, really means.

It may seem strange that simply telling people about Jesus is the appointed means by which such a momentous thing as this 'fellowship' can be extended to include new members. But John is very much aware that the opening move in the whole game was made by God himself as an act not of silent display but of verbal communication. Jesus was not only life-in-person: he was (verse 1) 'the **Word** of Life', Life-as-Word, Life-turned-into-speech, God's speech, God's self-communication to his people and, through them, to the wider world. In John's gospel, of course, he refers to Jesus simply as 'the Word', the Word who became flesh. The point is this. God has spoken in Jesus; and God now speaks, through the words which Jesus' friends speak and write about him, to others also, in the intention and hope that they will come to share this same 'fellowship'. That is the point of the letter. That should be our prayer as we read it.

1 JOHN 1.5—2.2

God's Light and Our Darkness

⁵This is the message which we have heard from him, and announce to you: God is light, and there is no darkness at all in him. ⁶If we say that we have fellowship with him and walk in the dark, we are telling lies, and not doing what is true. ⁷But if we walk in the light, just as he is in the light, we have fellowship with one another, and the blood of Jesus his son makes us pure and clean from all sin. ⁸If we say that we have no sin, we deceive ourselves and the truth is not in us. ⁹If we confess our sins, he is faithful and just, and will forgive us our sins, and cleanse us from all unrighteousness. ¹⁰If we say that we have not sinned, we make him out to be a liar, and his word is not in us.

²·¹My children, I am writing these things to you so that you may not sin. If anyone does sin, we have one who pleads our cause before the father – namely, the Righteous One, Jesus the Messiah! ²He is the sacrifice which atones for our sins – and not ours only, either, but those of the whole world.

Elizabeth faced a difficult choice. She had moved into her new home a few weeks before, and her parents, who had been overjoyed when she got the new job and so could set up on her own, had been determined to do something special for her. They had bought a wonderful period armchair, of a sort they knew she admired, and had had it covered in exactly the right material to go in her new living room. They were glad to have done it; she was delighted to have it.

But then, the day before they were due to visit, disaster struck. Elizabeth and some friends were sorting out some books and pictures, when suddenly . . . nobody knew quite how it happened, but a mug of hot, strong coffee found itself spilled right across the new chair. They scrubbed and wiped and did all they could, but the ugly stain was there, plain for all to see. She knew her parents would be devastated, as she herself was. What should she do?

Of course, what she most wanted to do (apart from turn the clock back) was to hope they'd put their visit off. Maybe then there would be time to clean it up, or even commission a new cover. They need never know . . .

But it was no good. They were coming. One glance and they'd know. The only thing to do was tell the truth and see what could then be done.

We must leave the little domestic drama at that point – as with all storms in teacups, if you happened to be in that teacup, it felt very stormy at the time – and move to the cosmic drama that John is playing out. It's all very well for him to say, in his wonderful opening paragraph, that we have **fellowship** with God himself, with the father and the son. But what if we have already spoiled the wonderful gift that we've been given? What if we have already ruined our lives by carelessness, stupidity or downright wickedness?

If we don't have something of that reaction, it may be because we haven't really appreciated what the word 'God' means. Think back to some of the famous God-moments in the Bible. Moses sees God in the burning bush, and does all he can to escape, to avoid being caught up in God's great new project. Isaiah sees God in the **Temple**, and is scared for his life. Peter meets Jesus on the boat and tells him to go away because he, Peter, is a sinner. John sees the risen Jesus in glory and falls at his feet as though dead. That is the proper reaction to being told that we are being welcomed into fellowship with the father and the son. We have messed it up. We have already spoiled things. We are – or ought to be – ashamed. If only God would put it off until we'd had a chance to clean up!

But that's not how it works. Yes, God is light, and in him is no darkness at all. The darkness which encroaches upon our messy, rebellious, unbelieving lives cannot survive in his sight. One glance and he'll know. There's no point hiding: if we pretend to be in fellowship with him while 'walking in the dark' (in other words, behaving in the less-than-human way we often choose), we are telling lies. If we say we have no sin, we are simply deceiving ourselves. We certainly won't deceive God. In fact, if we tried to say that we were not sinners (verse 10), we would be making matters worse. We would be making God out to be a liar, since he has said, in scripture and in person, that he has come to rescue us, knowing us to be sinners.

But that is the answer. In terms of the storm in a coffee cup, it is as though – though this wasn't actually how it worked out – the parents just happened to have a wonderful new product which, by some chemical magic, was able to remove coffee stains so completely that you would never know anything had happened. Imagine the sequence of Elizabeth's emotions if that had been the case: from fear and shame, to deep embarrassment and sorrow, to sudden joy and delight. Too good to be true? Well, perhaps with coffee stains it is. But in the cosmic drama, extraordinarily, this is how it works.

The key is that God's future has been displayed, as we saw, in and as his son, Jesus. But Jesus is, of course, the one who died on the cross; and from the very earliest days of Christian **faith**, his followers believed that his death had been the very thing the world had been waiting for. It was the ultimate **sacrifice**. No more would pagans have to offer sacrifices to their gods, not that it did much good anyway. No more would even the Jews have to bring sacrifices to the Temple, even though that had been commanded in the **law**. The God who gave the law had now summed up his rescuing purposes, for which the Temple and its sacrifices were advance signs, in the glorious display of his love in Jesus. The blood that flowed from Jesus' body as he hung on the cross was somehow, strangely, the very lifeblood of God himself, poured out to deal with sins in the way that all the animal sacrifices in the world could never do.

And that blood, that sacrificial death, that God-**life** given on our behalf and in our place, is available for all who 'walk in the light'. That doesn't mean we have to get our act together, morally speaking, before God can do anything. What it means is that when we consciously turn to the light – when we face up to what's gone wrong in the past and don't try to hide it, and when we are determined to live that way from now on – two things happen. First, we find ourselves sharing that intimate God-life, not only with God himself but with one another. Second, we find that Jesus' blood somehow makes us clean, pure and fresh inside. It deals with the nasty stain, the residual dirtiness, the scratchy, ugly feeling that something went badly wrong and we can't get rid of it. All that is gone when we turn to the light and start to walk in it. All because of Jesus.

That's why John encourages us to face up to the past. No point hiding: he's going to see, he's going to know what's happened. In fact, he'll see and know more than we allow ourselves to remember. But if we make a clean breast of it, then he will forgive us and cleanse us. Why does John say at this point (1.9) that God is 'faithful and just'? Because God is faithful to his promises, the promises to forgive. And because, in the death of Jesus, he has shown himself to be 'just', to be in the right. This is the way he is putting the whole world to rights, and us with it.

Now it would be easy for someone to say – someone who hadn't grasped just how serious the whole situation really was – that if God was going to forgive people like that, one might as well go on sinning. You can tell when the true **message** of the **gospel** has got across, because someone will always draw that wrong conclusion from it. But that would be like Elizabeth saying, 'Well, that's fine; since my parents have a miracle cure for coffee stains, I'll throw coffee over all the furniture next time!' It doesn't make sense. So John says, 'I'm writing these things to you so that you may not sin.' It's a delicate balance. Sinners need to know that Jesus has died for them, and that they can be fully and freely forgiven. Forgiven sinners need to know that this is not a reason to go on sinning. Both are true, and are at the very heart of what it means to be a Christian.

One other thing, too, is very near the heart of it all. It seems that John is writing to Jewish Christians who might have been tempted to suppose that Jesus, as Israel's **Messiah**, was the remedy for their problems, for their sins, and for them alone. Not a bit of it, says John. Jesus' sacrifice atones for our sins, 'and not ours only, either, but those of the whole world'. Just as God didn't remain content to be in fellowship only with his own son, but wanted to extend that fellowship to all those who met and followed Jesus; and just as John is writing this letter so that its readers may come to share in that same divine fellowship; so now all who know themselves to be forgiven through Jesus' death must look, not at their own privilege, but at the wider task. God intends to call more and more people into this 'fellowship'.

Why not? Is the blood of Jesus somehow insufficient?

1 JOHN 2.3–14

God's New Commandment

³This is how we are sure that we have known him, if we keep his commandments. ⁴Anyone who says, 'I know him', but doesn't keep his commandments, is a liar. People like that have no truth in them. ⁵But if anyone keeps his word, God's love is truly made complete in such a person. This is how we are sure that we are in him: ⁶anyone who says, 'I abide in him', ought to behave in the same way that he behaved.

⁷My beloved ones, I am not writing a new command to you, but an old command which you have had from the very beginning. The old command is the word which you heard. ⁸Again, however, I am writing a new command to you: it is true in him and in you, because the darkness is passing away and the true light is already shining. ⁹Anyone who says, 'I am in the light', while hating another family member, is still in darkness up to this very moment. ¹⁰Anyone who loves another family member abides in the light, and there is no cause of offence in such a person. ¹¹Anyone who hates another family member is in the

darkness, and walks about in the darkness. Such people have no idea where they are going, because the darkness has blinded their eyes.

[12]I am writing to you, children,
because your sins are forgiven through his name.
[13]I am writing to you, fathers,
because you have known the one who is from the beginning.
I am writing to you, young people,
because you have conquered the evil one.

[14]I have written to you, children,
because you have known the father.
I have written to you, fathers,
because you have known the one who is from the beginning.
I have written to you, young people,
because you are strong,
and the word of God abides in you,
and you have conquered the evil one.

Sometimes when we sing hymns, the hymns tell a story. They move from one idea to another, in a linear fashion. There is something satisfying about this. We all like stories, and even when the 'story' is a sequence of ideas, it makes sense to us. We feel we have been on a journey. We have arrived somewhere where we were not before.

But sometimes, in some traditions at least, the things we sing in church are deliberately repetitive. We use them quite differently: as a way of meditation, of stopping on one point and mulling it over, of allowing something which is very deep and important to make more of an impact on us than if we just said or sang it once and passed on. Quite different traditions find this helpful: the Taizé movement in France, for instance, uses some haunting brief songs or chants; but you find the same thing in many branches of the modern charismatic movement, where repetition is an essential part of worship. True, some people find these tedious, and want to get back to old-fashioned hymns as quickly as possible. This may be partly a matter of personality. But it may also be that such people are unwilling to allow the truth of which the poem speaks to get quite so close to them. Repetition can touch, deep down inside us, parts that other, 'safer' kinds of hymns cannot reach, or do not very often.

If someone (like the present writer) has spent a long time studying St Paul, and then suddenly moves across to John, and particularly to this letter, the effect is a bit like someone moving suddenly from old-fashioned narrative hymns to the repetitive sort. One is tempted to be a bit frustrated. Surely, we think, he should get on with it, say what he means, and move on to the next point? But that isn't John's style, and perhaps the analogy of the hymns may help to explain why. He is mulling it all over, and wants his hearers to do so too. And sometimes, as in verses 12–14, he seems as it were to break into song himself, into a sing-song, repetitive formula, which we shouldn't perhaps try to analyse in strict terms (why does he say *this* to the 'children' the first time, and *that* to them the second time? and so on) but should rather appreciate it for what it is: a meditation, a long, lingering gaze at his audience and what they need, at the way God works in people's lives. Stay with this, he seems to be saying. Children, your sins are forgiven. Fathers, you have known the one who is from the beginning. Young people, you have conquered the evil one. Now let's say it again. And so on. Perhaps it's only as we give ourselves to the strange, haunting repetition that the meaning will begin to sink down into us.

But it isn't just in these verses that John writes in a different way from people like Paul. His whole letter is repetitive – and yet it is also on the move. He keeps coming back to very nearly the same point, but at the same time he is moving forward. There is some kind of an ongoing narrative, but it isn't the type that moves from A to B to C to D in strict order. It's A with a bit of B; then A and B with a bit of C; then A, B and C with a bit of D; and so on. So we shouldn't be surprised if we think we've heard it before. We probably have. The question is, what is the particular point that John is making this time?

The new major theme in this passage is that of God's commandments. We may think of 'the commandments' in terms of the Ten Commandments, which for some will send us back in imagination to Moses, and for others to an antique sign-board, with old-style lettering, hanging on the church wall as a dire warning to anyone thinking of transgressing. And we might wonder what a Christian writer is doing referring to the commandments, and to the duty to keep them. Haven't we just been told that we are forgiven? Isn't part of the point of the New Testament that we are free from the **law**?

Yes and no. The commandments were a kind of advance signpost, a sketching out at long range of what a genuine, lovely, fruitful human life would look like. They became a terror to many because people realized they couldn't and didn't keep them. But they remained, looking forward to God's coming day. And now, as we found out in the first chapter, God's coming day, the **Life** of his New Age, has come rushing forward to meet us in the present time, in the person of Jesus himself! So we should expect that, in him, we will discover the reality to which the commandments were an advance signpost.

And we do – but it doesn't look, perhaps, like everyone would have imagined. For John, as for Paul, and above all as for Jesus, the commandments are all summed up in one word: Love. The Life of God's

New Age is revealed as the Love of God's New Age. All other commandments – the detail of what to do and not to do – are the outflowing of this love, the love which has been newly revealed in Jesus, the love which God now intends should be revealed in and through all those who follow Jesus.

Much of the rest of the letter will be devoted to exploring and explaining what this means. But for the moment let's look at the way John links this commandment with what has gone before – both what has gone before in the long story of Israel, and what has gone before in the letter.

In Israel: this, he says, is actually the 'old command' which they had from the beginning. It isn't, in that sense, 'new'. If Moses had heard Jesus talk about love, he would have said, 'That's it! That's the heart of what these commandments were all about.' But, as John has already said in the letter (A plus B and now C), this command is also 'new' in a particular sense, because it is coming into the present, with Jesus himself, as a gift from God's future. Love is the word that best describes the life of God's new age, and we get to taste it and practise it in the present time.

That's why, of course, it's difficult. It's so much easier to collapse back into living the old way, the way of suspicion and hatred. But that means going back into the darkness (verses 9 and 11), whereas the life of love means going forward into the light. That is both the command and the promise of these verses.

It is, of course, costly and difficult. Perhaps that's why the other new element in these verses, which occurs in the two addresses to 'young people' in verses 13 and 14, is that 'you have conquered the evil one'. There will be more to say about this presently. But we note this element, just in case everything should sound cosy or easy. Love – God's kind of love – isn't like that at all. It demands a victory, a victory over the old enemy who does his best work through human hatred. Love shines out the more brightly against a dark backcloth; which is just as well, because that's what's there.

1 JOHN 2.15-29

People of the Lie

¹⁵Do not love the world, or the things that are in the world. If anyone loves the world, the father's love is not in them. ¹⁶Everything in the world, you see – the greedy desire of the flesh, the greedy desire of the eyes, the pride of life – none of this is from the father. It is from the world. ¹⁷The world is passing away, with all its greedy desires. But anyone who does God's will abides for ever.

¹⁸Children, it is the last hour. You have heard that 'Antimessiah' is coming – and now many Antimessiahs have appeared! That's how we know that it is the last hour. ¹⁹They went out from among us, but they were not really of our number. If they had been of our number, you see, they would have remained with us. This happened so that it would be made crystal clear that none of them belonged to us. ²⁰You, however, have the anointing from the Holy One, and you all have knowledge. ²¹I am not writing to you because you don't know the truth, but because you do know it, and you know that no liar is of the truth.

²²Who is the liar? Is it not the one who denies that Jesus is the Messiah? Such a one is the Antimessiah – who denies the father and the son. ²³Nobody who denies the son has the father. One who acknowledges the son has the father too. ²⁴As for you: let what you heard from the beginning abide in you. If what you heard from the beginning abides in you, you too will abide in the son and in the father. ²⁵And this is the promise which he himself promised us: the life of the age to come.

²⁶I am writing to you about the people who are deceiving you. ²⁷You have received the anointing from him; it abides in you, and you do not need to have anyone teach you. That anointing from him teaches you about everything; it is true, it isn't a lie. So, just as he taught you, abide in him.

²⁸And now, children, abide in him, so that when he is revealed we may have boldness and may not be put to shame before him at his royal appearing. ²⁹If you know that he is righteous, you know that everyone who does what is right has been fathered by him.

The late psychotherapist M. Scott Peck once wrote a book called *People of the Lie*. It wasn't, perhaps, as famous as his remarkable (though still controversial) book *The Road Less Traveled*, but I found it more thought-provoking.

In *People of the Lie*, Peck described and discussed some cases of extreme dysfunctional behaviour that had come his way. In much of his work, he said, he could track, to a lesser or greater extent, the causes of unhappiness in the people who came to consult him. Bad things had happened to them; people had ill-treated them, often in their early childhood; they had made wrong decisions and were reaping the consequences. Those problems are the stock in trade of the psychotherapist. But there were other cases where something radically different seemed to be at work. Something much darker, more sinister.

Peck had not been prepared for this. All his training in secular psychiatry and psychotherapy, all the textbooks, had ruled out the e-word from their vocabulary. There was no such thing as evil, they declared; merely different levels of human malfunctioning, different problems and perceptions that people had. 'Evil' as such didn't enter into it. But these other cases convinced Peck that this was wrong. The people he wrote about in that book had taken a few more steps than most of us down a particular road. They had lied to themselves; they had lied to others, not least to other family members; they had started believing and living by those lies. Somehow, dark and incomprehensible though it might appear, they had thereby invoked a kind of anti-power, the power of the lie, an 'evil' which was more than the sum total of their own deceits. And this power then went to work around them with devastating effects.

It is 'people of the lie' that John is now warning against. He isn't a psychotherapist; he isn't offering the kind of careful or complex analysis of human motivation that we would expect from a professional in that field today. But he is putting his finger on one great lie above all, and warning that those who accept this lie and live by it are a corrupting and dangerous influence. Those who do not believe the lie must learn to trust God's work in them, the work because of which they believe the truth. They must hold onto it firmly.

The 'anti-power' in question is described as the 'Antimessiah'. We perhaps know this word better in its Greek form, 'Antichrist'; but since that word has been tossed around, sadly, by many people over many centuries, and has been used to refer to various different people and organizations, it may help us to get behind that and into John's mind if we keep the Hebrew form, 'Antimessiah'.

But what is an 'Antimessiah'? Jesus had warned that 'false **Messiahs**' would arise after him and deceive many people, perhaps even some from among his own followers. At this point it's easy for us to make a mistake. We might well think Jesus (and John, for that matter) were referring to what we would call a 'religious' phenomenon. But the complex world of first-century Judaism, particularly in Palestine itself, was full of men and movements claiming that God was acting at last in this way, in that way, through this movement, through that man. This was as much what we would call 'political' as what we would call 'religious', though in fact you couldn't get a razor blade between them in those days. This is bewildering to the historian trying to understand it all today, and it must have been far more bewildering in real life at the time.

And many of the early Christians must have wondered, as they heard about a new movement in a neighbouring town: can this be Jesus, back again? Should I go and see? Or even: perhaps this is the real thing, and all that extraordinary business about Jesus was just a preliminary, a warm-up act? After all, since he left us nothing much seems to have happened. Just a few people being healed . . .

And, it seems, some of those who had been with Jesus' followers did indeed go off after these new movements. That is what is causing the problem which John is now addressing. He is in no doubt. These movements are antimessianic movements! They may have started out within our **fellowship**, but they left, because the heart of the matter was not in them.

This could look dangerously like a self-justifying position (anyone who leaves us is by definition 'not one of us'), but John has something much more important in mind. The true follower of Jesus the Messiah has been 'anointed' by his **holy spirit** (verse 20), so that a real change of heart and character has happened. One of the key symptoms of that change is precisely the recognition that Jesus is indeed the Messiah. He truly is the **son of God**.

The 'antimessianic' movements are bound to deny this. If they don't, they have no reason to set up a new movement in the first place! And this is what ties them in to the idea of 'people of the lie'. The greatest lie of all is 'to deny the father and the son' (verse 22).

As John insists, to do this – to deny that Jesus really is God's son – is to cut off access to the father as well, since we only truly know the father through the son. But the antimessianic folk are saying, of course, that *this* is a lie – that the basic Christian confession itself is a mistake! Jesus wasn't really God's last **word** to his people. There is someone new. Give it all up and come with us!

Don't do it, says John. These people are deceiving you (verse 26). And, actually, you know this deep down, because that 'anointing' remains within you, so that without anyone teaching you from the outside, as it were, you know the truth deep within. And be assured, despite what they're saying: it isn't a lie (verse 27). It's the truth.

There is another level to what John is saying at this point. The word for 'anointing' is, in the Greek, the same root word as 'Messiah'. 'The Messiah', after all, is 'the anointed one', God's anointed king, his one and only 'son'. We should, therefore, perhaps think of it like this. Here are the 'Antimessiah' people (the 'anti-anointed-one' people); but you have been 'Messiah-ed', you have been 'anointed', so you must not be deceived by their denials. They are not only denying that Jesus is the Messiah; they are denying everything that makes you, now, who you truly are. This is the lie that will, if given its head, eat its way like rust into the imagination and heart of a Christian, or a church.

The whole passage, with these stark warnings, is framed within two short paragraphs which set the discussion in its proper context. This is the expectation of Jesus' return, his 'royal appearing' (verse 28). When he 'appears' (think of it as his 'coming', if you like, but don't be misled by that into imagining that he is at present far away from you; rather, he is very near, but hidden), then he will utterly transform the whole creation. And when that happens, the way of the present world will disappear (verse 17). That is why we are commanded 'not to love the world' (verse 15).

But what does that mean? Generations of Western Christians have supposed that Christians are meant to renounce 'the world' in any and every sense: natural enjoyments, the pleasures of food and drink, the created order itself. Perhaps, they think, 'the world' – this world of space, time and matter – is actually evil! Perhaps we should try to live as though we were pure **spirits**?

No: that's not what John has in mind. As in some other early Christian writings, 'the world' here, like the word 'flesh' when Paul uses it, means 'the world as it places itself over against God'. The world remains God's good creation, and as such is to be enjoyed with thanksgiving, as Paul says (1 Corinthians 10.25–26; 1 Timothy 4.4–5). Do not collapse into what we sometimes call 'dualism', the idea that God is good and creation is bad! That way lies catastrophe. Indeed, that (as we shall see) is part of the problem with the people who are denying that Jesus can truly be God's son. How can he have come, they think, in human flesh? So demeaning. So degrading. Not at all, replies John. This is at the heart of it all.

So the command 'not to love the world' refers not to the physical stuff of this world, but to 'the world' as it is in rebellion against God: 'the world' as the combination of things that draw us away from God. The flesh, the eyes, life itself – all can become idols, and like all idols they demand more and more from those who worship them. And all idolatry draws us into the lie, or if we're not careful into The Lie. We must celebrate all the goodness of the world, all God's goodness to us within his creation. But we must not worship it. We must thank God for it – and pray and watch for the day when it will be transformed by the royal appearing of his son.

1 JOHN 3.1–10

Born of God

¹Look at the remarkable love the father has given us – that we should be called God's children! That indeed is what we are. That's why the world doesn't know us, because it didn't know him. ²Beloved ones, we are now, already, God's children; it hasn't yet been revealed what we are going to be. We know that when he is revealed we shall be like him, because we shall see him as he is. ³All who have this hope in him make themselves pure, just as he is pure.

⁴Everyone who goes on sinning is breaking the law; sin, in fact, is lawlessness. ⁵And you know that he was revealed so that he might take away sins, and there is no sin in him. ⁶Everyone who abides in him does not go on sinning. Everyone who goes on sinning has not seen him, or known him.

⁷Children, don't let anyone deceive you. The person who does righteousness is righteous, just as he is righteous. ⁸The person who goes on sinning is from the devil, because the devil is a sinner from the very start. The son of God was revealed for this purpose, to destroy the works of the devil. ⁹Everyone who is fathered by God does not go on sinning, because God's offspring remain in him; they cannot go on sinning, because they have been fathered by God. ¹⁰That is how it is clear who are the children of God and who are the children of the devil: everyone who does not do what is right is not of God, particularly those who do not love their brother or sister.

There are many stories about people who are blind who then receive the gift of sight. One of the most remarkable, of course, is found in chapter 9 of John's gospel, where Jesus heals a man who had been born blind. But there are plenty more such stories in recent history. One I heard not long ago concerned a man who had gone blind in early adult life. He had then, subsequently, got married and had children. They could all see him, but he had never set eyes on them. Then, one day, the medical breakthrough came, the operation was a success, and he could see at last. What an amazing moment! To come face to face, eye to eye, with the people he had loved but never seen. There is something transformative about eye contact. People who spend a lot of time looking at one another sometimes come to resemble each other. Perhaps this is because they are instinctively copying one another's facial expressions until their muscles and tissue begin to be reshaped in that way. Imagine beginning that process at last after years of love which had been expressed through words and touch but never before through sight.

Something like that is evoked in a lovely line from a Christmas carol: 'And our eyes at last shall see him, through his own redeeming love.' There ought to be a catch in our voice when we say or sing that. If we have any love for Jesus right now, our deepest longing ought to be that we would come face to face with him at last, to see his smile, to catch his facial expression, to begin to know him in a whole new way. And that, of course, is what's promised here in verse 2, with a mysterious twist to it. 'It hasn't yet been revealed', says John, 'what we are going to be. We know that *when he is revealed we shall be like him, because we shall see him as he is.*' Everything John says, throughout the letter, hinges on this promise. Take it away, and you lose the whole point.

So what don't we know about our future state? Well, thinking about the **resurrection**, or about God's whole new world in which our resurrection will take place, is very difficult. We can say it's not quite like this, or it's more like that. We know that, because the present world is God's good creation, it will be like this only more so: without corruption, decay, death, injustice, illness, sorrow and shame. There will be no tears. There will be no barbed wire. But . . . what will *we* be like?

Perhaps we should say: like we are, only much more so. More gloriously physical, not less. Embodied but not subject to sickness or death. Able to celebrate the joys of God's world but no longer lured or seduced into abusing them, into lusting after them, into worshipping them as though they were divine.

All that is, I believe, true. But far more important is to say: we will be like Jesus. Think of the risen Jesus: the same, yet strangely different (or why did they want to ask him, 'Who are you?' in John 21.12?). He had gone through death, and still bore the marks of the nails, yet he was never going to die again. He seemed to belong in both worlds, **heaven** and earth, at once – and that, of course, will be appropriate for the new world, since then heaven and earth will have come together completely and for ever. But I suspect this is just the start of it. I reckon that when it happens the reality will stand in relation to these pointing-ahead-into-the-fog kind of statements in roughly the same way as the real Windsor Castle stands in relation to the symbolic brown signs, with their silly little picture of a castle, that point you to it off the main road. The real risen Jesus, when he meets us, will far outshine any pictures we might have formed of him in advance. When our blindness is cured, we will gaze and gaze on the face through which God has loved us so much. And perhaps – maybe this is the point of what John is saying – perhaps his look will transform our faces. Perhaps we will begin to copy his expressions . . .

So what's the point of all this speculation? Quite simply this: that we constantly need to be reminded that there is a glorious future ahead. Of course, we also need reminding that the present, too, is glorious, since it is into this present world that Jesus has come to display God and the **life** of his new age. That already is enough to tell us how much God loves us (verse 1); if Jesus is the **son of God**, God's love in Jesus has made us, too, his children, his sons and daughters. And if that's just the start, who knows what the ultimate end will be.

We need to be reminded of all this for a number of reasons, which will grow to a crescendo over the next two chapters. But before we get to the positive impact of this future hope, we need to come face to face with the negative one. Actually, I should have written 'with what seems to us to be the negative one', though in fact it is enormously positive. What do I mean?

If we have a hope like that up ahead of us, we should make every effort in the present time to be pure in the same way as he is pure. That is quite a challenge, but it makes all the sense in the world. If you are going to meet a very important colleague in another country, you might think it worth making the effort to learn at least some of their language in advance. If you are going to meet a future employer, you want to make sure you have learned enough about the business to make the right impression. And if you are going to meet *Jesus himself*...

You would want to make yourself 'pure'. But how? In verses 4–10 John issues what feels to us a very worrying challenge. 'Everyone who abides in him does not go on sinning.' What does this mean?

John is quite clear, and we can't get away from it. Following Jesus, 'abiding in him' (one of John's regular ways of saying 'belonging to him', implying that kind of life-sharing we saw earlier), means a transformed character. John knows, of course, that Christians do still sin from time to time; there is a remedy for that (see 2.1). What he is talking about here is the whole habit of life, 'going on sinning', sinning as the regular mode in which we live. We should be doing our best to avoid all kinds of sin, all the time, though we shall surely fail; but the failures must take place within a settled habit of life in which sin is no longer setting the tone. We are playing a different piece of music now, and even if our fingers slip sometimes and play some wrong notes, notes that belong to the music we used to play, that doesn't mean we are going back to play that old music for real once more.

It's not surprising that John says 'don't let anyone deceive you', because there have been many, and there are many today, who teach that sinning is perfectly all right. It isn't. To carry on as though no change of life was required is to show whose side you are on, and it isn't God's. God, as he says in verses 1 and 2, has made us his children in a whole new way, and being fathered by God means that our new selves, our new real selves, cannot and will not sin habitually, as our way of life.

And the greatest sin, it seems, is the failure to love. That points ahead to much of the rest of the letter.

1 JOHN 3.11—4.6

The Challenge of Love

> [11]This is the message which you heard right from the start, you see, that we should love one another. [12]We should not be like Cain, who was of the evil one, and murdered his brother. Why did he murder him? Because his deeds were evil, while his brother's were right.

¹³Don't be surprised, my brothers and sisters, if the world hates you. ¹⁴We know that we have passed from death to life, because we love the family. Anyone who doesn't love abides in death. ¹⁵Everyone who hates their brother or sister is a murderer, and you know that no murderer has the life of the coming age abiding in them. ¹⁶This is how we know love: he laid down his life for us. And we too ought to lay down our lives for our brothers and sisters. ¹⁷Anyone who has the means of life in this world, and sees a brother or sister in need, and closes their heart against them – how can God's love be abiding in them? ¹⁸Children, let us not love in word, or in speech, but in deed and in truth.

¹⁹Because of this, we know we are of the truth, and we will persuade our hearts of this fact before him, ²⁰because if our hearts condemn us, God is greater than our hearts. He knows everything. ²¹Beloved, if our hearts do not condemn us, we have boldness before God, ²²and we receive from him whatever we ask, because we keep his commands and give him pleasure when he sees what we are doing. ²³And this is his command, that we should believe in the name of his son Jesus the Messiah, and should love one another, just as he gave us the commandment. ²⁴Anyone who keeps his commandments abides in him, and he in them. This is how we know that he abides in us, by his spirit that he has given us.

⁴·¹Beloved, do not believe every spirit. Rather, test the spirits to see whether they are from God. Many false prophets, you see, have gone out into the world. ²This is how we know God's spirit: every spirit that agrees that Jesus the Messiah has come in the flesh is from God, ³and every spirit that does not confess Jesus is not from God. This spirit is actually the spirit of the Antimessiah. You have heard that it was coming, and now it is already in the world.

⁴But you, children, are from God, and you have overcome them, because the one who is in you is greater than the one who is in the world. ⁵They are from the world, and that is why they speak from the world, and why the world listens to them. ⁶We are from God; people who know God listen to us, but people who are not from God do not listen to us. That is how we can tell the spirit of truth from the spirit of error.

One of my favourite stories from the Old Testament is found in the book of 2 Kings, chapter 6. The context is one of continual skirmishing, and sometimes open warfare, between Israel, the northern half of the people of God, and Syria, their northern neighbour. The Syrian king has discovered that all his plans and deliberations are being revealed to the king of Israel because Elisha, the prophet in Israel, is being granted secret knowledge of them. So the king of Syria sends his army to track down Elisha and take him captive.

The next day, Elisha's servant discovers that there, all round their city, is an army with horses and chariots. He runs back to Elisha in a panic. What are they going to do? Elisha's answer is rightly famous: 'Don't be afraid', he says. 'There are more with us than there are with them.' What does he mean? Then he prays that God would open the young man's eyes. He does so, and the lad sees the reality: the mountain is full of horses and chariots of fire all around Elisha. From then on things naturally take a very different turn.

This sense of discovering that the forces with us are greater than the forces on the other side, despite initial appearances, comes again and again in scripture, and what John says here is one more instance. It always takes **faith** to see and know this reality, of course. Like Peter trying to walk on the water, it's all too easy to begin to doubt, and then we're in trouble. But, as John says here (4.4), 'the one who is in you is greater than the one who is in the world'. He has already warned us against loving 'the world'. Now we see something of the inner reality of 'the world', and how it goes to work. But we also see, more powerfully, the reality of God's presence with us, giving us the strength to overcome.

What is this battle, and why do we need this encouragement? Clearly the people to whom John is writing are in danger of being at best thoroughly confused, and at worst blown right off course, by all the different ideas, different claims, different would-be prophets with their various oracles, and so on, that are swirling all around them. We know so little of the first century, comparatively speaking, and can hardly begin to tell what precisely was going on. But from the hints in this passage and elsewhere we can figure out enough to see what John's readers might see as they, like Elisha's servants, came out of the house in the morning and stared in dismay at the forces ranged against them.

In particular, they are once again confronted with 'false prophets'. As we noted before, the problem about false prophets is that you can't tell them apart from the true ones – at first sight. They seem devout; they seem reasonable; they claim to have a word from God; so who are we to disagree? But John knows, as indeed Jesus himself had warned, and as we in our day need to learn all over again, that not everyone who claims to be a prophet is a prophet in fact. So how can you tell? How can you 'test the spirits', as he says?

The answer is that you need to listen carefully, and sift and weigh what you hear. Such people are unlikely to come out directly with curses or absurd teaching that is obviously absurd. That would give the game away. But gradually, as you listen, you may discern a fatal flaw. *They don't really believe that Jesus the **Messiah** has come in the flesh.* That is the criterion John offers in verse 2.

We can't be sure, because there were so many 'religious' movements, as well as political ones, in the first century that it's quite possible the 'false prophets' John has in mind didn't belong to any particular group that we know of from elsewhere. But to reject that Jesus had come in the flesh looks suspiciously like one branch at least of what came to be known as 'gnosticism' – a kind of religion that specialized in secret 'knowledge' (*gnosis*), and thought that by gaining this knowledge one might escape entirely from the physical world, and enter a realm of pure **spirit**.

For people who embraced this teaching – and it can be made to sound, for a while at least, quite like some bits of the genuine Christian **message** – it was out of the question that Jesus, the Messiah, should really have come 'in the flesh'. He was surely, they thought, a spiritual being. He couldn't have compromised that spiritual identity by having anything to do with 'flesh', the sordid, dirty, physical stuff, that needed to eat and drink, to urinate and defecate, to sleep and even – horror of all horrors! – to die.

And so, when they talked about 'Jesus', it wasn't the real Jesus they were referring to. It was someone who only 'seemed' to be a human like the rest of us. They made up stories about how he hadn't really died, because he hadn't really been a genuine, fleshly human all along. He was a spiritual being who came to reveal to others, to people who had a spark of the same 'spirit' already in them, that they were 'spiritual' too, and that by following his way they could escape this world altogether. There are many religious movements today, including some major ones, that similarly deny that Jesus could actually have been an ordinary 'fleshly' human being, and died a cruel death.

So, as I said, this message could sound quite like the genuine thing – hasn't John just said that we should not 'love the world'? – but at the crucial point it is radically different. Agreeing that Jesus the Messiah has come in the flesh is the crucial test, because that is not, actually, an extra bit added on to the Christian message; as John saw in writing his **gospel**, it was the vital, central point. 'The **word** became flesh and lived among us.' Take that away, and true Christian faith crashes to the ground. That's why any spirit that is making someone deny that Jesus has come in the flesh is the spirit of the 'Antimessiah'. Stop people believing, at all costs, in the incarnation of the Word! That spirit has been alive and active in our own day, as many people have poured scorn on the very idea of incarnation, of God actually becoming human. It remains a huge claim, as it always was. But it's central. It's non-negotiable.

At the moment, then, for John and perhaps for us, there is a conflict. People who speak 'from the world', going with the grain of popular opinion, will always find it easy to poke fun at the genuine beliefs of Christian faith. They will gain a hearing (verse 5). Sometimes all a Christian can do, faced with that, is to cling on to the bald and basic statement that, so far as we can tell, the meaning of the word 'God' is actually defined in relation to the Jesus who, we believe, came from this God and became flesh in our midst. Take that away, and we simply don't know who God is any more. That's why we are bound to claim, stark though it sounds, that 'people who know God listen to us, but people who are not from God do not listen to us.'

No doubt, in our own day, such a statement sounds impossibly arrogant. But John doesn't mean it like that. He is putting it sharply, almost telegraphically. His whole letter, as we see right at the end, is about holding on to the true God and rejecting the claims of idols. And the way we know the true God is through Jesus. You can't get round that.

That's why he needs to reassure his hearers, like Elisha with his servant. If the true God is indeed the source of our **life**, then you have already won the victory! The one who is in you is greater than the one who is in the world. It may not look or feel like that. But that's where faith comes in. Faith that the living God did indeed take flesh, our flesh, in Jesus. When that message is coming across, the spirit of truth is at work.

1 JOHN 4.7–21

God's Love

[7]Beloved, let us love one another, because love is from God, and all who love are fathered by God and know God. [8]The one who does not love has not known God, because God is love. [9]This is how God's love has appeared among us: God sent his only son into the world, so that we should live through him. [10]Love consists in this: not that we loved God, but that he loved us and sent his son to be the sacrifice that would atone for our sins. [11]Beloved, if that's how God loved us, we ought to love one another in the same way. [12]Nobody has ever seen God. If we love one another, God abides in us and his love is completed in us. [13]That is how we know that we abide in him, and he in us, because he has given us a portion of his spirit. [14]And we have seen and bear witness that the father sent the son to be the world's saviour. [15]Anyone who confesses that Jesus is God's son, God abides in them and they abide in God. [16]And we have known and have believed the love which God has for us.

God is love; those who abide in love abide in God, and God abides in them. [17]This is what makes love complete for us, so that we may have boldness and confidence on the day of judgment, because just as he is, so are we within this world. [18]There is no fear in love; complete love drives out fear. Fear has to do with punishment, and anyone who is afraid has not been completed in love. [19]We love, because he first loved us. [20]If someone says, 'I love God', but hates their brother or sister, that person is a liar. Someone who doesn't love a brother or sister whom they have seen, how can they love God, whom they haven't seen? [21]This is the command we have from him: anyone who loves God should love their brother or sister too.

Statistics aren't everything, but sometimes they are quite revealing. The word 'love', or some form of it, occurs no fewer than twenty-seven times in these fifteen verses. No need to ask, then, what the subject-matter is here. In fact, we seem to be at the very heart of the letter. This is what John most wants to say. Everything that has gone before leads up to this; everything that follows, in the final chapter, solidifies it and rounds it off. 'Love' is what John has on his mind.

The vital connection of thought here goes like this. John has just stressed that Jesus, the **Messiah**, has indeed come in the flesh, and that to deny that is to reveal oneself as a false prophet. But this is no mere dogmatic shibboleth, a meaningless formula which people have to learn in order to pass some arbitrary doctrinal test. It is a symptom of what Christianity is all about. The Christian **faith** grows directly out of, and must directly express, the belief that in Jesus the Messiah the one true God has revealed himself to be – love incarnate. And those who hold this faith, and embrace it as the means of their own hope and **life**, must themselves reveal the self-same fact before the watching world. Love incarnate must be the badge that the Christian community wears, the sign not only of who they are but of who their God is.

How easy to write, how hard to achieve. Only today I was talking to someone who, commenting gloomily on various experiences of actual church life, suggested that churches should have a 'danger' sign outside, warning people to expect nasty, gossipy, snide conversation and behaviour if they came in. That, sadly, has always been a reality in church life. That is why, from St Paul onwards, Christian writers have been at pains to insist that it should not be like that with us. The rule of love, I say again, is not an optional extra. It is of the very essence of what we are about. If this means we need some new reformations, so be it.

Follow the argument through. Basic to it all, in verses 7–10, is the fact that God's love is revealed precisely in sending Jesus, his son, into the world to be the **sacrifice** that would atone for our sins. Standing at the foot of the cross, gazing on the length to which God's love has gone for us, it's impossible (unless we are particularly hard-hearted; unless, as he says, we simply haven't known God at all) not to sense the power and possibilities within that love. This is the force that has changed the world, and could still change the world if only the followers of Jesus would really come on board with it.

Therefore, 'if that's how God loved us, we ought to love one another in the same way' (verse 11). This is, if anything, an even stronger statement than many might imagine. You could hear it as simply saying, 'There: God has set us an example; we should copy it.' That is true. But the next verse shows a greater depth. 'Nobody has ever seen God. If we love one another, God abides in us and his love is completed in us.' To get the point, stand that statement in parallel with the concluding verse (1.18) in the majestic Prologue to St John's **gospel**: 'Nobody has ever seen God. The only-begotten God, who is intimately close to the father – he has brought him to light.' The meaning of that statement is striking: we don't really know who 'God' is – until we look at Jesus. Now we see the meaning of our present statement in 1 John 4.12: people don't really know who 'God' is – until they see it revealed in the life of Christians. Until, that is, 'his love is completed in us'. What God launched decisively in Jesus, he wants to complete in and through us. As Jesus unveiled God before a surprised and unready world, so must we. Love is that important.

All this can and must come about because of the gift of God's **spirit**. The spirit enables us to bear witness to what the father has done in sending the son. Again, the witness must of course come not in word but in deed, as John says in 3.18. Our love must 'come in the flesh', just as God's love did.

That's why, at the end of this passage, John comes back to the same point. If you say you love God, but don't love your brother or sister (he means a fellow member of the Christian community), you are quite simply telling lies. The same door that opens to let out your love to God is the door that opens to let out love to your neighbour. If you're not doing the latter, you're not doing the former. It's as simple – and as devastating – as that.

We may well find this daunting. Who can live up to it? But in verses 17 and 18 John moves into almost lyrical mode as he talks not about the fear that we should have of being found out, of failing to come up to the mark, but of the boldness and confidence that we shall have on the day of judgment. He does not say, as we might expect, that we have this boldness and confidence because we look away from ourselves and simply trust in God's all-powerful, all-conquering love. No. He says that 'just as he is, so are we within this world'. What does he mean? He means, it seems, that if God revealed himself in the world by turning his love into flesh and blood, when we do the same we should realize that we are 'completing' God's love. What will be operating through us will be the true love of the true God.

When that happens, there is no need to fear any longer. Love that has been made complete in this way leaves no room for fear. Once you learn to give yourself to others as God gave himself to us, there is nothing to be afraid of any more, just a completed circle of love. No doubt this, like some other things John says, leaves us breathless, wondering if we will ever attain to that simplicity of faith and life. But did we expect that having the true, living God come to make his dwelling with us, inviting us to make our dwelling with him (verse 16), would be a kind of easy-going, half-hearted, hobby-religion? God has taken us utterly seriously. How can we not do the same with him?

At the heart of this passage we find, repeated, a little word which means a whole world to John, as in his gospel it means so much to Jesus himself. 'Those who *abide* in love *abide* in God, and God *abides* in them' (verse 16). This comes in various other places, including the previous verse, but this is its fullest expression. The word is a simple one, meaning 'dwell' or 'remain' or 'make one's home'; but the reality is profound, going to the heart of what Christian faith is all about. This is the meaning of the **'fellowship'**, the sharing of a common life, between the father, the son and all those who belong to the son, who confess 'that Jesus is God's son' (verse 15). It is a mutual indwelling: we in God and God in us. Once more, this is easy to say, but huge and hard to take in. Harder still to keep your balance, to maintain this life, day by day and year by year, with the dangerous winds of false prophecy blowing around our heads and the pull and drag of 'the world' at our feet. Only powerful love can keep us upright. And that powerful love is to be found, as always, as we gaze at the cross (verses 9–11).

1 JOHN 5.1–12

Faith Wins the Victory

[1]Everyone who believes that the Messiah is Jesus has been fathered by God. Everyone who loves the parent loves the child as well. [2]That is how we know that we love the children of God, because we love God and do what he commands. [3]This is what loving God means: it means keeping his commandments. His commandments, what's more, are no trouble, [4]because everything that is fathered by God conquers the world. This is the victory that conquers the world: our faith.

[5]Who is the one who conquers the world? Surely the one who believes that Jesus is God's son! [6]It was he who came by means of water and blood, Jesus the Messiah, not by water only but by the water and the blood. The spirit is the one who bears witness, because the spirit is the truth. [7]There are three that bear witness, you see, [8]the spirit, the water and the blood, and these three agree together. [9]If we have received human witness, God's witness is greater. This is the witness of God, the testimony he has borne to his son. [10]All those who

believe in the son of God have the witness in themselves, but anyone who does not believe God has made a liar of him, because they have not believed in the witness which God bore concerning his son. [11]This is the witness: God has given us the life of the age to come, and this life is in his son. [12]Anyone who has the son has life. Anyone who does not have the son of God does not have life.

The first time I went snorkelling on a tropical reef, I was overwhelmed by the sight. Face down in the water by the Great Barrier Reef, off the north-east coast of Australia, I knew at once that this was a totally new experience. All around me, some within a few inches, were dozens, hundreds of fish of all shapes and sizes, and particularly colours. Colours! It was like a kaleidoscope. Electric blues, vivid yellows, bright reds, and many, many more. They were getting up to all kinds of tricks, too, each behaving (I learned afterwards) in ways characteristic of their particular species.

After a few minutes of having my mind blown by this, I thought: I must go back to the boat, get a notebook, and write down what I've just seen. I knew that I would forget – how could I possibly remember! – the brilliant display and huge variety I had been watching. And then I thought: typical scholar, wanting to record everything. Just relax and enjoy the show. So I did. And, as a result, what I've written above is about as much as I can manage. But this is only a tiny fraction of the impression those fish made on me.

By this stage of the first letter of John, the reader may well be starting to feel rather as I did on that occasion. There are so many points coming and going, in this seemingly infinite spiral of John's discourse, that it is by now hard to keep track of where we've got to. The themes are repeating and double-repeating. John is producing variations on what he's already said, and then variations on the variations. Why not just sit back and enjoy what is now the familiar music? That, indeed, may be part of the point of the way he's writing. He is trying to teach his readers to make the connections for themselves; to see, and to enjoy seeing, the way in which each part of the picture leads more or less directly to every other part.

But then, just when we might be in danger of thinking, 'Yes, yes, you've said this before', a striking new idea emerges, not over against the others but drawing out yet another new dimension of them. He has spoken of our believing in Jesus, believing that he is the **Messiah**, that he has come in the flesh, that people who believe this are the children of God, bound by God's own love to keep God's commandments, which means primarily that one should love both God himself and one's neighbour. These are the brilliantly coloured creatures that now swim before our eyes. But here is the new element: everything fathered by God conquers the world (verse 4). What is this about? Why should we want not just to resist the blandishments of the world but to 'overcome' it? What does that mean, and how does it happen?

Why, to begin with, does he say 'everything' rather than 'everyone'? We can only guess; but my guess is that he is referring not only to the human beings who, as in verse 1, have been 'fathered by God', but to that which results from their life and work: the things they do, as well as the people they are.

So what is this 'conquest', and how does it come about? John seems, here, to be very close to a seam of thought we find in the **gospel** of John, a seam which emerges (for instance) at 12.31, where Jesus speaks of 'the world's ruler' being 'thrown out'; at 14.30, where he declares that 'the ruler of this world' has 'nothing to do with me'; and at 16.33 where, after warning the **disciples** that they will face persecution in the world, concludes, 'But cheer up; I have conquered the world!'

In the gospel, all this is meant, so it seems, to draw the eye up to the two dramatic chapters 18 and 19, in which an odd, unbalanced conversation takes place between Jesus, Pontius Pilate and the **chief priests**. Jesus and Pilate argue about the great themes of **kingdom**, truth and power, with the chief priests accusing Jesus and finally persuading Pilate to have him crucified. Somehow, we are meant to understand, these events and their aftermath, more particularly Jesus' death as 'king of the Jews', are in fact the moment when, and the means by which, 'the world's ruler' is being 'thrown out'. They are the means by which Jesus is in fact conquering the world, even though it looks for the moment as though the world is conquering him. There is a deep mystery here, and this is not the place to explore it further.

Except to this extent: that it is precisely then, in John's gospel, that the writer emphasizes that, at Jesus' death, water and blood came out of his side when the centurion pierced it with his spear (19.34). This, says the writer, is something he can personally vouch for. His 'witness' is true. And suddenly we realize that we are in exactly the same seam of thought as in our present passage, 1 John 5.4–9. *The victory that conquers the world is the saving death of Jesus.* And those who by **faith** cling on to the God who is made known personally in and as the Jesus who died on the cross – they share that victory, that conquest of 'the world'.

'The world', it seems, is not just the source of temptation and distraction. It is a positive power for evil, resenting the arrival of its own creator to claim his rightful lordship over it. ('He was in the world,' said John in the gospel, 'and the world was made through him, and the world did not know him.') It will fight back – a fight which, in the gospel, comes to its head when Jesus, representing God's kingdom, faces Pilate, representing Caesar's kingdom, the supreme power in the world. And the death of Jesus, with the water and the blood already separated, showing beyond doubt that his death had been real, gives the lie to any who might say that he didn't really die, or that he wasn't really fully human, 'come in the flesh'.

(At this point there is a quite different problem which will be obvious to anyone using the Authorized [King James] Version. That translation used a manuscript in which someone had added, in verse 7, words which are found nowhere else, introducing the 'trinitarian' formula: 'there are three that bear witness in **heaven**, the father, the **word** and the **holy spirit**; and these three are one.' It is important to say both that these words form no part of the original letter and that John would undoubtedly have agreed with them.)

John is now coming back to his controversy with the 'antimessianic' teachers, who denied that Jesus had truly come 'in the flesh'. They were prepared, it seems, to acknowledge that a figure called 'Jesus' had been baptized by **John the Baptist**. They could interpret that in terms of some kind of manifestation of a 'Jesus' who seemed to be human, even if he was not fully so. But they couldn't allow that this 'Jesus' would actually die, be really dead. And that is the point to which 'the **spirit**' bears witness – through the testimony in the gospel narrative, and in the work of the spirit in the individual hearts and minds of believers. God has given this witness, by his spirit, to make the point that the world has indeed been overcome. No other god, no other power, no other being in all the world loves like this, gives like this, dies like this. All others win victories by fighting; this one, by suffering. All other gods exercise power by killing; this one, by dying.

It is quite possible – though we can't be sure of this – that John expects his hearers themselves to face actual persecution. If so, the 'witness' or 'testimony' that they are to bear, welling up within themselves by the work of the spirit, might well turn into that other kind of 'witness', namely martyrdom. The word is the same in Greek. If so, this will be seen by John as further confirmation of the whole point. But his summary in verses 11 and 12 draws the whole thing together so well that it is hard to do other than repeat it. This is the witness – the witness that God has borne to his son, and that the spirit bears within us: God has given us the **life** of the **age to come**, and this life is in his son. This is what we saw right at the start of the letter. Therefore, dramatically and categorically: anyone who has the son has life. Anyone who does not have the **son of God** does not have life. Whether or not we like stark and plain conclusions, there are times when they matter, and this is one of those times.

1 JOHN 5.13-21

The True God

¹³I am writing these things to you so that you may know that you, who believe in the name of the son of God, do indeed have the life of the age to come. ¹⁴This is the bold confidence we have before him: if we ask for something according to his will, he hears us. ¹⁵And if we know that he hears us in whatever we ask, we know that we already possess the requests we have asked from him.

¹⁶If anyone sees a brother or sister committing a sin which is not deadly, they should ask, and God will give life to the people who are sinning in a way which is not deadly. There is such a thing as deadly sin; I do not say that one should pray about that. ¹⁷All sin is unrighteousness, and there is a sin which is not deadly.

¹⁸We know that everyone fathered by God does not go on sinning. The one who was fathered by God keeps them, and the evil one does not touch them. ¹⁹We know that we are from God, and the whole world is under the power of the evil one. ²⁰We know that the son of God has come and has given us understanding so that we should know the truth. And we are in the truth, in his son Jesus the Messiah.

This is the true God; this is the life of the age to come. ²¹Children, guard yourselves against idols.

Sometimes a short story will play a trick on its readers. Sometimes the author has told the story cleverly so as to lead us in one direction throughout the narrative, and then, with the last sentence, will reveal something which changes everything. This forces the reader to think quickly back through the whole story once more, eager to discover any earlier clues that might have given the game away. I remember, for example, an engrossing short story in which one was led to assume all along that the hero was a man, only to discover in the very last sentence that she was a woman. Suddenly everything looked, to say the least, radically different.

I don't think John was intending to play a trick on his readers, but all the same the final sentence of this remarkable little letter may well cause us to think back through what he has written to see where this apparently new idea had come from. 'Children,' he says, 'guard yourselves against idols.' What does he mean?

We might imagine that he was warning against idol worship, which of course flourished right across the ancient world, with temples to every god you could think of, including new temples to the newest gods, Julius Caesar, his successors, and their families. Certainly John would not want his readers to have anything to do with pagan worship as such. But I think he means something more subtle than that, more in keeping with what he has been saying all through.

The point of insisting on God's love, on the vital importance of loving one another, and above all on Jesus the **Messiah** having come in the flesh, is that this isn't just one necessary truth among many, part of the coherent structure of Christian belief. It is the sign that we are actually worshipping the true God *rather than some man-made idol.*

The idol in question, however, would not be one that was actually carved and placed in a temple. The idol in question would be one that would be called 'God', and might well be worshipped by some people who called themselves 'Christians'. But it would be a different god, not the true one at all. The true God is known, as far as John is concerned, by the fact that he sent his son to come into the world in human flesh and to die a genuine human death. Deny that, and you're not just denying something about Jesus. You're denying something about God.

This, then, is 'the true God', and this **life** which we have in him is indeed 'the life of the **age to come**'. The creator has brought his future purposes up into the present. That is why something radically new has been launched upon the world, even at the drastic cost of God's own son. This is why sharp conflict has come into being, between those who represent this new life and those who are desperately trying to contain the new wine in old bottles, to insist that nothing quite so drastic has actually happened.

What then for those who find themselves caught up in this extraordinary and unprecedented overlap of the two ages? Here, in verses 13–15, John amplifies what he said earlier in 3.22; he is echoing, too, promises made by Jesus in John 14.13, 15.7 and elsewhere. Those who believe in Jesus, who abide in God, can pray with a new, bold confidence. They stand at the place where **heaven** and earth meet, and are encouraged to draw down the blessings of heaven into the life of earth, and to know as they make their requests that they have already been granted – even though, as scripture itself and Christian experience both teach, they may be granted in ways one had not expected. The fact that one naturally tends to add that kind of qualifying remark is telling. Perhaps, instead, one should just start praying a bit more thoroughly for more specific things, quoting this promise back at the God who does not want us to make him a liar (4.10).

One of the things we are to pray for is for those who are wandering from the path. It's hard to know where exactly John draws the line between deadly and non-deadly sin. Perhaps he means that those who have denied that Jesus is come in the flesh have committed a sin which puts them beyond the reach of **redemption**, since they have cut off the branch from which the fresh shoots of rescue-promises are growing. But one of the comforting things about this strange little passage is the light it sheds on verse 18. Without this, we might suppose that John thinks all Christians have stopped sinning altogether; with it, it is clear that he does indeed mean, as I have translated it, 'everyone fathered by God *does not go on sinning*'. It is the continuous habit of life that here concerns him. Clearly he would rather one did not sin at all, but occasional sins, a blip on the chart as it were, can be prayed for, can be confessed and forgiven. They are quite different from the hard-hearted sin which carries on regardless, and which, as in Romans 1.32, even comes to see the action in question as not sinful at all.

Central to the assurance of these verses is the promise in the second half of verse 18, which links Jesus himself closely to the believer. Believers are everyone fathered by God, but Jesus is the one *par excellence* who is fathered by God; and he, Jesus, will keep believers under his protection, so that the evil one, who for the moment retains power over the world, cannot do them harm. It may not always feel like that. But part of the victory which consists in **faith** (5.4) is believing that Jesus has in fact defeated all the powers that might endanger us, and that we are 'in him', and so 'in the truth' as opposed to being 'in the lie', the lie of which the world has done its best to persuade us.

The true God. The one Jesus. The life of the age to come. Love given, love passed on. This is where we stand. This is the witness of John.

2 JOHN

2 JOHN 1-6

The Sign of Life

¹From the Elder to the Chosen Lady and her children, whom I love in truth – as indeed, in addition to myself, do all those who know the truth, ²because of the truth that abides in us and is with us for ever. ³Grace, mercy and peace from God the father and from Jesus the Messiah, the son of the father, be with us in truth and love.

⁴I was delighted when I found some of your children walking in the truth, just as we received the commandment from the father. ⁵And now, dear Lady, I am writing to you, not indeed a new commandment, but the one we had from the very beginning, that we should love one another. ⁶This is love: that we should behave in accordance with his commandments. And this is the commandment, just as you heard it from the very start, that we should behave in accordance with it.

When I was doing research on life after death, and on what people believed about it, I came across some disturbing material from the nineteenth century. People had realized that sometimes the doctors made a mistake, supposing someone to be dead when they were only in fact in some kind of a coma. Breath and pulse can be so faint that you wrongly suppose they've gone altogether. Sometimes coffins were discovered in which the supposedly dead inhabitants had been trying to claw their way out, to scratch the lid with their fingernails, until inevitably dying of suffocation. Being naturally afraid of this possibility, some people gave orders that their coffins should be fitted with either a speaking tube or a bell rope or some other means through which they could, if necessary, indicate that they were still alive.

We are perhaps a little better at detecting the signs of **life**, and the clear signs of death, these days, though the fears persist. But the question of how you can tell whether someone is really alive or not persists in other spheres, too. What are the signs – the moral and spiritual equivalents of breath and pulse – which enable you to tell whether someone is truly alive in the **spirit**, that they are a true Christian?

John the Elder – which seems to have been a title some in the early church gave to the ageing **apostle** – is writing here to another church, addressing it cryptically as the 'Chosen Lady'. At the end of the letter he refers to the church where he himself is based as the 'Chosen Sister'. We have no idea which churches these were: one may have been in Ephesus, and another in a city either near at hand or far away. They could even be two churches within the same large city; the population of Ephesus in this period was in the tens of thousands, perhaps even larger, and there might well be two or more churches of a dozen or two at some distance from one another. Why he referred to them in this way we can only guess, but the best guess is that danger was at hand, and the more he could make the opening and closing of the letter look like an ordinary message within a family, the safer he and his readers might be.

But the point of what he is saying in this first part of the letter is that he has seen the vital signs, the signs of life, in some members of this other church. He is delighted (verse 4) because he has 'found some of your children walking in the truth'. This, indeed, is the major theme of the first part of this short letter, as the introduction makes clear, mentioning 'truth' no fewer than four times in three verses.

But what (as Pontius Pilate famously asked Jesus) is 'truth'? For John it is very simple, and very profound. At one level 'truth' simply means 'Jesus the **Messiah** as the full revelation of God the father'. Everything else will flow from that. But this 'everything else' gets us into all sorts of areas. Already in these verses we find John speaking of loving in truth, of knowing the truth, of the truth abiding in us and with us, and God's grace, mercy and peace being with us in truth and love. Then, as the key 'sign of life', he finds some members of the other church who are 'walking in the truth', who are (that is) behaving in accordance with the truth.

Truth, for John, seems to be something to do with a wholeness, a completeness, of human life, from the first stirrings of thought and imagination through to every detail of practical living. He believes that in Jesus the Messiah the creator God has both displayed the form and pattern of this truth and, by dealing with all the untruth in the world, all the lies that distort and deface humans and the world, has enabled men and women to rediscover truth-in-action, truth-in-the-heart, truth-in-real-life. Truth has to do with integrity. And integrity has to do with God's redeeming purposes for the whole world, with God's plan for the new creation.

Truth, then, isn't just a matter of saying things which correspond to reality, saying 'today it is cold' when it really is. That is simply surface-level truth. Truth, for John, is something that goes down deep and spreads out wide. It is what happens when humans, redeemed in the Messiah and renewed by the **spirit**, think, speak and act in a way which corresponds to God's plan to renew the whole creation – and, indeed, which sets that renewal forward in whatever way they are called to do.

Untruth (telling lies), by contrast, is therefore what happens when people think, speak and act as though the present unredeemed world is all that there is; as though 'the way things are' sets the pattern and boundary for 'the way things should be'. This is the foundation for what will be said in the second part of the letter, where the Deceiver denies the great new truth which must shape all perceptions of reality, all actions within the world.

And the great 'truth' which is unveiled in the **gospel** of Jesus is of course that the powerful, redeeming love of God is the motor that drives the cosmos – and that those who are discovering the truth, or rather being discovered by it, must learn to let that love flow through them to their fellow Christians and to the world around. This is the 'commandment' above all others, emphasized as such by Jesus himself and by one early Christian writer after another. Love is what matters. If only the church had allowed this to sink in and transform its life from generation to generation. Thank God it still happens all over the place; but please God, may it do so on a larger scale.

Love is not, then, the optional extra to be added when everything else is sorted out. It is the thing that goes on round and round, like blood circulating in a healthy living body, or to and fro, like good strong breathing. That's actually how John's writing works, here and elsewhere. Breathe out: the commandment is that we should love one another (verse 5); breathe in: love means keeping the commandments (verse 6a). And, underneath this, there is the further commandment – that you should keep on living in accordance with it (verse 6b)! He can't say it enough. And we can't hear it enough. These little letters may be small, and may not attract much attention in comparison with their better-known neighbours. But they carry the same explosive charge.

2 JOHN 7–13

Don't Be Deceived!

⁷Many deceivers, you see, have gone out into the world. These are people who do not admit that Jesus the Messiah has come in the flesh. Such a person is the Deceiver – the Antimessiah! ⁸Watch out for yourselves, so that you won't lose what we have worked for, but may receive the full reward.

⁹Anyone who goes out on their own, and does not abide in the teaching of the Messiah, does not have God. One who abides in the teaching – such a one has the father and the son. ¹⁰If anyone comes to you and does not bring this teaching, don't receive them into the house; don't even give them a greeting. ¹¹Anyone who utters a greeting to such a person shares in their wicked deeds.

¹²I have many things to write to you, but I did not wish to write with pen and ink. I am hoping instead to come to you, and to speak face to face. That will complete our joy.

¹³The children of your Chosen Sister send you greetings.

I was going to quote a Beatles song, but then I remembered that you have to pay a lot of money even to quote a single line. But the song is well enough known, declaring that the only thing one might need is love. It's ironic, of course, that you have to pay through the nose to quote a song whose whole message is that love matters and money doesn't.

That irony haunts the mood, and the philosophy, of a large swathe of Western culture over the last forty or fifty years. 'Make love, not war', ran the slogan from those who were protesting against the war in Vietnam. Nobody was going to say that love was a bad thing. Surely life would be simpler and better if we all agreed to love each other and not fight any more. But the protests, insisting that love is better than war, contained a dark note of hatred against Western governments and ways of life, a hatred which easily spilled over into a different type of violence. What happened to all that love?

The trouble is, of course, that 'love' covers far too many things in our language today. Yes, as Peter says, 'love covers a multitude of sins' (1 Peter 4.8, quoting Proverbs 10.12). But it is clear throughout the whole New Testament, not least in the teaching of Jesus himself, that 'love' was never meant to mean one of the main things which, sadly, it has come to mean today.

Today, 'love' is regularly supposed to mean 'tolerance'. You should never insist on anything, but always 'love' the other person who does things differently. You should never say that anything is actually wrong: that's 'unloving' to the person who is not only doing it but claiming that it's the right thing to do. You should never say, either, that *this* way of doing things is 'right', still less that it is the *only* 'right' way to live: how 'intolerant', how 'arrogant', how 'unloving'. That is where a large part of our culture now stands. So strongly is this view held that if a Christian attempts to challenge it they are accused of being, well, unChristian.

But, as with protest movements, this passion for 'tolerance' only extends so far. Such a position is in fact extremely 'intolerant' of people who take a more definite stance – which includes the mainstream adherents of many traditional faiths. This shows up the cult of 'tolerance' for what it is: the moralistic invention of the modern secular world, borrowing Christian language to refer to something very different. Underneath the nice language this view is just as 'arrogant', just as 'intolerant', as those it opposes. If anything, more so, because it effortlessly claims the high moral ground without taking seriously the claims of other world-views.

We need to bear all this in mind when reading a passage like this, because our modern cult of 'tolerance' is bound to react sharply against what John has to say in this letter. This is hard on John, one of the greatest Christian minds and hearts there ever was, one of the most attuned to Jesus his master. Here, when he gets down to business, he is about as 'intolerant' as it's possible to be. Don't be taken in by the Deceiver, the Antimessiah! Don't be hoodwinked by those who follow him! Watch out for yourselves too; if you're not careful, all the work of building up the church might go to waste. Fancy going through all you've gone through and then not receiving the full reward (verse 8)!

As in the longer letter, 1 John, the critical question here is about Jesus the **Messiah** actually 'coming in the flesh'. This was such a scandalous idea in the ancient world, as it has been in the modern world, that people will do anything to avoid having to believe it or live by it. And, as we saw in 1 John, this is not a mere 'dogmatic' point, to be insisted on even though it's abstract and unrelated to real life. God's love in the flesh, in Jesus, is the source and framework for God's love coming in human flesh in those who follow Jesus. That is how the two halves of this little letter belong so closely together. Anything that waters down this truth is not to be 'tolerated'.

What's more, this great central truth is to determine the limits of Christian **fellowship**. We today bend over backwards to be 'hospitable' and 'inclusive' – only up to a point, of course, as we saw before. As Paul says when facing similar questions, we must of course maintain civil and courteous relations with 'those outside' (1 Corinthians 5.10; 10.27). But if someone is claiming to be a Christian, and does not keep to this central teaching – then they should not be welcomed. They should not even be greeted in the street. If this seems harsh, as indeed it does, we need to remember the way in which even casual greetings, let alone hospitality, can then be used and are indeed regularly used as a sign that such people are approved of: 'Well, so-and-so had them to dinner, so they can't think it's so bad after all.'

Is it, after all, 'unloving' or 'intolerant' to shout to people that the house is on fire? Ought we to 'tolerate' people who come into someone else's house and throw lighted matches around the room? Is it 'intolerant' to warn people that they should not drive down that road, because the bridge has been weakened by floods and might collapse? Is it 'unChristian' to insist that if we are to worship the God we know in Jesus we can't simultaneously be worshipping one of the very different gods who are on offer elsewhere? Of course not. Is it a failure of Christian charity if we warn people that certain styles of behaviour lead to ruin rather than to **life**?

Of course not – though, naturally, we need to be sure we are standing on the firm ground of the **gospel**, not on a point that just happens to embody our particular prejudices. All of that has to be worked out.

No doubt this challenge is too hard for some. And, yes, it is difficult to know where to draw the line today. It's quite unlikely that we will be faced with people teaching what John's opponents were teaching. There may well be other issues which, when we understand what's at stake, function as flash points. And, yes, it is always tempting to draw the line just a bit more tightly than one should, boosting one's own sense of rightness at the cost of someone who, in their own way, may be moving closer to the light. But just because that danger exists, that doesn't mean that these verses have nothing to say to us. A word to the wise.

The letter ends with a sign of that embodied love which John has been expounding. A letter is a poor substitute for a personal, face-to-face meeting, and he's going to stop here because he is looking forward to being together again. This is, perhaps, a reminder to us today, with our multiple electronic communications making even letters, for many, a thing of the past, that full human life involves full, bodily, facial contact and meeting. We are in danger today of adopting, without reflection, styles of behaviour which devalue the deep truth of genuine humanness. John would gently urge us to take every opportunity to put this right.

3 JOHN

3 JOHN 1-8

Hospitality for God's People

¹The Elder to beloved Gaius, whom I love in truth.

²Beloved, I pray that all is going well with you, and that you are every bit as healthy physically as you are spiritually. ³I was absolutely delighted, you see, when some of the family arrived and bore witness to your truthfulness, since clearly you are walking in the truth. ⁴Nothing gives me greater joy than this, to hear that my children are walking in the truth.

⁵Beloved, when you are doing all that you do for family members, even when they are strangers, you are doing a faithful work. ⁶These people have borne witness to your love in the presence of the assembly, and you will do well to send them on their way in a manner worthy of God. ⁷They went out for the sake of the Name, not accepting help from outsiders. ⁸We ought to support people like that, so that we may become fellow-workers with the truth.

One of the more exciting and entertaining parts of the internet revolution is the kind of software that lets you zoom in, all the way from satellites in space, on a particular country, then a particular town, then a particular street, and finally on just one house. Sometimes there are photographs of the house which enable you to recognize someone's car in the street, or a familiar object outside the building. When my daughter looked up her house on one occasion, we could even see her cat, a white blob in the back garden. And when my wife and I were house-hunting not long ago, it was a marvellous way of narrowing down our search before we had even got in the car to visit particular properties.

The three letters of John have this zooming-in effect. The first letter could be addressed to almost any church, and indeed from the beginning was relevant to a large number of churches, probably (but not certainly) in the western part of ancient Turkey. And it could be taken and applied at once to churches anywhere else in the ancient or the modern world. Then, in the second letter, it's clear that John is writing to a particular church. He doesn't say where, but obviously he has met some members of that church and is writing to the leadership to congratulate them on the way in which his people are 'walking in the truth'. Now, in the third letter, he is writing to one particular church leader, someone called Gaius about whom, sadly, we don't know anything else. We don't know which church he belonged to, or why he received this short letter. But we do know enough to be able to learn a couple of much-needed lessons from what John has to say to him.

As in the previous letter, John is delighted to know that someone is 'walking in the truth', behaving with that integrity which both reflects and embodies the truth of the **gospel** itself. We can take it that this involves not just correct doctrine and proper outward behaviour, but that love for God and for one's fellow believers which, for John, is the sign that the truth of the gospel has really been grasped, not as an abstract idea but as what it is, the very **life** of God himself at work in his people.

It is this love which must then flow out into hospitality to fellow believers. This was even more important in the early church, where all that most people 'knew' about this new movement was that it was bizarre, crazy and socially undesirable. If that was the probable context, we can understand that travelling missionaries, or even Christians who were simply travelling on ordinary business, would be very much dependent on local groups of believers for board and lodging. So common was this practice that, not long after this letter was written, another early Christian writing called 'The Teaching' (known as the *Didache*) had to lay down regulations for such travellers. '**Apostles**' could stay at most two days, and ordinary Christians a maximum of three. If generous love was to be the rule for the hosts, the guests needed clear boundaries so as not to abuse that love. As we see in 1 and 2 Thessalonians and 1 Timothy, the church had to make clear that its obligation to care for one another was not the same thing as an invitation to lazy spongers.

But Gaius, it seems, had gone out of his way to be generous. Those from John's church who had visited Gaius had come back with a glowing report, and part of the reason for this letter seems to be to thank him. This is love in action, as John was urging in 1 John 3.18: not in word only, but in deed and in truth. In fact, as we have seen in other New Testament passages, 'love' for the early Christians was not primarily something you did with your heart and emotions. It was something you did with your whole life, not least your money and your home. So it had been with Gaius.

John is quite clear: the travelling missionaries had gone out 'for the sake of the Name', the great and powerful name of Jesus himself. This would at once put them at risk, and, partly for that reason, they had determined not to receive help from non-Christians. Like Ezra in his journey to Jerusalem (Ezra 8.21–23), they were trusting in God's protection, and God provided through the hospitality of his people. Yes, says John (verse 8): this is how our **faith** is supposed to work. We are meant to be 'fellow-workers with the truth'.

Truth, as always in John, is not simply a fact or a quality. It is an energy, a power, the living and dynamic quality that transforms people, communities and ultimately the world. We are privileged to be caught up in the work of Truth, turning our misguided and often wicked world into a place where once again the creator God is honoured and glorified. And this collaboration in the work of the Truth comes right down to the practical details of a meal, a bed for the night and a good start in the morning.

Apart from the journeys of Paul, we know very little of the movements of other Christian leaders, teachers and missionaries in the first two or three generations. Yet, from the evidence we have, such people seem to have been numerous, and often on the move. It is worth pondering the vast difference between their world, where most people hadn't even heard of Jesus, and those who only knew that his followers were a strange and dangerous bunch of people, and ours, where 'the church' as an institution is all too well known, even in countries which try to ban or severely limit the practice of Christian faith.

Precisely because of the differences, we have a lot to learn from those early days. The cheerful courage and faith both of such first-century missionaries and of those who gave them hospitality (perhaps arousing suspicious questions from neighbours) ought to remind us that following Jesus is expected to be an adventure. New things will happen. New people will come into our lives, and even though they were strangers a moment before, suddenly we realize we are part of the same family (verse 5).

That, indeed, is perhaps the main lesson of these verses. If I were to turn up unexpectedly on the doorstep of a close family member, I would expect them to welcome me and see how they could help. At the heart of the New Testament vision of the church is that sense of *family*, of being brothers and sisters. I have sometimes been privileged to see this sense coming alive in local churches, even in our cynical Western world where the church so often reflects the hyper-individualism of our culture. When it happens, it is a lovely thing. It's like being back with John, Gaius and the rest, trusting in the Truth and walking in it.

3 JOHN 9-15

Authority and Example

⁹I have written something to the assembly. But Diotrephes, who wants to be the most important person there, refuses to acknowledge us. ¹⁰So, then, if I come, I will refer back to what he has done, and the slanderous words he has spoken against us. Not being satisfied with that, he doesn't welcome family members himself; and, when others want to do so, he forbids them and throws them out of the assembly.

¹¹Beloved, don't imitate evil; imitate good! Someone who does good is from God; someone who does evil has not seen God. ¹²Demetrius has been well attested by everybody, and by the truth itself. We join in this testimony, and you know that our testimony is true.

¹³I have much to write to you, but I don't want to do it with pen and ink. ¹⁴I am hoping instead to see you very soon, so that we can talk face to face.

¹⁵Peace be with you. All the friends greet you. Greet all the friends by name.

One of the many things I relished about serving as a bishop was the way in which my life would swing sharply from dealing with national and international issues one minute to dealing with small, sharp and tricky problems in this church here or that group there. Or even with one person in particular. Perhaps it's always like that in ministry: the big, fuzzy issues that it's hard to get clear in your mind but which you know matter enormously for the wider church, and the small, brightly lit storms in this or that teacup.

As with so much else in the early church, we don't know anything about Diotrephes except what we read here. There has been a fashion of late for 'mirror-reading' the New Testament letters, like someone trying to reconstruct the other end of a telephone conversation from what we could hear at this end. Perhaps, for all I know, someone somewhere has tried to rehabilitate Diotrephes, to see the thing from his point of view.

After all, hadn't John himself said elsewhere that you had to be very careful about people coming in who might be bringing different teaching? Wasn't Diotrephes simply making doubly sure that the church for which he was responsible was 'pure'? Yes, some might be upset that he wouldn't let their guests come to share in worship; but wasn't that the price you had to pay to be firmly and foursquare 'walking in the truth', as old John had always said? And as for the idea that he was always looking for the limelight: well, someone has to take a lead, and since in a small group not many people have intellectual or speaking gifts, it looks like it's got to be him. In any case (one can imagine him and his friends saying), John is now very old, and he really should stop trying to control what everyone else is doing. It's all very well for him to write letters about this and that, but if only he was here on the ground he'd see that it wasn't that easy . . .

Yes, it's quite easy to sketch a plausible scenario in which Diotrephes appears, if not as a polished saint, at least not so much the villain of the piece as you might think from reading these verses. Perhaps we can only hear what the letter is saying when we have made the effort to get inside his skin.

Part of the problem in any human dispute, in fact, is that only very rarely is one party completely and utterly in the right, and the other one completely and utterly in the wrong. It takes two to have a dispute, people say. That is not, actually, always the case: there really are some bullies out there, and one of the most damaging things they do is to make their victims imagine that they themselves are to blame. And yet judgments have to be made, decisions have to be taken, and not everyone is going to like them.

And those who really have been entrusted by God with oversight and care of churches have to exercise that ministry even when it's difficult. They will have to give an account of it to God himself. John knows, none better, just what he has seen and heard, what it meant to meet and know and love the living embodiment of God's **Word**. That knowledge has left him deeply humble, deeply convinced that love, love of God's own sort, is the one thing that matters. Like Moses, who was also accused of high-handedness, he is actually a very meek person. That is the secret of his pastoral strength; you can feel it between every line in these three letters. He has to say what he has to say, even though some independent-minded leaders in some of the local churches may not like being reminded either of the **message** or of the fact that he, John, really was chosen and equipped for a unique and vital ministry. He gets on and says it.

So John has to warn Gaius about Diotrephes. Diotrephes loves to be in the front of everything, much as James and John in the gospels had hoped they would be. He likes to throw his weight around, as the Corinthians did when they informed Paul, their founder, that he would have to produce letters of reference if he wanted to visit them again. He has slandered John himself behind his back; he has refused to welcome bona fide fellow Christians into the church, and has dealt harshly or even violently with those who have tried to bring them in. Sadly, most of us know people like that. If it's John's word against that of Diotrephes, I know who I would find it easier to believe.

Another thing we don't know about the scenario is what the relationship was between Gaius and Diotrephes. Why is John warning Gaius about what he will have to say if he comes to the church where Diotrephes is, or is trying to be, in charge? Presumably Gaius needs to know this, either because he is part of that church himself, or because he is a near neighbour. Either way, it is not a happy picture. The only thing one can say is this. There are some churches where people are too 'nice' (in other words, nervous or embarrassed) to confront problems, with the result that the problems get worse and worse until people leave in disgust. John is not going to go that cowardly route. He is determined, if he can, to nip this problem in the bud.

The contrast with the other man named here, Demetrius, is sharp. Demetrius is almost certainly carrying this letter to Gaius, and so needs a formal introduction (as, for example, with Phoebe in Romans 16.1–2). No problem: John regards him very highly, and so does everybody else. So, he says, does 'the truth itself' (verse 12): in other words, Demetrius is one of those in whom 'the truth of the **gospel**' has made its way into the bloodstream of his thinking, his believing, his acting, his whole personality. There is an integrity about him which shines out for all to see. John adds his witness to those of others, commenting, as in the gospel story (John 19.35; 21.24), 'you know that our testimony is true'. The best index of reliability is not the heaping up of oaths, but the power of a life known to have integrity through and through. John would not lie, about Demetrius or anything or anyone else.

As with the previous short letter, this one stops abruptly, with the remark that John would prefer a face-to-face conversation. No doubt this was a standard thing to say in letters. No doubt, though, this was truly what he found in his heart. Someone for whom love, and the truth which shines through the whole person, are as important as they are for John is not going to be satisfied for long with anything other than full human relationships where sight, sound, touch and even smell (the ancients were more aware of this than we usually are) all played their part.

Why do the closing greetings mention 'friends' rather than 'family'? It's hard to say. Perhaps this letter, too, has an element of secrecy about it. Perhaps John wants anyone who glances at it to think it's just an ordinary letter. It isn't, of course. Even though it's the shortest document in the Bible (219 words as against 245 in 2 John), and even though, remarkably, the name 'Jesus' is nowhere in it (though he does refer to 'the Name' in verse 7), it breathes the **spirit** of Jesus just as strongly as its much longer cousins. It speaks, as in the closing verse, of 'peace': not the easy peace that comes from ignoring the problems, but the deeper peace that comes from confronting them in the knowledge that truth and love are the two arms with which God in Jesus now enfolds both church and world in one embrace.

JUDAH

JUDAH 1-4

Contend for the Faith

¹Judah, slave of Jesus the Messiah, brother of James, to those who are called, the people whom God loves and whom Jesus the Messiah keeps safe! ²May mercy, peace and love be multiplied to you.

³Beloved, I was doing my best to write to you about the rescue in which we share, but I found it necessary to write to you to urge you to struggle hard for the faith which was given once and for all to God's people. ⁴Some people have sneaked in among you, it seems, who long ago were marked out for this condemnation – ungodly people, who are transforming God's grace into licentiousness, and denying the one and only master, our Lord Jesus the Messiah.

In my teens and my early twenties, one of my passions was rock-climbing. I wouldn't say I was an utterly fearless climber; I had a proper respect for danger, and didn't try to do things which were too far outside my competence. But I relished the challenge, and have many happy memories of the exhilaration that comes when you're stuck halfway up a bare rock with nothing above or below you and spend twenty minutes looking for the next foothold.

In any case, I had no fear of heights. I could stand on the edge of a massive cliff and look down without a tremor. I could climb up the tower of a cathedral and look over the parapet at the people far, far below. On the one occasion in that period when I visited New York, the skyscrapers were a natural attraction. Looking down thousands of feet was no problem, and I felt patronizingly sorry for those who, as the saying goes, 'have no head for heights'.

Imagine my chagrin, in middle life, when I discovered that it was my turn to feel queasy when faced with a rock face, or even a narrow mountain path. I can date this discovery more or less exactly to a family holiday in Switzerland, when my sons were happily walking along a path two or three feet wide with a sheer wall on one side and a sheer drop the other, while I, feeling a complete fool, wanted to hug the wall for dear life. On another occasion I actually felt so dizzy I thought I might faint. It all may have had something to do with my needing by then to wear spectacles, and so not being able instantly to adjust my balance. But it felt like a loss of innocence, of spontaneity, of ease and enjoyment.

I have something of that sense as I come to the letter of Judah.

(As so often, we are not absolutely sure who he is. He describes himself as 'brother of James', which probably means James the brother of Jesus. There is a 'Judah' who is mentioned among those brothers in Mark 6.3. But, since Jesus was taken from them perhaps three or more decades earlier, it may seem more natural to speak of himself as brother of the leader who is either still alive or else only recently dead. In any case, he calls himself 'slave of Jesus'; even if he, too, was a son of Mary he would not presume to describe himself as Jesus' brother. It's interesting, isn't it, that we tend to call him 'Jude', thereby distinguishing him from two others who had the same name: Judah the patriarch, the ancestor of Jesus, and Judas Iscariot. Why have we done that? He has a royal and ancient name, and I prefer that he should keep it.)

Anyway, as I was saying: I have something of that sense of a loss of innocence when I read this letter. We would prefer, I think, to be able to take the **gospel** forward, to explain and expound it, to speak of the glorious achievement of God in Jesus the **Messiah**, to encourage people to a clear and powerful witness and to lives of **faith**, hope and love. That is the exhilarating task. But Judah represents a moment where we sense a change of mood. Things are going wrong. What seemed easy before now seems dark and difficult.

It appears that Judah sensed this as well. He had been going to write, he says, about 'the rescue in which we share' – God's rescue of us in Jesus the Messiah, the great saving acts which all Christian teachers love to celebrate. But he had to put those plans on hold, because it appears that the church has been infiltrated with people teaching what is basically a different **message** altogether. And the ordinary Christians, with no long centuries of experience behind them in the church, are deeply vulnerable. If new teaching sounds exciting and fun, why not give it a try?

No, says Judah: it's time to put your climbing ropes on. These rocks are dangerous and difficult. It's time to 'struggle hard for the faith which was once and for all given to God's people'. The very heart of Christian faith and practice is under direct attack, and unless those who are grasped by the truth of the gospel do their best to maintain it those who are heading in another direction are going to take a lot of people with them. You may have been able to climb the high rocks of Christian teaching before; now things appear more dangerous, people are getting dizzy and giddy, and we have to take precautions.

That, we assume, is why even in the opening greeting Judah speaks of Jesus the Messiah keeping his people safe. He guards them. That is among the great truths of Jesus' present ministry, interceding for his people before the father (see Romans 8.34). But, as ever, what God loves to do he loves to do *through others*, calling and equipping people to take his work forward. And the way Jesus guards his people is, not least, by prayerful and accredited teachers encouraging them, warning them, sketching for them the bigger picture within which they can make sense of the puzzling things that are happening to them. That is what Judah is doing right now.

He is clear and explicit about the twin dangers the church now faces – dangers which we can hardly hear about without realizing that this letter is very contemporary. On the one hand, people are 'transforming God's grace into licentiousness'. On the other hand, they are 'denying the one and only Master, our Lord Jesus the Messiah'.

Find people who today are saying that God loves everyone exactly as they are, so everyone must stay exactly as they are, doing all the things they want to do, because God is so full of generosity that obviously he wants them to do that. Find such people, and you've found those of whom Judah is writing. Find people who today are saying that Jesus is one religious teacher among others, one way of **salvation** among others, that there might well be a variety of paths up the mountain of which Jesus' path is only one, that it's important not to make exclusive claims or we'll become arrogant; find such people, and you've found those of whom Judah is writing.

These were, of course, problems right across the early church. Paul addresses the problem of 'cheap grace' several times in his letters, notably in Romans 6 and Galatians 5. But Judah has seen that these are no longer just incidental dangers, to be dealt with on the side of another argument. People have come into the church who are teaching these things full on. The only possible answer is direct confrontation.

Part of the task of the teacher, as I said, is to sketch the bigger picture within which puzzled or worried Christians can understand where they are and what's going on. We may feel we're lost, but if you will show us a map and point out where we are on that map, we can get our bearings and find our way through the mist on to a safe path. So what Judah determines to do is to sketch the bigger picture of the way in which God's people have always had a struggle to follow in God's way, and at every turn some have tried to pull them off the right track. This, in other words, is not something strange or outlandish. It doesn't mean you've taken a wrong turn somewhere. It merely means you are experiencing the typical struggle which God's people must learn to expect. Get ready for the big picture. It's not a pretty sight, but we need to understand it if we're to keep our balance and see the way through to safety.

JUDAH 5-16

False Teachers

⁵I do want to remind you, even though you know it all well, that when the Lord once and for all delivered his people out of the land of Egypt, he subsequently destroyed those who did not believe. ⁶In the same way, when some of the angels did not keep to their rightful place of

authority, but abandoned their own home, he kept them under conditions of darkness and in eternal chains to await the judgment of the great day. ⁷In similar fashion, Sodom, Gomorrah and the cities round about, which had lived in gross immorality and lusted after unnatural flesh, are set before us as a pattern, undergoing the punishment of endless fire.

⁸However, these people are behaving in the same way! They are dreaming their way into defiling the flesh, rejecting authority and cursing the Glorious Ones. ⁹Even Michael the archangel, when disputing with the devil about the body of Moses, did not presume to lay against him a charge of blasphemy, but simply said, 'The Lord rebuke you.' ¹⁰These people, however, curse anything they don't know. They are like dumb animals; there are some things they understand instinctively – but it is these very things that destroy them. ¹¹A curse on them! They go off in the way of Cain; they give themselves over for money into Balaam's deceitful ways; they are destroyed in Korah's rebellion. ¹²These are the ones who pollute your love-feasts; they share your table without fear while simply looking after their own needs. They are waterless clouds blown along by the winds. They are fruitless autumn trees, doubly dead and uprooted. ¹³They are stormy waves out at sea, splashing up their own shameful ways. They are wandering stars, and the deepest everlasting darkness has been kept for them in particular.

¹⁴Enoch, the seventh in line from Adam, prophesied about these people. 'Look!' he said. 'The Lord comes with ten thousand of his holy ones, ¹⁵to perform judgment against all, and to charge every human being with all the ungodly ways in which they have done ungodly things, and with every harsh word which ungodly sinners have spoken against him.' ¹⁶These people are always grumbling and complaining, chasing off after their own desires. From their mouths come arrogant words, buttering people up for the sake of gain.

One of the great examples of sheer, multiple, many-sided wickedness in recent history is of course the Nazi regime, which, under Adolf Hitler, produced six years of bitter and costly war and the Jewish Holocaust at the same time. All of this, like a massive and complex earthquake, caused enormous social and political repercussions, the aftershocks of which are still being felt.

It is hard for those of us born after the war, who grew up with the tales of Nazi atrocities, to understand just how many people in Britain, America and elsewhere completely failed to realize just what was going on. They refused to believe that anyone could be so utterly, demonically wicked.

On the contrary, many people admired the way Hitler had turned Germany round, and instilled a sense of national pride after the awful experiences of the 1920s. Neville Chamberlain, the British Prime Minister, met Hitler shortly before the war, and spoke of the splendid agreement they had reached. The Duke and Duchess of Windsor, it seems, were hoping that maybe if Germany won the war they would be able to return to Britain as king and queen. Before Pearl Harbor brought the Americans into the war on the Allied side, there were plenty of people in the United States who thought that, if they joined the war at all, it ought to be alongside the Germans. People simply found it impossible to believe things were as bad as they really were. Tales leaked out from Germany about the persecution of Jews, but most people disbelieved them or suggested they were being exaggerated for political effect. Only when the liberating forces finally reached the death camps did the full, awful truth come out. Bit by bit, as Europe took a deep, shuddering, post-war breath, a wave of revulsion swept the Western world which, within a few years, redrew the entire moral landscape. It was a shame it took such atrocities to make people realize just how appalling idolatrous nationalism and racism really are.

Part of our dilemma in reading Judah 5–16, which I have put all together in one long passage for reasons that may become obvious, is that we have real difficulty believing that things could have been, or could be again, quite as bad as he is making out. We hear passages like this in the way that people heard tales of Nazi behaviour, and we think, 'Well, perhaps there's a problem of sorts; but do you really need to go on about it at such length? Aren't you getting a bit obsessive? Aren't you just demonizing people you happen not to like that much? Can they really be as bad as all that?' And the danger, of course, is that we distance ourselves from what Judah has perceived as the enormous danger facing the church, opening up in front of the little community like a huge hole in the road into which, unless they watch out, they will stumble to their doom.

The other difficulty we have with this passage is that it refers, with breathtaking speed, to all kinds of (to us) out-of-the-way biblical and other stories. This is Judah's method of sketching the large picture within which the present threat is to be imagined. 'Look!' he's saying. 'This is what has always happened! Don't be surprised that it's happening again!' To feel the point of this, we need to slow down, and remind ourselves of the force of these various stories.

In the first paragraph (verses 5–7), he reminds his readers that God can and does judge and condemn those who presume to rebel against his way. It happened with some of those who came out of Egypt at the **Exodus** (verse 5). It happened as well, though this story is not in the Bible but in later Jewish tradition, to the angels who rebelled against God's ordering of their different ranks and duties (verse 6). It happened too, in a better-known story in Genesis, to the cities of Sodom and Gomorrah, whose eagerness to use unexpected visitors as sexual playthings (Genesis 19) was apparently typical of their regular life, just as their awful punishment was seen as typical of the fate that might be in store for other gross sinners (verse 7).

All this, Judah is saying, is well known. But the thrust of the second paragraph (verse 8–13) is that the people he is now worried about are simply ignoring these stories! At this point we in the modern church might well feel slightly shamefaced: we, perhaps, have ignored them as well. But I hope we haven't ignored them to the extent that these teachers had done. Having noted two of their key wrongdoings back in verse 4 – they treat God's grace as an excuse for licentiousness, and they deny Jesus himself – Judah here lists three, the first of which belongs with the first of the earlier pair: they defile the flesh, they reject authority, and they curse the Glorious Ones (angels who hold authority from God).

This third charge seems remote to us. Most people today either ignore angels or treat them as cute, vaguely religious, feel-good symbols. But for Judah the angels were real, and powerful – and not to be taken lightly as these teachers were doing. He harks back to a story which emerges in the Bible in Zechariah 3, but was developed in various places. In this story, Michael the archangel comes face to face in a dispute with **the satan**, and simply invokes the Lord's own rebuke against him. Michael won't curse the satan himself; he will hand the problem over to the Lord. But, says Judah, these people curse anything they don't know – a familiar enough phenomenon, as people today hurl abuse at Christian **faith,** and indeed any faith at all, revealing their ignorance with every paragraph they write.

The first two charges go closely with this. Once you reject supernatural authority, it's easy to reject human authorities as well, whether in the church or the wider world. And once you do that, the most obvious thing is to cast off restraint in any and every aspect of behaviour, not least in relation to sex. It would be amusing if it were not so tragic to see people imagining that sexual immorality is a comparatively 'modern' invention, so that the inevitable march of 'progress' in our own day means that less and less sexual restraint is required. All that such people succeed in doing is going right back to one of the oldest forms of dehumanizing behaviour known to human beings.

That leads Judah into a bewildering catalogue of biblical villains of whom these false teachers remind him: Cain the murderer, Balaam the false prophet, Korah the leader of a rebellion against Moses. Rebellion, in fact, is near the heart of the problem. The teachers are overthrowing or ignoring the proper structures of authority, and the result is moral chaos and pollution, signalled by a further bewildering list of metaphors: waterless clouds, fruitless trees, splashing waves, wandering stars. These all have in common the fact that they appear to promise something but don't deliver it: no rain from the clouds, no fruit from the trees, no safe passage on the stormy sea, no regular movement of stars across the sky. The teachers appear to offer a way of life which is exciting, different and liberating; but the only thing they achieve is shame, darkness and chaos.

The third and final paragraph in the section quotes a Jewish text well known at the time, which puts into the mouth of the ancient figure Enoch all kinds of prophecies, including this one. Here, as in verse 9, Judah echoes Zechariah, this time 14.5: the Lord is coming with his holy ones. Judgment is on the way, not least for the ungodly (Judah repeats the word three times, a solemn signal that this is at the heart of the whole problem). But the teachers in question simply grumble, complain, and go off on yet another round of pleasure-seeking, supporting their behaviour with arrogance and greed.

A horrible catalogue. We would much rather not have to notice such things at all, just as ordinary peace-loving people would much rather not notice that another nation is preparing not only for war but for genocide. But the reality of false teaching, especially the rejection of authority, the denial of the uniqueness of Jesus, and the encouragement of sexual immorality, is with us today every bit as much as it was in the first century. We take a deep sigh for sorrow, and pray that Jesus the **Messiah** will indeed keep us safe. Part of the answer to that prayer will be that we have been alerted to the problem, so when it appears again, as it surely will, we will be able to recognize it for what it is.

JUDAH 17–25

Rescued by God's Power

> ¹⁷But you, my beloved ones, remember the words that were spoken before by the apostles of our Lord Jesus the Messiah. ¹⁸'In the last time,' they said to you, 'there will be scornful people who follow their own ungodly desires.' ¹⁹These are the people who cause divisions. They are living on the merely human level; they do not have the spirit. ²⁰But you, beloved ones, build yourselves up in your most holy faith. Pray in the holy spirit. ²¹Keep yourselves in the love of God, as you wait for our Lord Jesus the Messiah to show you the mercy which leads to the life of the age to come.
>
> ²²With some people who are wavering, you must show mercy. ²³Some you must rescue, snatching them from the fire. To others you must show mercy, but with fear, hating even the clothes that have been defiled by the flesh.

> [24]Now to the one who is able to keep you standing upright, and to present you before his glory, undefiled and joyful – [25]to the one and only God, our saviour through Jesus the Messiah our Lord, be glory, majesty, power and authority before all the ages, and now, and to all the ages to come. Amen.

Sometimes a quick burst of biblical dialogue catches a truth in sharp relief. After many generations in which the people of Israel had gone from bad to worse, led by a succession of wicked kings, God finally sends the prophet Elijah to sort it all out. He prays for, and prophesies, a great drought, which comes upon the land. Then, when it is time for it to end, Elijah appears before King Ahab (1 Kings 18.17–18).

'Is it you', asks Ahab, 'you troubler of Israel?'

'I have not troubled Israel,' replies Elijah. 'It is you, and your father's house, who have done that, by leaving YHWH's commands and following the Baals.'

There have been many times in recent history when that snatch of conversation has come back to me, as different groups in the church have charged one another with being 'divisive', with causing trouble. It is at best ironic, and at worst flatly hypocritical, to tell the prophet off for troubling Israel when what he has done is to blow the whistle on wickedness that had been going on unchecked. That, of course, is often the fate of whistleblowers. The problem is that people don't want to make a fuss. They don't want to seem out of line or behind the times. So they don't say anything, even when they may find new developments disturbing. Then, when someone with courage finally stands up and speaks out, they are labelled as 'divisive'. It was ever thus.

So here we have it in Judah verse 19: 'These are the people who cause divisions.' No doubt the teachers would have said that it was people like Judah himself who caused divisions, by dragging them back to an old-fashioned morality, based on funny old stories in the ancient scriptures rather than on the freedom they had discovered through what they took to be God's grace. But Jesus and his early **apostles** had given the same warning as those ancient scriptures: scornful people will come, mocking you for your silly little rules, eager to follow whichever desires happen to be uppermost at the time. Such people, says Judah, simply do not have God's **spirit**, for all they may claim to do so. They are living at the merely human level.

But then, after all the warnings and denunciations, comes the **word** we need to hear, the word of strengthening, of promise, of holiness. This is what we must do in order not only to be on our guard but to brace ourselves for the shock. Once again Judah puts his ideas together in quick succession: build yourselves up in **faith**, pray in the spirit, keep yourselves in God's love, and wait for the ultimate mercy of Jesus' return (verses 20–21). A word about each of these.

First, build yourselves up in 'your most holy faith'. This is the 'faith' for which he said, in verse 2, that they were to struggle hard. 'The faith', meaning both a body of teaching and a heart-level commitment to it, is the firm ground on which we stand, and we must learn to stand tall at that point.

Second, pray in the **holy spirit**. Prayer remains a mystery, but it is the mystery to which we are totally committed as Christians. One of the most important works of the spirit is to call out prayer from the depths of our hearts, even if – particularly if, as in this letter! – it may be a prayer of lament on the one hand and a prayer for protection on the other. It is God's lament we share as we look in sorrow at human wickedness and arrogance invading the church itself. It is God's protecting power and love we draw down as we pray by his spirit in the midst of turmoil.

Third, keep yourselves in the love of God. This sounds strange: surely it's God's job to keep us in his love? But, granted that, it is also our job not to wander away. The good shepherd doesn't keep us locked up. He wants us to learn to follow him because we love and trust him. Don't give him more work to do by going and getting yourself lost somewhere.

Fourth, wait patiently for the mercy, leading to God's new age and its promise of new **life**, which will come when Jesus is revealed. All Christian discipleship has this forward look. As we see moral and religious disarray all around us, we long and pray for that 'mercy', for ourselves and for the church, which will come at the last and, please God, will also come, in a measure, in times of healing and renewal in advance of that day if it is delayed.

These are the very simple, but very powerful, steps we can take in the present. Judah does not say, 'Take up the cudgels and fight these false teachers on their own ground.' He simply wants his readers to recognize the grave danger they are in, and to learn the heart-habits of genuine Christian discipleship which will mean that the storm, though it may rage, will not overwhelm them.

Then, from the great spiritual disciplines, he turns to the pastoral needs. Verses 22 and 23 sound like a team of rescuers arriving on the scene of a disaster – a train crash or a tsunami. There are people in all kinds of trouble, and those who are firm in their faith need to go to the rescue. The three instructions here are probably not exhaustive. Judah is just saying, 'Make sure you look carefully to see what condition people are in, and apply the mercy of God appropriately in each case.' There are people out there who have been carried off by this strange teaching, with its moral (or rather immoral) practices. They need res-cuing. Some are teetering on the brink of moral collapse; don't sneer at them or harry them, but show them mercy, the mercy we expect from Jesus himself. Others are already in the flames, and need rescuing. It's hard, particularly if they claim they are enjoying the warmth of the fire, but the effort must be made. Others again are deeper into sin, and it has left its mark on them, and on everything about them. In rescuing them with mercy you must also beware. Their very clothes may carry the memory, and the moral stain, of the life they have been living.

But Judah will not end there. His instincts as a writer grow straight out of his instincts as a Christian: that whatever joys and sorrows have come to pass, all must in the end be gathered up again in praise to the one true God. The form his concluding praise takes embodies in itself, in verse 24, the particular thrust of the letter: the God who deserves all praise is 'the one who is able to keep you standing upright'.

Many translations put this more negatively, 'to keep you from falling'. That expresses truth as well, but the word Judah uses is a bit more positive: 'to keep you unstumbling'. The image is of someone walking along who might have tripped over, but has not done so in fact. That is what we should pray for, and that is what we should praise God for when it happens.

And the unstumbling walk is going towards a definite destination. The goal towards which we are moving is that moment when we shall be presented before God's glory, undefiled and joyful. The letter has had much to say about defilement, and the whole tone has been gloomy as a result. Looking into the murky pit of human wickedness is always like that. The alternative to the licentious and Jesus-denying teaching of the infiltrators isn't, though, a gloomy, kill-joy religion. The very opposite! It is about glory, about purity, about glad and thrilling celebration. This, after all, is what we were made for.

Judah then gathers the whole thing up in one of the all-time classic bursts of Christian praise, praise which wells up when the holy spirit has flooded the heart with the knowledge of God in Jesus and of the rescue which he has accomplished. 'To the one and only God, our saviour through Jesus the **Messiah** our Lord, be glory, majesty, power and authority before all the ages, and now, and to all the ages to come. Amen.' If the book of Revelation had not been written, this last verse would not have been a bad way to conclude the whole New Testament.

GLOSSARY

age to come, *see* **present age**

apostle, disciple, the Twelve

'Apostle' means 'one who is sent'. It could be used of an ambassador or official delegate. In the New Testament it is sometimes used specifically of Jesus' inner circle of twelve, but Paul sees not only himself but several others outside the Twelve as 'apostles', the criterion being whether the person had personally seen the risen Jesus. Jesus' own choice of twelve close associates symbolized his plan to renew God's people, Israel (who traditionally thought of themselves as having twelve tribes); after the death of Judas Iscariot (Matthew 27.5; Acts 1.18), Matthias was chosen by lot to take his place, preserving the symbolic meaning. During Jesus' lifetime they, and many other followers, were seen as his 'disciples', which means 'pupils' or 'apprentices'.

ascension

At the end of Luke's **gospel** and the start of Acts, Luke describes Jesus 'going up' from earth into **heaven**. To understand this, we have to remember that 'heaven' isn't a 'place' within our own world of space, time and matter, but a different *dimension* of reality – God's dimension, which intersects and interacts with our own (which we call 'earth', meaning both the planet where we live and the entire space-time universe). For Jesus to 'ascend', therefore, doesn't mean that he's a long way away, but rather that he can be, and is, intimately present to all his people all the time. What's more, because in the Bible 'heaven' is (as it were) the control room for 'earth', it means that Jesus is actually in charge of what goes on here and now. The way his sovereign rule works out is of course very different from the way earthly rulers get their way: as in his own life, he accomplishes his saving purposes through faithful obedience, including suffering. The life and witness of the early church, therefore, resulting in the spread of the gospel around the world, shows what it means to say that Jesus has ascended and that he is the world's rightful Lord.

baptism

Literally, 'plunging' people into water. From within a wider Jewish tradition of ritual washings and bathings, **John the Baptist** undertook a vocation of baptizing people in the Jordan, not as one ritual among others but as a unique moment of **repentance**, preparing them for the coming of the **kingdom of God**. Jesus himself was baptized by John, identifying himself with this renewal movement and developing it in his own way. His followers in turn baptized others. After his **resurrection,** and the sending of the **holy spirit,** baptism became the normal sign and means of entry into the community of Jesus' people. As early as Paul, it was aligned both with the **Exodus** from Egypt (1 Corinthians 10.2) and with Jesus' death and resurrection (Romans 6.2–11).

chief priests, *see* priests, high priest

Christ, *see* Messiah

circumcision, circumcised
The cutting off of the foreskin. Male circumcision was a major mark of identity for Jews, following its initial commandment to Abraham (Genesis 17), reinforced by Joshua (Joshua 5.2–9). Other peoples, e.g. the Egyptians, also circumcised male children. A line of thought from Deuteronomy (e.g. 30.6), through Jeremiah (e.g. 31.33), to the **Dead Sea Scrolls** and the New Testament (e.g. Romans 2.29) speaks of 'circumcision of the heart' as God's real desire, by which one may become inwardly what the male Jew is outwardly, that is, marked out as part of God's people. At periods of Jewish assimilation into the surrounding culture, some Jews tried to remove the marks of circumcision (e.g. 1 Maccabees 1.11–15).

covenant
At the heart of Jewish belief is the conviction that the one God, **YHWH**, who had made the whole world, had called Abraham and his family to belong to him in a special way. The promises God made to Abraham and his family, and the requirements that were laid on them as a result, came to be seen in terms either of the agreement that a king would make with a subject people, or of the marriage bond between husband and wife. One regular way of describing this relationship was 'covenant', which can thus include both promise and **law.** The covenant was renewed at Mount Sinai with the giving of the **Torah;** in Deuteronomy before the entry to the promised land; and, in a more focused way, with David (e.g. Psalm 89). Jeremiah 31 promised that, after the punishment of **exile,** God would make a 'new covenant' with his people, forgiving them and binding them to him more intimately. Jesus believed that this was coming true through his **kingdom**-proclamation and his death and resurrection. The early Christians developed these ideas in various ways, believing that in Jesus the promises had at last been fulfilled.

day of Pentecost
A major Jewish festival, 50 days after Passover and the feast of Unleavened Bread (Leviticus 23.9–14). By the first century this had become associated with the time, 50 days after the Israelites left Egypt, when Moses went up Mount Sinai and came down with the **law.** It was on the day of Pentecost that the **holy**

spirit came powerfully upon the early **disciples**, 50 days after the Passover at which Jesus had died and been raised (Acts 2). Whether or not we say that this was 'the birthday of the church' (some would use that description for the call of Abraham in Genesis 12, or at least the call of the first disciples in Mark 1), it was certainly the time when Jesus' followers discovered the power to tell people about his **resurrection** and lordship and to order their common life to reflect his saving **kingdom**.

Dead Sea Scrolls

A collection of texts, some in remarkably good repair, some extremely fragmentary, found in the late 1940s around Qumran (near the north-east corner of the Dead Sea), and virtually all now edited, translated and in the public domain. They formed all or part of the library of a strict monastic group, mostly likely Essenes, founded in the mid-second century BC and lasting until the Jewish–Roman war of 66–70. The scrolls include the earliest existing manuscripts of the Hebrew and Aramaic scriptures, and several other important documents of community regulations, scriptural exegesis, hymns, wisdom writing, and other literature. They shed a flood of light on one small segment within the Judaism of Jesus' day, helping us to understand how some Jews at least were thinking, praying and reading scripture. Despite attempts to prove the contrary, they make no reference to **John the Baptist**, Jesus, Paul, James or early Christianity in general.

demons, *see* **the satan**

disciple, *see* **apostle**

Essenes, *see* **Dead Sea Scrolls**

exile

Deuteronomy (29—30) warned that if Israel disobeyed YHWH, he would send his people into exile, but that if they then repented he would bring them back. When the Babylonians sacked Jerusalem and took the people into exile, prophets such as Jeremiah interpreted this as the fulfilment of this prophecy, and made further promises about how long exile would last (70 years, according to Jeremiah 25.12; 29.10). Sure enough, exiles began to return in the late sixth century BC (Ezra 1.1). However, the post-exilic period was largely a disappointment, since the people were still enslaved to foreigners (Nehemiah 9.36); and, at the height of persecution by the Syrians, Daniel 9.2, 24 spoke of the 'real' exile lasting not for 70 years but 70 *weeks* of years, that is, 490 years. Longing for the real 'return from exile', when the prophecies of Isaiah, Jeremiah, etc. would be fulfilled, and **redemption** from pagan oppression accomplished, continued to characterize many Jewish movements, and was a major theme in Jesus' proclamation and his summons to **repentance**.

Exodus

The Exodus from Egypt took place, according to the book of that name, under the leadership of Moses, after long years in which the Israelites had been enslaved there. (According to Genesis 15.13f., this was itself part of God's covenanted promise to Abraham.) It demonstrated, to them and to Pharaoh, King of Egypt, that Israel was God's special child (Exodus 4.22). They then wandered through the Sinai wilderness for 40 years, led by God in a pillar of cloud and fire; early on in this time they were given the **Torah** on Mount Sinai itself. Finally, after the death of Moses and under the leadership of Joshua, they crossed the Jordan and entered, and eventually conquered, the promised land of Canaan. This event, commemorated annually in the Passover and other Jewish festivals, gave the Israelites not only a powerful memory of what had made them a people, but also a particular shape and content to their **faith** in YHWH as not only creator but also redeemer; and in subsequent enslavements, particularly the **exile**, they looked for a further **redemption** which would be, in effect, a new Exodus. Probably no other past event so dominated the imagination of first-century Jews; among them the early Christians, following the lead of Jesus himself, continually referred back to the Exodus to give meaning and shape to their own critical events, most particularly Jesus' death and **resurrection**.

faith

Faith in the New Testament covers a wide area of human trust and trustworthiness, merging into love at one end of the scale and loyalty at the other. Within Jewish and Christian thinking, faith in God also includes *belief*, accepting certain things as true about God, and what he has done in the world (e.g. bringing Israel out of Egypt; raising Jesus from the dead). For Jesus, 'faith' often seems to mean 'recognizing that God is decisively at work to bring the **kingdom** through Jesus'. For Paul, 'faith' is both the specific belief that Jesus is Lord and that God raised him from the dead (Romans 10.9) and the response of grateful human love to sovereign divine love (Galatians 2.20). This faith is, for Paul, the solitary badge of membership in God's people in **Christ**, marking them out in a way that **Torah**, and the works it prescribes, can never do.

fellowship

The word we often translate 'fellowship' can mean a business partnership (in the ancient world, businesses were often run by families, so there's a sense of family loyalty as well), or it can mean a sense of mutual belonging and sharing in some other corporate enterprise. Within early Christianity, 'fellowship' acquired the sense not just of belonging to one another as Christians, but of a shared belonging to Jesus **Christ**, and a participation in his life through the **spirit**, expressed in such actions as the 'breaking of bread' and the sharing of property with those in need.

forgiveness

Jesus made forgiveness central to his **message** and ministry, not least because he was claiming to be launching God's long-awaited 'new **covenant**' (Jeremiah 31.31–34) in which sins would at last be forgiven (Matthew 26.28). Forgiveness doesn't mean God, or someone else, saying, of some particular fault or sin, 'it didn't really matter' or 'I didn't really mind'. The point of forgiveness is that it *did* matter.

Gehenna, hell

Gehenna is, literally, the valley of Hinnom, on the south-west slopes of Jerusalem. From ancient times it was used as a garbage dump, smouldering with a continual fire. Already by the time of Jesus some Jews used it as an image for the place of punishment after death. Jesus' own usage blends the two meanings in his warnings both to Jerusalem itself (unless it repents, the whole city will become a smouldering heap of garbage) and to people in general (to beware of God's final judgment).

Gentiles

The Jews divided the world into Jews and non-Jews. The Hebrew word for non-Jews, *goyim*, carries overtones both of family identity (i.e. not of Jewish ancestry) and of worship (i.e. of idols, not of the one true God YHWH). Though many Jews established good relations with Gentiles, not least in the Jewish Diaspora (the dispersion of the Jews away from Palestine), officially there were taboos against contact such as intermarriage. In the New Testament, the Greek word *ethne*, 'nations', carries the same meanings as *goyim*. Part of Paul's overmastering agenda was to insist that Gentiles who believed in Jesus had full rights in the Christian community alongside believing Jews, without having to become **circumcised**.

good news, gospel, message, word

The idea of 'good news', for which an older English word is 'gospel', had two principal meanings for first-century Jews. First, with roots in Isaiah, it meant the news of YHWH's long-awaited victory over evil and rescue of his people. Second, it was used in the Roman world of the accession, or birthday, of the emperor. Since for Jesus and Paul the announcement of God's inbreaking **kingdom** was both the fulfilment of prophecy and a challenge to the world's present rulers, 'gospel' became an important shorthand for both the message of Jesus himself and the apostolic message about him. Paul saw this message as itself the vehicle of God's saving power (Romans 1.16; 1 Thessalonians 2.13).

The four canonical 'gospels' tell the story of Jesus in such a way as to bring out both these aspects (unlike some other so- called 'gospels' circulated in the second and subsequent centuries, which tended both to cut off the scriptural and Jewish roots of Jesus' achievement and to inculcate a private spirituality rather than confrontation with the world's rulers). Since in Isaiah this creative, life-giving good news was seen as God's own powerful word (40.8; 55.11), the early Christians could use 'word' or 'message' as another shorthand for the basic Christian proclamation.

gospel, *see* **good news**

heaven

Heaven is God's dimension of the created order (Genesis 1.1; Psalm 115.16; Matthew 6.9), whereas 'earth' is the world of space, time and matter that we know. 'Heaven' thus sometimes stands, reverentially, for 'God' (as in Matthew's regular **kingdom of heaven**'). Normally hidden from human sight, heaven is occasionally revealed or unveiled so that people can see God's dimension of ordinary life (e.g. 2 Kings 6.17; Revelation 1, 4—5). Heaven in the New Testament is thus not usually seen as the place where God's people go after death; at the end, the New Jerusalem descends *from* heaven *to* earth, joining the two dimensions for ever. 'Entering the kingdom of heaven' does not mean 'going to heaven after death', but belonging in the present to the people who steer their earthly course by the standards and purposes of heaven (cf. the Lord's Prayer; 'on earth as in heaven', Matthew 6.10), and who are assured of membership in the **age to come.**

hell, *see* **Gehenna**

high priest, *see* **priests**

holy spirit

In Genesis 1.2, the spirit is God's presence and power *within* creation, without God being identified with creation. The same spirit entered people, notably the prophets, enabling them to speak and act for God. At his **baptism** by **John the Baptist**, Jesus was specially equipped with the spirit, resulting in his remarkable public career (Acts 10.38). After his **resurrection**, his followers were themselves filled (Acts 2) by the same spirit, now identified as Jesus' own spirit; the creator God was acting afresh, remaking the world and them too. The spirit enabled them to live out a holiness which the **Torah** could not, producing 'fruit' in their lives, giving them 'gifts' with which to serve God, the world and the church, and assuring them of future resurrection (Romans 8; Galatians 4—5; 1 Corinthians 12—14). From very early in Christianity (e.g. Galatians 4.1–7), the spirit became part of the new revolutionary definition of God himself: 'the one who sends the son and the spirit of the son'.

John (the Baptist)

Jesus' cousin on his mother's side, born a few months before Jesus; his father was a **priest**. He acted as a prophet, baptizing in the Jordan – dramatically re-enacting the **Exodus** from Egypt – to prepare people, by **repentance**, for God's coming judgment. He may have had some contact with the **Essenes**, though his eventual public message was different from theirs. Jesus' own vocation was decisively confirmed at his **baptism** by John. As part of John's message of the **kingdom**, he outspokenly criticized Herod Antipas for marrying his brother's wife. Herod had him imprisoned, and then beheaded him at his wife's request (Mark 6.14–29). Groups of John's disciples continued a separate existence, without merging into Christianity, for some time afterwards (e.g. Acts 19.1–7).

jubilee

The ancient Israelites were commanded to keep a 'jubilee' every fiftieth year (i.e. following the sequence of seven 'sabbatical' years). Leviticus 25 provides the basic rules, which were expanded by later teachers: land was to be restored to its original owners or their heirs, and any fellow Jews who had been enslaved because of debt were to be set free. It was also to be a year without sowing, reaping or harvesting. The point was that YHWH owned the land, and that the Israelites were to see it not as a private possession but as something held in trust. People debate whether the jubilee principle was ever put into practice as thoroughly as Leviticus demands, but the underlying promise of a great remission of debts was repeated by Isaiah (61.1–2) and then decisively by Jesus (Luke 4.16–21). It is likely that this underlies the action of the first Christians in sharing property and giving to those in need (Acts 4.32–35, etc.).

justification

God's declaration, from his position as judge of all the world, that someone is in the right, despite universal sin. This declaration will be made on the last day on the basis of an entire life (Romans 2.1–16), but is brought forward into the present on the basis of Jesus' achievement, because sin has been dealt with through his cross (Romans 3.21—4.25); the means of this present justification is simply **faith**. This means, particularly, that Jews and **Gentiles** alike are full members of the family promised by God to Abraham (Galatians 3; Romans 4).

kingdom of God, kingdom of heaven

Best understood as the king*ship*, or sovereign and saving rule, of Israel's God YHWH as celebrated in several psalms (e.g. 99.1) and prophecies (e.g. Daniel 6.26f.). Because YHWH was the creator God, when he finally became king in the way he intended this would involve setting the world to rights, and particularly rescuing Israel from its enemies. 'Kingdom of God' and various equivalents (e.g. 'No king but God!') became a revolutionary slogan around the time of Jesus. Jesus' own announcement of God's kingdom redefined these expectations around his own very different plan and vocation. His invitation to people to 'enter' the kingdom was a way of summoning them to allegiance to himself and his programme, seen as the start of God's long-awaited saving reign. For Jesus, the kingdom was coming not in a single move, but in stages, of which his own public career was one, his death and **resurrection** another, and a still future consummation another. Note that 'kingdom of **heaven**' is Matthew's preferred form for the same phrase, following a regular Jewish practice of saying 'heaven' rather than 'God'. It does not refer to a place ('heaven'), but to the fact of God's becoming king in and through Jesus and his achievement. Paul speaks of Jesus as **Messiah**, already in possession of his kingdom, waiting to hand it over finally to the father (1 Corinthians 15.23–28; cf. Ephesians 5.5).

last days

Ancient Jews thought of world history as divided into two periods: 'the **present age**' and 'the **age to come**'. The present age was a time when evil was still at large in its many forms; the age to come would usher in God's final reign of justice, peace, joy and love. Ancient prophets had spoken of the transition from the one age to the other in terms of the 'last days', meaning either the final moments of the 'present age' or the eventual dawning of the 'age to come'. When Peter quotes Joel in Acts 2.17, he perhaps means both: the two ages have overlapped, so that Christians live in the 'last days', the time between God's **kingdom** being launched in and through Jesus and it being completed at Jesus' return. The New Testament gives no encouragement to the idea that we can calculate a precise timetable for the latter event, or that the period of history immediately before Jesus' return will be significantly different (e.g. more violent) than any other (see Matthew 24.36–39).

law, *see* Torah

life, soul, spirit

Ancient people held many different views about what made human beings the special creatures they are. Some, including many Jews, believed that to be complete, humans needed bodies as well as inner selves. Others, including many influenced by the philosophy of Plato (fourth century BC), believed that the important part of a human was the 'soul' (Gk: *psyche*), which at death would be happily freed from its bodily prison. Confusingly for us, the same word psyche is often used in the New Testament within a Jewish framework where it clearly means 'life' or 'true self', without implying a body/soul dualism that devalues the body. Human inwardness of experience and understanding can also be referred to as 'spirit'. *See also* **holy spirit**; **resurrection**.

message, *see* good news

Messiah, messianic, Christ

The Hebrew word means literally 'anointed one', hence in theory either a prophet, **priest** or king. In Greek this translates as *Christos*; 'Christ' in early Christianity was a title, and only gradually became an alternative proper name for Jesus. In practice, 'Messiah' is mostly restricted to the notion, which took various forms in ancient Judaism, of the coming king who would be David's true heir, through whom YHWH would bring judgment to the world, and in particular would rescue Israel from pagan enemies. There was no single template of expectations. Scriptural stories and promises contributed to different ideals and movements, often focused on (a) decisive military defeat of Israel's enemies and (b) rebuilding or cleansing the **Temple**. The **Dead Sea Scrolls** speak of two 'Messiahs', one a priest and the other a king. The universal early Christian belief that Jesus was Messiah is only explicable, granted his crucifixion by the Romans (which would have been seen as a clear sign that he was not the Messiah), by their belief that God had raised him from the dead, so vindicating the implicit messianic claims of his earlier ministry.

Mishnah

The main codification of Jewish law (**Torah**) by the **rabbis**, produced in about AD 200, reducing to writing the 'oral Torah' which, in Jesus' day, ran parallel to the 'written Torah'. The Mishnah is itself the basis of the much larger collection of traditions in the two Talmuds (roughly AD 400).

parables

From the Old Testament onwards, prophets and other teachers used various storytelling devices as vehicles for their challenge to Israel (e.g. 2 Samuel 12.1–7). Sometimes they appeared as visions with interpretations (e.g. Daniel 7). Similar techniques were used by the **rabbis**. Jesus made his own creative adaptation of these traditions, in order to break open the world view of his contemporaries and to invite them to share his vision of God's **kingdom** instead. His stories portrayed this as something that was *happening*, not just a timeless truth, and enabled his hearers to step inside the story and make it their own. As with some Old Testament visions, some of Jesus' parables have their own interpretations (e.g. the sower, Mark 4); others are thinly disguised retellings of the prophetic story of Israel (e.g. the wicked tenants, Mark 12).

Pharisees, lawyers, legal experts, rabbis

The Pharisees were an unofficial but powerful Jewish pressure group through most of the first centuries BC and AD. Largely lay-led, though including some **priests**, their aim was to purify Israel through intensified observance of the Jewish law (**Torah**), developing their own traditions about the precise meaning and application of scripture, their own patterns of prayer and other devotion, and their own calculations of the national hope. Though not all legal experts were Pharisees, most Pharisees were thus legal experts.

They effected a democratization of Israel's life, since for them the study and practice of Torah was equivalent to worshipping in the **Temple** – though they were adamant in pressing their own rules for the Temple liturgy on an unwilling (and often **Saducean**) priesthood. This enabled them to survive AD 70 and, merging into the early rabbinic movement, to develop new ways forward.

Politically they stood up for ancestral traditions, and were at the forefront of various movements of revolt against both pagan overlordship and compromised Jewish leaders. By Jesus' day, there were two distinct schools, the stricter one of Shammai, more inclined towards armed revolt, and the more lenient one of Hillel, ready to live and let live.

Jesus' debates with the Pharisees are at least as much a matter of agenda and policy (Jesus strongly opposed their separatist nationalism) as about details of theology and piety. Saul of Tarsus was a fervent right-wing Pharisee, presumably a Shammaite, until his conversion.

After the disastrous war of AD 66–70, these schools of Hillel and Shammai continued bitter debate on appropriate policy. Following the further disaster of AD 135 (the failed Bar-Kochba revolt against Rome), their traditions were carried on by the rabbis, who, though looking to the earlier Pharisees for inspiration, developed a Torah-piety in which personal holiness and purity took the place of political agendas.

present age, age to come, the life of God's coming age
By the time of Jesus many Jewish thinkers divided history into two periods: 'the present age' and 'the age to come' – the latter being the time when YHWH would at last act decisively to judge evil, to rescue Israel, and to create a new world of justice and peace. The early Christians believed that, though the full blessings of the coming age lay still in the future, it had already begun with Jesus, particularly with his death and **resurrection**, and that by **faith** and **baptism** they were able to enter it already. For this reason, the customary translation 'eternal life' is rendered here as 'the life of God's coming age'.

priests, chief priests, high priest
Aaron, the older brother of Moses, was appointed Israel's first high priest (Exodus 28—29), and in theory his descendants were Israel's priests thereafter. Other members of his tribe (Levi) were 'Levites', performing other liturgical duties but not sacrificing. Priests lived among the people all around the country, having a local teaching role (Leviticus 10.11; Malachi 2.7), and going to Jerusalem by rotation to perform the **Temple** liturgy (e.g. Luke 2.8).

David appointed Zadok (whose Aaronic ancestry is sometimes questioned) as high priest, and his family remained thereafter the senior priests in Jerusalem, probably the ancestors of the **Sadducees**. One explanation of the origin of the Qumran **Essenes** is that they were a dissident group who believed themselves to be the rightful chief priests.

rabbis, *see* Pharisees

redemption
Literally, 'redemption' means 'buying-back', and was often used in the ancient world of slaves buying their freedom, or having it bought for them.

The great 'redemption' in the Bible, which coloured the way the word was heard ever afterwards, was when God 'bought' his people Israel from slavery in Egypt to give them freedom in the promised land. When, later, the Jews were exiled in Babylon (and even after they returned to their land), they described themselves as undergoing a new slavery and hence being in need of a new redemption. Jesus, and the early Christians, interpreted this continuing slavery in its most radical terms, as slavery to sin and death, and understood 'redemption' likewise in terms of the rescue from this multiple and tyrannous slavery, which God provided through the death of Jesus (Romans 3.24).

repentance

Literally, this means 'turning back'. It is widely used in Old Testament and subsequent Jewish literature to indicate both a personal turning away from sin and Israel's corporate turning away from idolatry and back to YHWH. Through both meanings, it is linked to the idea of 'return from exile'; if Israel is to 'return' in all senses, it must 'return' to YHWH. This is at the heart of the summons of both **John the Baptist** and Jesus. In Paul's writings it is mostly used for **Gentiles** turning away from idols to serve the true God; also for sinning Christians who need to return to Jesus.

resurrection

In most biblical thought, human bodies matter and are not merely disposable prisons for the **soul**. When ancient Israelites wrestled with the goodness and justice of YHWH, the creator, they ultimately came to insist that he must raise the dead (Isaiah 26.19; Daniel 12.2–3) – a suggestion firmly resisted by classical pagan thought. The longed-for return from **exile** was also spoken of in terms of YHWH raising dry bones to new **life** (Ezekiel 37.1–14). These ideas were developed in the second-**Temple** period, not least at times of martyrdom (e.g. 2 Maccabees 7). Resurrection was not just 'life after death', but a newly embodied life *after* 'life after death'; those at present dead were either 'asleep' or seen as 'souls', 'angels' or 'spirits', awaiting new embodiment.

sacrifice

Like all ancient people, the Israelites offered animal and vegetable sacrifices to their God. Unlike others, they possessed a highly detailed written code (mostly in Leviticus) for what to offer and how to offer it; this in turn was developed in the **Mishnah** (*c.* AD 200). The Old Testament specifies that sacrifices can only be offered in the Jerusalem **Temple**; after this was destroyed in AD 70, sacrifices ceased, and Judaism developed further the idea, already present in some teachings, of prayer, fasting and almsgiving as alternative forms of sacrifice. The early Christians used the language of sacrifice in connection with such things as holiness, evangelism and the eucharist.

Sadducees

By Jesus' day, the Sadducees were the aristocracy of Judaism, possibly tracing their origins to the family of Zadok, David's **high priest**. Based in Jerusalem, and including most of the leading priestly families, they had their own traditions and attempted to resist the pressure of the **Pharisees** to conform to theirs. They claimed to rely only on the Pentateuch (the first five books of the Old Testament), and denied any doctrine of a future life, particularly of the **resurrection** and other ideas associated with it, presumably because of the encouragement such beliefs gave to revolutionary movements. No writings from the Sadducees have survived, unless the apocryphal book of Ben-Sirach (Ecclesiasticus) comes from them. The Sadducees themselves did not survive the destruction of Jerusalem and the **Temple** in AD 70.

salvation

Salvation means 'rescue', and the meanings of the word have depended on what people thought needed rescuing, and from what. Thus, where people have imagined that the human plight was best seen in terms of an immortal **soul** being trapped in a mortal and corrupt body, 'salvation' was seen in terms of the rescue of this soul from such a prison. But for most Jews, and all early Christians, it was death itself, the ending of God-given bodily **life**, that was the real enemy, so that 'salvation' was bound to mean being rescued from death itself – in other words, the **resurrection** of the body for those who had died, and the transformation of the body for those still alive at the Lord's return (e.g. 1 Corinthians 15.50–57). For Paul and others, this 'salvation' was extended to the whole of creation (Romans 8.18–26). But if 'salvation' refers to this ultimate rescue of God's created order, and our created bodies, from all that distorts, defaces and destroys them (i.e. sin, sickness, corruption and death itself), we should expect to find, and do in fact find, that often in the New Testament 'salvation' (and phrases like 'being saved') refers not simply to people coming to **faith** and so being assured of eternal life, but to bodily healing and to rescue from awful plights (e.g. Acts 16.30–31; 27.44). Jesus' resurrection remains the foundation for a biblical view of salvation for the whole person and the whole creation, a salvation which, though to be completed in the future, has already begun with the mission and achievement of Jesus.

the satan, 'the accuser', demons

The Bible is never very precise about the identity of the figure known as 'the satan'. The Hebrew word means 'the accuser', and at times the satan seems to be a member of YHWH's heavenly council, with special responsibility as director of prosecutions (1 Chronicles 21.1; Job 1—2; Zechariah 3.1f.). However, it becomes identified variously with the serpent of the garden of Eden (Genesis 3.1–15) and with the rebellious daystar cast out of **heaven** (Isaiah 14.12–15), and was seen by many Jews as the quasi-personal source of evil standing behind both human wickedness and large-scale injustice, sometimes operating through semi-independent 'demons'. By Jesus' time, various words were used to denote this figure, including Beelzebul/b (lit. 'Lord of the flies') and simply 'the evil one'; Jesus warned his followers against the deceits this figure could perpetrate. His opponents accused him of being in league with the satan, but the early Christians believed that Jesus in fact defeated it in his own struggles with temptation (Matthew 4; Luke 4), his exorcism of demons, and his death (1 Corinthians 2.8; Colossians 2.15). Final victory over this ultimate enemy is thus assured (Revelation 20), though the struggle can still be fierce for Christians (Ephesians 6.10–20).

scribes

In a world where many could not write, or not very well, a trained class of writers ('scribes') performed the important function of drawing up contracts for business, marriage, etc. Many scribes would thus be legal experts, and quite possibly **Pharisees**, though being a scribe was compatible with various political and religious standpoints. The work of Christian scribes was of initial importance in copying early Christian writings, particularly the stories about Jesus.

son of David

An alternative, and infrequently used, title for **Messiah**. The messianic promises of the Old Testament often focus specifically on David's son, for example 2 Samuel 7.12–16; Psalm 89.19–37. Joseph, Mary's husband, is called 'son of David' by the angel in Matthew 1.20.

son of God

Originally a title for Israel (Exodus 4.22) and the Davidic king (Psalm 2.7); also used of ancient angelic figures (Genesis 6.2). By the New Testament period it was already used as a **messianic** title, for example, in the **Dead Sea Scrolls**. There, and when used of Jesus in the **gospels** (e.g. Matthew 16.16), it means, or reinforces, 'Messiah', without the later significance of 'divine'. However, already in Paul the transition to the fuller meaning (one who was already equal with God and was sent by him to become human and to become Messiah) is apparent, without loss of the meaning 'Messiah' itself (e.g. Galatians 4.4).

soul, *see* life

spirit, *see* life, holy spirit

Temple

The Temple in Jerusalem was planned by David (*c.* 1000 BC) and built by his son Solomon as the central sanctuary for all Israel. After reforms under Hezekiah and Josiah in the seventh century BC, it was destroyed by Babylon in 587 BC. Rebuilding by the returned **exiles** began in 538 BC, and was completed in 516, initiating the 'second Temple period'. Judas Maccabaeus cleansed it in 164 BC after its desecration by Antiochus Epiphanes (167). Herod the Great began to rebuild and beautify it in 19 BC; the work was completed in AD 63. The Temple was destroyed by the Romans in AD 70. Many Jews believed it should and would be rebuilt; some still do. The Temple was not only the place of **sacrifice**; it was believed to be the unique dwelling of YHWH on earth, the place where **heaven** and earth met.

Torah, Jewish law

'Torah', narrowly conceived, consists of the first five books of the Old Testament, the 'five books of Moses' or 'Pentateuch'. (These contain much law, but also much narrative.) It can also be used for the whole Old Testament scriptures, though strictly these are the 'law, prophets and writings'. In a broader sense, it refers to the whole developing corpus of Jewish legal tradition, written and oral; the oral Torah was initially codified in the **Mishnah** around AD 200, with wider developments found in the two Talmuds, of Babylon and Jerusalem, codified around AD 400. Many Jews in the time of Jesus and Paul regarded the Torah as being so strongly God-given as to be almost itself, in some sense, divine; some (e.g. Ben-Sirach 24) identified it with the figure of 'Wisdom'. Doing what Torah said was not seen as a means of earning God's favour, but rather of expressing gratitude, and as a key badge of Jewish identity.

word, *see* good news

YHWH

The ancient Israelite name for God, from at least the time of the **Exodus** (Exodus 6.2f.). It may originally have been pronounced 'Yahweh', but by the time of Jesus it was considered too holy to speak out loud, except for the **high priest** once a year in the holy of holies in the **Temple**. Instead, when reading scripture, pious Jews would say *Adonai*, 'Lord', marking this usage by adding the vowels of *Adonai* to the consonants of YHWH, eventually producing the hybrid 'Jehovah'. The word YHWH is formed from the verb 'to be', combining 'I am who I am', 'I will be who I will be' and perhaps 'I am because I am', emphasizing YHWH's sovereign creative power.

STUDY GUIDE

INTRODUCING THE STUDY

James, Peter, John and Judah for Everyone is one in a series of commentaries written by N. T. Wright, noted Pauline and New Testament scholar, who intended these to be guides for readers ready to delve deeper into the scriptures. Suitable for group or individual study, Wright provides his own translation of the early Christian letters covered in this volume. He notes that the letters are full of practical advice for the earliest Christians and that these letters 'breathe the fresh air of delight' in a newfound faith. 'Full of wonder' at the fact of Jesus, they are realistic in their view of challenges to be faced both within and outside of the church. 'They are a vital resource for every church and every Christian' Wright proposes (page xii).

The commentary on each letter includes Wright's translation of the biblical text divided into small sections, accompanied by insights into its context and in-depth explanation of each segment. Notice that Wright provides a glossary for key words at the end of the volume. Your personal preparation for each session might include studying the selected texts in different translations as well as praying for guidance in understanding and relating those scriptures to your own life. Listen for the Spirit's encouragement to you as you encounter the letters to early believers and churches, and recall Wright's reminder to us in the introduction: 'On the very first occasion when someone stood up in public to tell people about Jesus, he made it very clear: this message is for everyone'.

If Using the Guide for Individual Study

In addition to your copy of *James, Peter, John and Judah for Everyone*, you may wish to read Wright's translations alongside other translations, which you can find online or perhaps in a local library. Did you study a second language in school? Consider finding a copy of the New Testament in that language, as the additional insights coming from the unfamiliarity of that language can be spiritually revealing. Completing the questions for each text in writing (never mind complete sentences;

bullet points get full marks) and completing the suggested activities as if a good friend was by your side will enrich your experience.

If Using the Guide as a Group Member

- Be prepared by reading the scriptures before the sessions.
- Be on time for each session.
- Be encouraging to everyone.
- Be willing to contribute to group discussions.
- Be prayerful that great things will come from this study.

If Serving Others by Facilitating a Group

God bless you! This guide was prepared with you in mind, in the hope and prayer that spiritual blessings are abundant for you as well as those you lead. Every group is unique, so take this guide as a starting place, adapting and using the resources provided. Written for four one-hour sessions, you could adapt the length of your study to meet your needs. As an extra consideration, since these seven letters are significantly different in length, this guide will explore them in order while arranging the sessions into manageable lengths. In addition, the last session concludes with a culminating activity session covering all of the scriptures studied.

Suggested Session Format

Opening Prayer (1 minute)
Group Opening (5 minutes)
Exploring the Scriptures (30 minutes)
Applying the Scriptures (15 minutes)
Sharing 'Oh Wow' Moments (5 minutes)
Closing Prayer (1 minute)
Ticket Out the Door (3 minutes)

Readings for Each Session

Session One—James 1.1—5.20
Session Two—1 Peter 1.1—5.14; 2 Peter 1.1—3.18
Session Three—1 John 1.1—5.21
Session Four—2 John 1.1–13; 3 John 1.1–15; Judah 1.1–25

Helpful Hints for Facilitators

- Set up the room where you will meet early. Create expectations for learning by changing the usual appearance of the room. (Be sure to get permission before making any changes!)
- Ask others to lead a part of the session.
- Allow time for reflection. Silence may improve the quality of group responses.
- Involve as many persons as possible. Extend conversations by replying, 'Yes, and ...'
- Engage the group to reset the room to its original condition, building a sense of purpose for the group.
- Pray for the members individually and as a group. The message of these letters will change hearts and lives, as well as churches.

SESSION 1: JAMES 1.1—5.20
'HOW-TO' INSTRUCTION FOR EARLY CHRISTIANS
FROM 'OLD CAMEL KNEES'

(PAGES 3–32)

Opening Prayer (1 minute)

Holy God, in these few minutes our comfortable ways will be challenged and our priorities will be stood on their heads by God's message to us. Focus our ears to listen, our minds to perceive and our hands to act on what we learn. In the name of Jesus, we pray. Amen.

Group Opening (5 minutes)

In the tradition of the early church, James the brother of Jesus (Mark 6.3, Matthew 13.55) became the leader of the Christian church in Jerusalem. He spent so much time in prayer that his nickname was 'Old Camel Knees', so when he wrote in James about prayer and its importance, he wrote from experience. As the leader of one of the central churches in early Christianity, he likely had abundant experience in guiding believers through challenges and temptations. James wrote for a community composed of Jewish Christians, so his letter contains more references to the Jewish scriptures than other writers, distinguishing his message from that of Paul, the apostle to the Gentiles. James's central message is that faith must be lived, for living faith means living actions. Modern commentators regard James as the most socially conscious book in the New Testament, guiding the reader to compare the warnings of James to the behaviour of modern Christians and the attitudes of the modern church. Prayer, patience, faith in the face of trials and wise speech are other topics James explores in his instructions to believers and churches.

Exploring the Scriptures (30 minutes)

These questions are offered as starting points for your group's discussion. Feel free to pick and choose from the following list to best meet the needs of your members.

1. James's first 'how-to' is actually a 'how-not-to'! The challenge to faith, Wright says, is the 'challenge not to be a wave' (page 3). How does Wright describe the origin of testing and its forms?
2. What should be the result of such testing in the life of a believer? James asserts that out of trials and tribulations come patience. How many synonyms do you know for 'patience'? Make a list and choose a favourite, and then every time you encounter the word 'patience' in the text, substitute your word and see if the verse comes more alive for you.
3. Another meaning for 'patience' comes from the Arabic word *sabr*, translated commonly as 'patience', coming from the word *sabbar*, the name for the aloe vera plant. Requiring only minimal water and tolerating poor soil, that plant flourishes in conditions which would kill most plants, yet its shallow roots and extensive water storing system allow it to survive.
4. How do you know if God will give you patience? 'God, after all,' Wright translates, 'gives generously and ungrudgingly to all people' (James 1.5).
5. What two snares does James warn against in this passage? Where can we place our trust in this world?
6. What substance does Wright compare to the word of God, and how does it heal us?
7. What temptation develops its own family tree? How does that temptation play out?
8. In his discussion of James 1.9–18, Wright suggests we listen for echoes of Isaiah 40, especially the promise that 'the word of our God will stand for ever' (Isaiah 40.8).
9. In James 1.19–27, James introduced an important theme of his letter – the dangerous power of the human tongue. God's word causes things to happen, good things bringing about new joys. Human words sometimes take things in the opposite direction, especially in the specific case of which emotion?

10. What happens when we reach the end of our patience and must
say something? In Wright's brilliant insight, we always imagine that
when the world is out of joint, a little bit of our own anger will put
things straight. What should we do, however, when the world goes
wrong, according to Wright?
11. Wright says that 2.1–13 rules out any question of which behaviour
within the church?
12. What is the 'paradox of mercy'? Why can't God's mercy apply to
those who engage in arrogance, corruption, blasphemy, favouritism, law-bending for personal advantage and lawbreaking?
13. At the center of Jewish religious practice is the Shema, the daily
confession of faith: 'Hear, O Israel: the LORD our God, the LORD is
One. Love the LORD your God with all your heart and with all your
soul and with all your strength' (Deuteronomy 6.4–5, NIV). Jesus
added to this confession the royal law: 'and you shall love your
neighbour as yourself'. James is driving home his point that there
is no reason to be satisfied with saying 'God is One' without living
out the meaning of that statement.
14. How does the story of Abraham in Genesis 15 and Genesis 22 illustrate James's assertion about faith and works?
15. Rahab is also named as an example of one whose faith lived in her
actions. Who was she, what did she do and how was she mentioned
in the New Testament? (See Joshua 2.11.)
16. Wright states that translating faith into action, even when it seems
impossible or dangerous, is the faith that justifies (2.24) and the
faith that saves (2.14). Share with the group, or later with a friend, a
time when you lived out your faith courageously.
17. So what exactly does James expect from Christians? Does Jesus
expect the same behaviour from Christians? Convince the others
in the group by using relevant examples of your answer.
18. The topic of discussion in James 3.13–18 is true and false wisdom.
What is the challenge identified by Wright for modern Christians
seeking to tell the truth about the world?
19. What kind of wisdom does God give the believer who asks? In
verse 17 of chapter 3, James lists the characteristics of true religion:
it is 'holy, then peaceful, gentle, compliant, filled with mercy and
good fruits, unbiased, sincere'. How would the rich and powerful
of today's world react to such a description of wisdom? How does
the author describe the personal acquisition of these traits by the
believer?
20. In the Bible, Wright explains, marriage is used as a metaphor for
the exclusive claim that God makes on the loyalty of followers.

What point is James trying to make by calling some believers 'adulterers'? How does this relate to verse four of chapter 3: 'So anyone who wants to be friends with the world is setting themselves up as God's enemies'?

21. What is the characteristic means of solving a problem 'in the world'? Wright implies that to slide along as a 'normal' person in the world is to be a 'friend of the world' (page 20). Is it possible to be a Christian, then, without being so different from others that you are considered odd, out of touch, naive or damaged?
22. James emphasizes a personal trait especially lacking in his day: humility. Its opposite, arrogance, insists that *my* way is best, *my* desires come first, and *my* cause is so important that it is worth fighting and dying for. In what ways do you recognize this attitude in the church today?
23. The author identifies the antidote to this arrogance in verse 8 of chapter 4 in a double promise so stupendous as to defy belief. How would you go about incorporating that double promise in your own life?
24. In 4.13, James turns to a second metaphor concerning making judgments about life and our own opinions and desires. What is that metaphor, and how does it relate to the lessons of 4.11–12?
25. Who are the rich of James 5.1–6? What is the worst thing that they have done?
26. How did Jesus counter the stance of the rich toward the poor?
27. What is the significance in 5.3 of 'the last days'?
28. In James 5.7–12, he returns to the theme of patience, using a farmer as an example. Perhaps there are committed gardeners in your group and someone could clarify the connection between farming and patience. What is the role played by humility in this passage?
28. James ends with another discussion of patience and with a discussion of the power of prayer. The first connection mentioned between patience and prayer is sickness. One of the greatest challenges facing modern people is the need for patience in the treatment of illness. We all look for and pray for a 'magic bullet' for instantaneous relief when the best offer we have is patience for slow healing. Perhaps we could endeavour to learn patience through prayer before we reach the crises of end-of-life care.

Applying the Scriptures (15 minutes)

The purpose of this section of the study is to gather the threads discovered in the study and to weave them into a deeper understanding of the message of James. Use the suggested activities as time permits to consolidate what you have learned.

1. Divide into small groups or ask individuals to identify and clarify the themes in James's writing. Support your findings with reference to the text of James or to the written guidance given by the author. You can use whatever technology is at hand and easy to use to communicate your thoughts more effectively.
2. Perhaps you have known a person in real life who has embodied the teachings of James in a positive way. Encourage several members to share personal experiences with those saints.
3. Have you ever experienced a scene in a movie, book or work of art that incorporates the message of James? Again, encourage members to share those sorts of life-changing experiences.

Sharing 'Oh Wow' Moments (5 minutes)

In these brief moments, members of the group can share moments of realization or reproof that they experienced during this study.

Closing Prayer (1 minute)

Giver of all good gifts, thank you for your gift of instruction in faithful living found in the message of James. Help us to incorporate what we have learned into who we are for the sake of the kingdom of God. Amen.

Ticket Out the Door (3 minutes)

What do you already know about the letters called 1 Peter and 2 Peter? Write down as many as three lessons on a slip of paper and give them to the facilitator on your way out of the door.

SESSION 2: 1 PETER 1.1—5.14; 2 PETER 1.1—3.18 GUIDANCE FOR THE EARLY CHURCH
(PAGES 35–92)

Opening Prayer (1 minute)

Great Shepherd, we know that not a single person is out of your sight, not one is forgotten. We need that reassurance from you, especially when we feel separated from you and alienated by the society we live in. Help us to use Peter's guidance to remain on the right path and to take that path to wholeness in you. Amen.

Group Opening (5 minutes)

From the responses at the end of the first session, choose several to introduce the purpose and contents of Peter's epistles. Recall that the purpose of 1 Peter is to give encouragement to Christians in Asia Minor who are suffering. Also, remind the group that 2 Peter was a warning against the false teachers attempting to disrupt the message and growth of the early church. If anyone shared a favourite verse from Peter, be sure to share that with the group.

Exploring the Scriptures (30 minutes)

1. In chapter 1 of Peter's first letter, Wright identifies the width of the building being built by God for these believers, who are reminded of their new identity in Christ (verses 1–2). Chosen for a particular purpose, Christians are dual citizens of their residence as well as the kingdom of Jesus Christ. What does Wright say is the purpose of these believers?
2. What is the height of the Christian calling? How does he describe the new life created for the world in verses 3–5?
3. How does Wright describe the depth (verses 6–9) of the new Christian life? How does he apply this insight to those who first read this letter?
4. Those first readers, and those that followed, could live in the good news that we have been ransomed, bought back from abusive slavery, just like the Jewish people in Egypt at the time of the Exodus. We are redeemed by the sacrificial lamb of Passover, Jesus. Our new life is radically different from the life normally lived by others. Our lives should be characterized by straight thinking, certain of its content and not malleable into the shape of our former ignorance.
5. How does Peter utilize Psalm 34.8 to develop a new metaphor for the believers? What use does he make of verses 23 and 25 to instruct the reader? Why does Peter refer to Isaiah 40:6–8 and 55.10–13?
6. Perhaps a willing group member would agree to clarify the meaning of 2.4–10, which references Psalm 118.22, 2 Samuel 7.12–14 and Isaiah 8.14. Why is Peter using terms which refer to the Temple in Jerusalem to refer also to the Gentile churches scattered throughout Asia Minor? How do Exodus 19:3–6 and Hosea 2.23 bring additional depth to this description of a scattered Christian church?
7. In what important ways are we to take on the sufferings of the Messiah just as the Suffering Servant portrayed in Isaiah's prophecies did?

8. Wright asserts that the early Christian household code as portrayed in 3.1–7 is actually radical in its teaching. How does Wright justify that characterization?
9. In 3.8–16, Peter refers again to Psalm 34. Make a list of the ways that Psalm is needed today. Why, in particular, does Wright emphasize the necessity of a clear conscience for the believer?
10. List and explain the steps Wright takes to discuss 3.17–22, paying close attention to his use of 1 Enoch to introduce the example of Noah.
11. How does Wright focus suffering as essential to transformed Christian living in 4.1-2? Why does Wright single out 4.14 as central to the understanding of 4.12–19?
13. Peter characterizes the pastors of his day as shepherds. In our day, church leaders produce books on leadership with regularity. What point is Wright making when he suggests that 'leading' and 'shepherding' are not the same thing? (To the group facilitator: it might be wise to read this passage without comment unless the pastor of the group is present. The discussion of this passage could easily go astray if not guided sensitively.)
14. To the Christians in Asia Minor who were the first readers of this letter, it might have seemed that they had taken a wrong turn or even made a serious mistake in following Jesus. Facing persecution, experiencing alienation and called to be radically different from their neighbours, they might be excused for having doubts. Peter provides a direct charge to them and to us: 'You are indeed standing in the true grace of God' (5.12). None of these challenges are unexpected, and all necessary help will be provided. You are right where you should be.
15. How does the author describe the 'big picture' presented in 2 Peter 1.1–11?
16. List the four things God wants for his believers as presented by Wright in this passage.
17. What discipline must we learn, according to Wright, and what two actions does the writer of 2 Peter say must be taken to develop this discipline?
18. Second Peter 1.12–21 contains the only mention outside the first three gospels of what event? What is the Old Testament reference for this event? How does Wright explain verse 21?
19. On page 81, the author describes the devastating thing about false teachers and their teaching in what terms?
20. How did the writer of 2 Peter use the strange story of Genesis 6 to expose false teachers?

21. Balaam, the prophet in Numbers 15, is the next example the writer uses concerning false teachers. How does this story apply in this context?
22. How does Wright deal with the concept of a 'delay' in Christ's return in 3.1–10?
23. What is the writer's recipe for waiting on Christ's return as described in 2 Peter 3.11–18?

Applying the Scriptures (15 minutes)

The German people have a concept called *Bildung*, which is 'the combination of the education and knowledge necessary to thrive in your society, and the moral and emotional maturity to both be a team player and have personal autonomy', according to the European Bildung Network.[1] The writer of 2 Peter seems to be suggesting much the same idea, according to Wright, in 1.1–10, where Christians are called to 'become more fully human'. Divide the group into two, assigning to the first the question 'How does the writer describe the process in 2 Peter 1.1–10?' and to the second 'What practical steps could modern Christians take to create their own spiritual Bildung?'

Sharing 'Oh Wow' Moments (5 minutes)

In these brief moments, members of the group can share moments of realization or reproof they experienced during this study.

Closing Prayer (1 minute)

Holy God, we have a long way to go to be who we were chosen to be. Peter knew the hazards of that journey, and we too may find it easy to get lost. Use this study to keep us on the right path so that we can better serve others in your name. Amen.

Ticket Out the Door (3 minutes)

On your way out of the door, hand to the facilitator your slip of paper which lists a favourite verse or teaching from 1 John.

---

1. European Association for the Education of Adults, 'What Is Bildung?', https://eaea.org/wp-content/uploads/2021/02/What-is-Bildung-pdf-English.pdf.

SESSION 3: 1 JOHN 1.1—5.21
LIGHT, LOVE, LIFE

(PAGES 95–124)

Opening Prayer (1 minute)

God is light, God is love, and God is life! Help us, O God, to make these simple sentences into profound life. In the name of Jesus, we pray. Amen.

Group Opening (5 minutes)

During this time, review and share responses to the 'ticket out the door' activity from the second session.

Exploring the Scriptures (30 minutes)

1. What were the two ages referred to by ancient Jews, according to the author? (See page 95.)
2. Translating from one language to another is a difficult task, requiring a grasp of two or more languages as well as an intimate knowledge of how those languages are used in context. In the case of 1.2, Wright, leaning on a knowledge of Hebrew and Jewish custom, translates 'the life of God's coming age', rather than 'eternal life', as found in many translations. What misunderstanding of John's intent is Wright seeking to avoid?
3. What was the 'secret at the heart of the early Christian movement', and why was its name 'life'?
4. Read and reread Wright's treatment of the word 'fellowship' on pages 97–98. What is John, and Wright as well, trying to tell us? How can we believe that we have been accepted into the circle of those who were eyewitnesses of Jesus' ministry? How can we be blessed to that extent, given that we live two thousand years later?
5. Let Wright's inspired explanation resonate in your spirit: 'The point is this. God has spoken in Jesus; and God now speaks, through the words which Jesus' friends speak and write about him, to others also, in the intention and hope that they will come to share this same 'fellowship' (page 98).
6. 'We have messed it up', the author writes. What if we have made such a disaster of the planet, of the church, or of our own selves that God cannot redeem the situation? At a fair remove from the time of John and of Jesus, these are reasonable questions to ask. John says to us today, 'You don't understand! Jesus and his blood

is the sacrifice which atones for our sins and the sins of the world!'
Wright tells us what happens when we 'turn to the light' (page 100).
What does Wright say happens to us in our turning?

7. How does Wright explain the difference between the linear nature
of Paul's writings compared to the repetition and interweaving
nature of John's writings?

8. What new major theme is found in 1 John 2.3–14? What is one
word that can be used to summarize the commandments given to
Israel?

9. Why and how does Wright use the term 'Antimessiah'? What is the
great attraction, and greatest sin, described by John in verse 22 of
chapter 2? How does the Hebrew meaning of the word 'anointed'
figure into this discussion?

10. Verse 15 of chapter 2 says, 'Do not love the world, or the things
that are in the world'. This, and what follows it immediately, were
sometimes taken to demand a hatred of natural things, physical
pleasures that are part and parcel of God's created world. How
does Wright explain the use of this language and its meaning for us
today?

11. John said explicitly that we are God's children. Stunning as it is to
contemplate, even more stunning is the assertion that when Jesus
is revealed we shall be like him. Take your time, and describe to
yourself, a neighbour, or the group how in the world we could be
like him. What does John say? 'We shall see him as he is'. Our con-
ceptions of him are shaped by our personal experiences, to some
extent, but much more by our reading of God's word. The understanding of who Jesus is, for individuals and for the church, is as
varied as the number of believing persons who have ever lived, and
yet we all will know Jesus because we 'see him as he is'.

12. What does John say the greatest sin is?

13. How does Wright relate the story of the prophet Elisha as told in
2 Kings 6 to 1 John 3.11—4.6?

14. Which false teachers was John warning his readers about? Wright
makes an educated guess about those teachers and their teaching,
based on John's description of them. How does Wright connect the
true nature of Jesus, the false teaching about him and the prologue
of the gospel of John?

15. With what statistic does Wright begin his discussion of 1 John
4.7–21?

16. How does Wright explain the 'knowing' of God in Jesus from
verse 7 through verse 12?

17. What distinction does the author make using the term 'brother or
sister' in verse 20?

18. What word is central to the meaning of verse 16? How does it relate to 'fellowship'?
19. The author of this commentary begins his study of 1 John 5.1–12 by relating a story about the first time he went snorkeling on a tropical reef. How did he compare that experience to his reading of this passage? Perhaps a member of the group has been on a similar trip or is an experienced scuba diver and can tell of a similar experience.
20. Wright comments on John's writing style by making a point that any teacher could love (page 119). Ask a teacher to explain and to share an instance in which she or he sought to create the same opportunity for learning.
21. On 1 John 5.4, Wright asks why John says 'everything' rather than the more natural 'everyone'. Then he continues, 'We can only guess' (page 120). It is amazing, isn't it, that even a thoroughly educated and brilliantly articulate scholar admits that the best he, or we, can do is to guess at the meaning of this verse.
22. John has taken his readers back to Old Testament stories and references many times in this letter. According to Wright, John now leads readers to the gospel of John and to an event described in John 19.34: 'Instead, one of the soldiers pierced Jesus' side with a spear, bringing a sudden flow of blood and water'. Wright's teaching style is especially inspired here: 'And suddenly we realize that we are in exactly the same seam of thought as in our present passage, 1 John 5.49. *The victory that conquers the world is the saving death of Jesus.* And those who by faith cling on to the God who is made known personally in and as the Jesus who died on the cross – they share that victory, that conquest of "the world"' (page 120).
23. Please be sure to notice the translation of verse 7 in this passage and Wright's explanation of how his own translation differs from that of the King James version.
24. Wright directs us to John's insistence that the 'Antimessiah' faction were teaching a false understanding of Jesus. The center of John's argument is that Jesus was born as a human, grew in stature and understanding as a human and suffered and died as a human. At no time in his life was Jesus anything but a man in form and understanding, and nothing done by Jesus was just an illusion of reality. Yet the 'mutual indwelling' of Jesus the son and God the father was divine in its completeness and in its relationship.
25. How was the world overcome by Jesus; how was it conquered? John paints an astounding picture, and Wright explains in poetic and powerful terms: 'No other god, no other power, no other being in all the world loves like this, gives like this, dies like this. All others

win victories by fighting; this one, by suffering. All other gods exercise power by killing; this one, by dying' (page 121).

26. Wright provides a wonderfully consoling thought in his comment on 1 John 5.18, which says, 'We know that everyone fathered by God does not go on sinning' (page 124). Wright points out that this verse assumes that each and every one of us will sin, but we will not make our sinning a continuous habit of life. God knows that I will never grow to be in a place where I will never sin, but I can be forgiven and restored by God. What good news!

27. The author uses the example of a short story to illustrate how an author can give the reader an entirely new insight into the truth of a story. The ending of 1 John is unlike the ending of any other letter or gospel in the New Testament. Seemingly out of nowhere, John writes, 'Children, guard yourselves against idols' (1 John 5.21). What in the world does this mean? How does Wright explain its possible meaning?

Applying the Scriptures (15 minutes)

These activities can be done by individuals, in groups or as a large group. Their purpose is to reinforce what you have learned in your study of 1 John. A wonderful way to extend your knowledge is to answer the questions raised here in 1 John with reference to other biblical texts.

1. 'Life, Love, Light' is the title of this session, taken from verses in 1 John wherein 'God is . . .' statements introduce a new topic in the outline. Create for one of these themes, or for all, a chart or table which includes the following elements: verses in which a specific L-word is mentioned, what actions that theme commands or suggests and the shades of meaning that theme has in 1 John, but also what it means to individuals in the group. Be prepared to report back to the large group your results and to lead a discussion about applying your discoveries to individual lives.

2. First John refers to Jesus, or God, in different ways. List and explore the meaning and relevance of as many of these as time permits. Examples might include the 'serving' God and the 'victorious' God. Be prepared to report back to the large group your results and to lead a discussion about applying your discoveries to individual lives.

3. Wright comments several times on the writing style of 1 John. What comparisons does he make to create an appreciation of John's style? From your own experience and interests, how would you describe John's writing style, and what parallels do you see with other fields such as poetry, music, film or art?

4. The author, commenting on 1 John 2.15–21, sets his comments
(pages 122–24) in the context of Jesus' return, his 'royal appearing'.
He writes, 'When he [Jesus] "appears" (think of it as his "coming",
if you like, but don't be misled by that into imagining that he is at
present far away from you; rather, he is very near, but hidden), then
he will utterly transform the whole creation. And when that happens, the way of the present world will disappear' (verse 17). What
do you make of this comment, particularly regarding the current
location of Jesus?

Sharing 'Oh Wow' Moments (5 minutes)

In these brief moments, members of the group can share moments of
realization or reproof they experienced during this study.

Closing Prayer (1 minute)

Dear Jesus, John's revelations about you overwhelms our brains and
our hearts. So much light, so much love, so much life and still we are
called 'the children of God'. Thank you for your mercy and grace! As
you reveal yourself to us in words, please also guide us to reveal you to
others in our deeds. Amen.

Ticket Out the Door (3 minutes)

Write down anything you know about 2 John, 3 John or Judah on the
slip of paper provided to you and give it to the group facilitator on your
way out the door.

SESSION 4: 2 JOHN 1–13; 3 JOHN 1–15; JUDAH 1–25
THE EARLY CHRISTIANS AND THEIR CHALLENGES

(PAGES 127–52)

Opening Prayer (1 minute)

Great Teacher, we don't know too much about these letters, so in your
grace, enlighten us with your word and show us how to apply our
learnings to our livings. Amen.

Group Opening (5 minutes)

During this time, review and share responses to the 'ticket out the
door' activity from the third session.

Exploring the Scriptures (15 minutes)

This session will begin with an introduction to these three short works and will then examine each work in turn. Because each of these is brief, we will then turn to a longer than usual 'Applying the Scriptures' to integrate and extend our understanding of *James, Peter, John and Judah for Everyone*. These three letters are the shortest and, most likely, the least consulted letters in the New Testament. According to some scholars, their brevity is based on the size of the piece of parchment on which they were written. They contain guidance from an authority figure in the early church and are chiefly concerned with false teachers and behaviours which disturbed local congregations. One is written using pseudonymous names, one is written to a person and not to a church, and the third does not designate its audience. Together, they share descriptions of the early church and the challenges that early believers faced.

2 John 1–13

1. The writer of 2 John, 'the Elder', presumably the apostle himself, is writing to the 'Chosen Lady and her children', probably a prominent local house church and other groups of believers in the orbit of the 'Chosen Lady'. The letter begins on a positive note of praise that some of her children were found 'walking in the truth' (2 John 4). How does Wright explain the meaning of that compliment?
2. Who does the Elder identify as the deceivers, and what have they done to earn such scorn?
3. Which of the many definitions of love in modern life does Wright single out for reproof? How would you apply his teaching to your own life situation? What are the dangers and blessings of following Wright's train of thought?
4. How does the author apply verse 12 to life today? How would you apply verse 12 to today's social communication?

3 John 1–15

1. Wright begins his commentary on this letter with a brief look at 'zooming in' software and compares it to the progression of the three letters of John being addressed to a large area of Asia Minor (Turkey), then to a specific church (the Chosen Lady), and finally to just one person (Gaius). The Elder narrows his focus on loving the family of believers to the specific case of providing hospitality for those persons who traveled for the benefit of a local church or group of churches. Providing such hospitality as lodging, meals and rest could become a burden, financially and physically, for

some. Gaius, however, excelled in his generosity, and travelers from John's church had returned with praise for this believer and his love as exhibited by his hospitality.

2. How does the author relate this open-handed behaviour to the truth? Wright notes that to undertake a journey, as portrayed in this brief account, was to live out an adventure in faith. It is difficult to imagine such courage in these days, isn't it? Perhaps we need to cultivate a deeper sense of faith's adventures.
3. Who was Diotrophes? After reading Wright's account of him, would you wish to be a part of his congregation?
4. Who was Demetrius? Why was he a good messenger to carry this letter? What do you suppose happened in this case?
5. Why are there so often conflicts in our churches? What can we do to avoid such conflict or to correct it if we cannot?

Judah 1–25

1. In what two ways described in the opening to this letter does Judah say Jesus guards his people?
2. Why does Wright refer to the writer of this letter as Judah? What historic person is the writer supposed to be, and where did he most likely live?
3. On page 145, Wright identifies people today who Judah would have accused of false teaching. Who are they?
4. What is the lesson contained in verses 5–7?
5. How does Judah use the story of Michael and the devil in verses 8–9? How does Wright explain them?
6. Verse 11 provides three examples of wickedness. Explain the references for each one.
7. How are believers in evil times to 'build themselves up' as described in verses 20–21?
8. How does Wright's translation of verse 24 differ from others, and how does he explain his own choice of words?

Applying the Scriptures (30 minutes)

Today's session is largely an opportunity to bring together all that we have learned in this study, so here are several activities to lead the group in that direction. You will not likely have time to complete them all, so choose among them as the Spirit leads, interest is shown and time permits.

1. From your study of *James, Peter, John and Judah for Everyone*, make a list of the common problems faced by early Christian churches and believers. Create a presentation, digital or traditional, to

describe these problems and to illustrate the similarities and differences in the way the writers of these seven letters recommended approaching them. Use specific examples to strengthen your presentation, and share a copy, if possible, with each member in your large group.

2. These letters were written to early Christian churches filled with mostly Gentiles. As an analogy, in our time those churches would be filled with people who have had no or limited exposure to our faith or our churches. Would the advice to today's new believers be different than that given to first-century Christians? Describe the differences, or compose your own letter of encouragement and warning to a new believer in your church.

3. After considering the persons and groups identified in at least one of the seven letters we have studied, create and explain a Venn diagram showing the connections between the groups. Note that these connections can be either positive or negative and could include persons named or referenced in the Old Testament.

4. Do you think that false teachers still exist today? Create a list of places where you might encounter a false teacher today. What kinds of teaching would 'false teaching' encompass today? Under what circumstances might you hear false teaching today? List examples you might share with a new Christian. Note: naming, displaying pictures of and vilifying living persons may not be in the proper spirit of this exercise. Generic examples, or examples of general types, may be the better idea here.

Sharing 'Oh Wow' Moments (5 minutes)

In these brief moments, members of the group can share moments of realization or reproof they experienced during this study.

Closing Prayer (1 minute)

Almighty God, in a world that has lost its way, we implore you to give us a spirit of discernment so that we may know what to do; a spirit of wisdom, so we may know how to live; and a spirit of love, so we may follow your commandments in spirit and in truth. Amen.

Ticket Out the Door (3 minutes)

Make a suggestion for the next volume in this study series to your facilitator. Volunteer to lead a study or one of the sessions in the next study!